Representing Death in the News

Representing Death in the News

Journalism, Media and Mortality

Folker Hanusch

First published 2010 by
PALGRAVE MACMILLAN

Palgrave Macmillan in the UK is an imprint of Macmillan Publishers Limited,
registered in England, company number 785998, of Houndmills, Basingstoke,
Hampshire RG21 6XS.

Palgrave Macmillan in the US is a division of St Martin's Press LLC,
175 Fifth Avenue, New York, NY 10010.

Palgrave Macmillan is the global academic imprint of the above companies
and has companies and representatives throughout the world.

Palgrave® and Macmillan® are registered trademarks in the United States,
the United Kingdom, Europe and other countries.

ISBN-13: 978–0–230–23046–0 hardback

This book is printed on paper suitable for recycling and made from fully
managed and sustained forest sources. Logging, pulping and manufacturing
processes are expected to conform to the environmental regulations of the
country of origin.

A catalogue record for this book is available from the British Library.

A catalog record for this book is available from the Library of Congress.

Printed and bound in Great Britain by
CPI Antony Rowe, Chippenham and Eastbourne

For my parents

Contents

Acknowledgments

Book projects are never strictly the work of one person alone, and this one is no different. I have been fortunate enough to have had the support of a number of people, without whom it is unlikely this book project would have come to fruition. First and foremost, I thank my wife and son, who have, especially over the last two months before completion of the manuscript, been an eternal source of encouragement and moral support. Most importantly, they have been more than understanding when I needed to shut myself away in order to work on the manuscript. Weekends with daddy will now return. Thanks also go to my parents, without whom none of this would have been possible. This book is dedicated to them, because they taught me to follow my dreams, which unfortunately meant I ended up living a long way away. To their credit, they have coped well. At Palgrave Macmillan I would like to thank everyone involved in this project, which began more than two years ago: Renee Takken, Catherine Mitchell and especially commissioning editor Christabel Scaife, who saw the potential in this project and encouraged me to develop it further. I owe my gratitude to the three anonymous reviewers; their constructive feedback alerted me to a number of issues and helped me refine the project. Special thanks is due to Levi Obijiofor, who has been a close mentor during my entire life in academia and who, despite the short notice, read through the entire manuscript to give me detailed and valuable feedback. His undying encouragement for my work has been a constant source of energy. I would further like to thank my boss Stephen Lamble, Head of the School of Communication at the University of the Sunshine Coast, who was extremely supportive of my project in many ways. My appreciation also goes out to Barbie Zelizer, who allowed me a look at the manuscript of her latest work, *About to die: How news images move the public*. I have the greatest admiration for her work on the way in which journalism deals with death. Finally, I would like to thank the journal *Media International Australia* for allowing me to re-use parts of a paper I wrote on Steve Irwin's death in this book. The article's publication details are:

Hanusch, Folker (2009) ' "The Australian we all aspire to be": Commemorative journalism and the death of the Crocodile Hunter', *Media International Australia*, 130, pp. 28–38.

1
Introduction

The news media these days seem to be full of reports about death and destruction. When *Time* magazine published its list of the top 10 news stories for 2009, all but two included tales of destruction and death. There was the ongoing war in Afghanistan, which experienced a dramatic surge in Coalition casualties. In Iran, a protester made worldwide news when her death was broadcast around the world on YouTube. A lone gun man rampaged through the US military base at Fort Hood, taking 12 lives in the process and wounding many others. Pakistan was an ongoing site for terrorist attacks and fighting between the Taliban and military forces. In the escalating drug war in Mexico 1800 murders were committed in the first nine months of 2009 alone. Then there was the swine flu pandemic, which killed well over 10,000 people worldwide and almost caused mass panic as governments around the globe attempted to stop it from spreading.

The year 2009 also saw the end of the civil war in Sri Lanka, which over the course of 26 years had killed more than 70,000 people. And finally, of course, there was one death that possibly generated the most amount of news coverage. In 2009, the 'King of Pop' Michael Jackson died, spawning countless stories, public expressions of grief, and completely dominating the news for days. These stories do not even include the 173 people killed in the most deadly bushfires in Australian history, or the more than 300 who perished in the devastating earthquake in the Italian town of L'Aquila. Nor do they feature the mysterious crash of an Air France airbus over the Atlantic Ocean, in which 228 people lost their lives, or the more than 1000 who died in an earthquake on the Indonesian island of Sumatra and the 115 who were killed when a tsunami hit the islands of Samoa. Not to mention over 4000 Americans who had died during Operation Iraqi Freedom by the end of 2009.

Death, it seems, is the new black of the modern media age. The old adage 'when it bleeds it leads' appears to be as true as ever, as we are seemingly surrounded by dead bodies wherever we look. Of course death, in particular that of a gruesome nature, is always a highly disruptive event in any society. And, because they meet a number of news criteria, stories about death often make the front pages of our newspapers or are the leading items in news bulletins. It seems, and the above examples appear to support this, that news coverage is saturated with death in all its shapes and forms. In fact, it is taken as fact by many scholars as well. Yet, is it really the case? How do the news media report on death? Has there been a shift towards an increased focus on death in the news as many claim? Can we really say that the news is full of blood and gore? Does the repeated portrayal of death on television and in pictures numb us to the pain and suffering of others? And, not to forget, what impact does it have on those who report the news? This book attempts to answer these questions by mapping the extant literature on the topic in order to synthesize a largely incongruent field.

Why is the study of death in the news important?

Death, or the end of life, constitutes a central component of all societies around the world, who have over thousands of years developed various elaborate rituals to deal with the passing of one of their own. Over time, the human experience of death has changed too. For the majority of humans' existence on the planet, death was experienced as a matter of course, as humans lived together in close environments and life-expectancy was relatively low. Death and dying was very much a communal affair during those days. Yet, as hunter-gatherers evolved into settler cultures and societies grew more complex, family units began to reduce in size and the end of life was a more and more individualized affair (Kellehear, 2007). Whereas death was quite public even up to the late nineteenth century, for much of the twentieth century it became a taboo subject, as the dying were moved to nursing homes and hospitals, out of the view of most. Death therefore moved to the private sphere, as a problem to be dealt with by medicine.

Yet, recent scholarship of death and dying in society has identified a return of death to the public sphere, most notably through the mass media. An increasing amount of literature argues that death is becoming omnipresent in the media, and that this is fast changing the way Western societies deal with the end of life. Some even believe these developments constitute a return to death-affirming societies (Staudt, 2009a).

The performance of the mass media is crucial in this context. In an increasingly globalized and technology-dominated world, we live in an environment where much of our knowledge is to a large extent shaped by the information we receive from the mass media. While we are constantly exposed to the lives of famous politicians, sportspeople and celebrities, very few of us have actually ever met them. Yet we believe we almost know them, based on the accounts we read, see and hear about them in the media. Similarly, many of us have never been to places like Iraq or Palestine, yet we believe we have a reasonably clear picture of what it must be like to live there, based on the news reports we see and hear. The media bring us into contact with experiences that we are generally not personally confronted with on a daily basis. So, as dying now takes place in the hospital or nursing home, rather than in the family home, much of what we know about death comes through the media. In fact, Carolyn Kitch and Janice Hume (2008, p. xvii) argue that 'the mediated sharing of the stories of strangers' deaths may be the most common death experience in modern culture'.

Indeed, there seems to be an increasingly visible level of death and dying around us. In particular, the arrival of new technologies appears to have made images and reports of death ubiquitous. On the Internet, a large range of memorial and grief websites now exists, dedicated to lost loved ones. In Germany, a new television channel devoted entirely to the issue of death and dying is due to begin broadcasting around the clock (Hawley, 2007). Aimed at the country's dramatically aging population, EtosTV plans to screen factual documentaries about cemeteries, programs on funeral cultures, as well as tips on retirement homes. Similarly, the entertainment industry has long been concerned with the issue of death and dying. Many major Hollywood movies deal with the topic, and television shows such as *CSI*, *Six Feet Under* and *Desperate Housewives* have followed suit. In the arts, the controversial Body Worlds exhibition of corpses was a major discussion point. Such developments may all be a sign of an increased awareness and problematization of death in Western society which had been hiding it for much of the twentieth century. In fact, Foltyn (2008, p. 170) suggests that 'perhaps shared grief about the passing of celebrities and fascination with their corpses are ways for everyday people to better familiarize themselves with death and the dead human body'. Even in tourism a new type of travel experience has found increasing attention from scholars. Here, the concept of Dark Tourism is used to describe 'sites, attractions or events linked in one way or another with death, suffering, violence or disaster' (Stone and Sharpley, 2008). All these developments suggest that death is becoming increasingly visible again and is making its way back into social consciousness. This book examines the ways in which the news media play a part in this, how they represent death and the role they play in the process of its mediation.

As mediated experiences of death are so important for our understanding of death in the modern age, it is crucial that we examine the way the news media deal with the topic. We actually possess a rich volume of scholarship that at least touches on the way death appears in the news. But at the same time, such scholarship has also rarely been able to provide a holistic overview of death in the media. Instead, studies have tended to focus only on certain aspects of the issue. Probably most popular in this regard have been examinations of the visual depiction of death, as well as how news media differentiate between 'our dead' and 'their dead'. Wars and disasters have attracted significant attention in this regard, as arguably these constitute sites of increased media coverage. More recently, the way in which journalism takes control of discourses of collective memory after high-profile deaths has also generated a considerable amount of scholarship. At the same time, other aspects of the relationship between the news and death have received relatively little attention. Most neglected here has been the way in which reporting death actually impacts on journalists themselves, as well as the specific ways in which audiences may extract meanings out of news coverage of death. In fact, there exists a variety of qualitative and quantitative studies drawing on a vast amount of disciplines and paradigms, and at times it seems that one doesn't speak to the other. As a result, there is an urgent need to try to draw together the divergent strands of the scholarship of death in the news, in order to provide an update on where the field stands, and where important gaps in our knowledge still exist.

This book seeks to answer these questions. It is the first attempt to distill the vast, and at times conflicting, amount of perspectives that focus on news coverage of death. The goal is to provide a holistic overview of the research that scholars have undertaken in a number of disciplines, primarily in journalism and communication studies, but also in cultural studies, sociology, literature, anthropology, psychiatry and psychology. In doing so, it takes a strongly inter-disciplinary view and aims to combine studies that may come from disparate paradigms, but tries to align them and arrive at a kind of synthesis in order to further our understanding of death in the news.

It is also important to point out that the book is not concerned with fictional representations of violence or death. This decision is made purposefully, as studies of audience perceptions of media displays of horror and death show that viewers do appear to distinguish between real-life representations in journalism and the fictional portrayals of television shows and Hollywood movies (Gould, 2001). The distinction is crucial, as the two areas of media representations are sometimes conflated. For example, Foltyn (2008) notes that body counts in television drama have steadily gone up in the past few years, while news representations are still largely censored. Hence, when I talk about the media in this study, it generally does not include fictional portrayals. This is not to say that fictional portrayals of death do not have a role to play in shaping or reflecting our attitudes to death. In fact, they play an immensely crucial role. Yet, including them would open up another, much more comprehensive field that is best left to others to examine on its own. The literature on news representations of death is already so large in itself, that even a book such as this can at times only sketch aspects of it.

The social construction of death in the news

One important aspect of media representations of death and dying that needs to be considered here briefly is the concept of reality and how news media play a role in constructing it. This is important as much of the literature discussed in this book takes this constructivist paradigm as its starting point. Journalism is essentially characterized by the selection and rejection of news items from the innumerable mass of news that reaches a media organization on any given day. Newspapers or broadcast bulletins cannot possibly report every event that happens on this planet, so journalists, guided by news criteria, choose from the flood of information that reaches their offices. This means that events that go unreported may appear not to have happened at all, as audiences are not aware of them. Death is an extremely disruptive event and therefore satisfies one of the prime news values, which relates to negativity. As the seminal study of news values by Norwegian researchers Johan Galtung and Mari Holmboe Ruge (1965) found decades ago, events that contain negative news are much preferred over positive news. After all, the saying goes, bad news sells. And if a death satisfies even more news criteria, for example when it is violent, comes unexpectedly, involves a famous person, or the audience can identify with the death, then its news value will be even higher. Deaths which are expected, or which strike people who are unknown and in unremarkable circumstances, may not satisfy enough news criteria in order to be reported. While we should bear in mind that, as cultural theorist Stuart Hall (1973, p. 181) has stated, news factors remain one of the most opaque structures in modern society, and journalists use them more or less subconsciously, they are still a useful way of exploring reasons behind media reporting. This notion is important, as this book investigates which deaths are deemed by the media as newsworthy and are therefore reported, as opposed to those which are unworthy of coverage and are rejected. Further, how news media report deaths, the language that is used and the pictures that are displayed, need to be taken into account, as they create certain views about death and attach values to it. This process in turn, it is argued, shapes the social reality of the audience.

The term 'social construction of reality' was first coined by Berger and Luckmann (1966), who referred to the relationship between the individual and the social structure surrounding that individual. Everyday life, which Berger and Luckmann saw as the paramount reality, is experienced as an ordered reality, an inter-subjective reality, shared with others, and also an objective reality which appears independent of one's own volition. Berger and Luckmann (1966) argued that the knowledge of everyday life is organized in zones around an individual, who is the center of his or her social world. Around this center, knowledge is arranged in zones of decreasing relevance. The closest and most important zone is the face-to-face situation, regarded by Berger and Luckmann (1966) as prototypical. In this case, reality is constructed by one's own direct experiences. The further away a zone is from the individual, however, the more reality is a typified one, where only characteristics interesting to the individual are selected, leading to a typified image (Berger and Luckmann, 1966). Therefore, an individual's reality is created through a process of socialization, where the individual constantly engages in a dialectical process in order to determine his or her own reality.

Adoni and Mane (1984) argued that the mass media play an important role in the construction of social reality. They identified three types of reality: Objective social reality is experienced as the objective world outside the individual and which confronts him or her as facts. Symbolic reality consists of any form of symbolic expression of objective reality such as media contents. Subjective social reality is the reality where the objective and the symbolic realities together determine the construction of an individual's own subjective reality (Adoni and Mane, 1984, pp. 325–6). Kepplinger (1979) also argued that individuals may have primary experiences, ('situationally-based knowledge') or secondary experiences ('media-relayed knowledge'). Secondary experiences could, under certain circumstances and up to a certain degree, be functional alternatives for primary experiences (Kepplinger, 1979, p. 165). The media's role is to build an information system which reduces the complexity of reality by providing selected information according to certain regulations (Kepplinger, 1979). In the absence of personal experiences, the way in which news portrays death may influence how audiences experience it – and their behavior when they do experience the death of someone close to them.

The background on the concept that news is socially constructed is useful, as it presents the theoretical starting point for many studies discussed in this book. Many are concerned with the way that journalists construct news about death and thereby create certain realities for audiences. This is evident, for example, when journalists choose to report some types of deaths over others. Research has found that murders are much more likely to be reported than deaths from natural causes. If such news coverage was the only basis for a reader or viewer's knowledge, they may get the impression that hardly anyone dies from natural causes anymore and that society is becoming ever more violent. But of course news content is only one of many resources in the social construction of knowledge, and most audience members would know from personal contacts that more people still die from natural causes.

A holistic perspective of news

As this study attempts to comprehensively map the scholarship on death in the news, a holistic approach is needed. Truly holistic approaches have been relatively rare in journalism and communication research, as most studies have specifically examined one of the following: producers, the content or its effect on audiences. As John B. Thompson (1995) has pointed out, mediated communication in general is always a contextualized social phenomenon, which is embedded in social contexts. He argues that these social contexts are structured in a number of ways, which again have a structuring impact on the communication. Thompson (1995, p. 11) says it is 'easy to focus on the symbolic content of media messages and to ignore the complex array of social conditions which underlie the production and circulation of these messages'. Similarly, Hamid Mowlana (1997) has called for comprehensive studies to include a careful consideration of four stages: the source, the process of production, the process of distribution and the process of utilization. To do so, he argues, researchers need to move beyond the existing political, economic and sociological models and incorporate anthropological, linguistic and socio-cultural frameworks (Mowlana, 1997, p. 231). Lie (2003) also advocates a media holistic perspective in research. 'The holistic perspective means that an element in a structure is studied as being an element in that structure. Thus the structure becomes more important than the separate elements. The whole is more than the sum of the parts' (Lie, 2003, p. 45).

This book therefore examines studies of death in the news media from all angles: the multiplicity of paradigms, the constituents of the communication process itself and perspectives on various time periods. Death in the news has been explored from a variety of paradigms and, as will become apparent from reading this book, the multiplicity of approaches to the topic in itself demonstrates the need for more inter-disciplinary work in this area, as past studies have tended to stay within one particular paradigm, neglecting insights from other areas. The study further aims to take a holistic approach to the field not only in terms of considering the complexity of various approaches and disciplines, but also by examining the entire communication process to create an overall picture of how death is reported in the media. In this way, it looks at studies of journalists and content (such as the reports and images of death), as well as the effects this content may have on the audience. In order to put the current state of scholarship and journalistic practice in context, the book furthermore provides background on what we know about how death has been represented in the public sphere over the ages. It also speculates about how changing societal attitudes and technology may affect the representation of death in the future. It is important to point out, however, that this study mainly examines representations of death in Western countries, predominantly in the Anglo-American world, as there is currently very little research available from non-Western countries' reporting of death. Wherever possible, non-Western studies are included, but there is in fact an important gap in the literature in this regard, an issue which will be discussed throughout the book.

The representation of death in the media is an extremely complex issue, which researchers have battled with somewhat in the past. In the words of Jean Seaton (2005, p. 227), 'death in the news – apparently a simple, verifiable fact – is in reality a many-faceted phenomenon, open to a thousand interpretations and presentations'. In order to map the divergent strands of research then, this book sets out to approach the research along thematic lines in order to eventually provide a synthesis of what we know about the coverage of death in the news and, more importantly, what we still need to find out.

Organization of the book

This book examines the vast amount of studies which in some way relate to non-fictional representations of death and dying in the news media. That includes a varied array of theoretical and methodological approaches. The aim of the book is to analyze them comprehensively in order to integrate existing knowledge. It was therefore decided to loosely base the book around the dominant scholarly approaches, focusing on production, content and reception of news media messages about death. Organizing the book in this way will also enable readers looking for a particular approach or a particular aspect of the coverage of death to use it as a reference work.

Before embarking on this analysis, however, it is necessary to provide some background to the representation of death today. In this vein, Chapter 2 provides a contextual account of how death has been represented over the ages. This includes early representations of violence in the Roman Empire through to accounts and drawings of death in early news pamphlets in Europe during the sixteenth and seventeenth centuries as well as the display of death in various forms during Victorian times. A common thread throughout this chapter is the notion that the seemingly ubiquitous presence of death in the mass media today is, as Seaton (2005, p. xix) has argued, 'only the latest manifestation of the long history of the public representation of cruelty'. In this regard the chapter examines and integrates the general debates about the presence of death in the public sphere. By examining and critiquing the differing viewpoints about the historical development of the presence or absence of death in the public sphere in the latter half of the twentieth century, a contextual groundwork is laid for Chapter 3, which examines research into the large variety of general representations of death in the news media.

These studies, which have been largely quantitative in nature, examined in quite some detail the representation of a variety of deaths in the news media. The aim of this chapter is to provide an overview of existing research, highlighting its strengths and weaknesses as well as pointing out the gaps that still exist. The chapter investigates representations of deaths based on how people died, as well as the growing literature on obituaries. The debate about an over-representation of unexpected and violent deaths leads to an analysis of whose deaths are more worthy of being reported, with special consideration given to the deaths of children. Particular attention is also paid to studies of foreign deaths. In this regard, the chapter examines notions of how these 'others' are represented in the reporting and whether the deaths of certain 'others' (for example those from proximate cultures) are more likely to be reported than deaths from people in distant cultures.

Chapter 4 moves forward from mere textual analyses to include the examination of the visual coverage of death, which has been at the forefront of many debates in the field. One crucial area of debate here is the disagreement over how graphic the reporting of deaths in Western news media actually is. While some scholars see a surfeit of gory images, quantitative assessments have actually found that the news media very rarely show anything beyond the bounds of taste and decency. The chapter also contributes to the discussion about how much space news reports about the deaths of others are given by examining the way in which news photographs draw distinctions between the dead from other countries. In particular, journalism's role in war is a point for special attention in this regard.

When reading much of the literature on the coverage of death and dying in the news media, one notices a certain preoccupation – in both quantitative and qualitative approaches – with the way in which death is displayed and what the consequences of this may be for the audience. Yet, little attention has been paid to the production side of the process. Chapter 5 addresses this previously neglected area of research. Very few studies have actually examined the content producers and how they might deal with the task of covering death on an almost daily basis. Even those studies that have included interviews with journalists (for example, Moeller, 1999; Hanusch, 2008a) have tended to be limited in scope, although they have been able to uncover some of the rationales behind news decisions in relation to death. Of primary concern in the production of news about death in recent years has, however, been the way in which journalists' work impacts on news producers themselves. A growing amount of research into post-traumatic stress in journalists has found consistent evidence that at least a significant minority of journalists suffer from such stress, which has even led some to commit suicide.

Chapter 6 moves the focus to the way in which news reporting of death may impact on audiences. Two primary areas of concern have been prevalent in this regard. One relates to the notion of an assumed surfeit of photographic displays of death and violence which leads to compassion fatigue in audience members. This view sees stereotypical and increasingly graphic portrayals of death as a reason that audiences do not sufficiently care about the fate of victims of disasters and wars.

Yet a number of scholars reject such claims and point to the fact that news actually shows very few graphic images and that the argument about a lack of compassion is not rooted in empirical evidence. While few in number, some surveys have investigated audience attitudes to the reporting of death, with most people claiming they did not want to see gory images of death in the news. That such images can indeed hurt people is evident in the discussion of research from trauma studies, which have looked at the correlation between secondary traumatic stress and television viewing of terrorist attacks. Effects are also believed to occur from the news reporting of suicides, where media organizations have in recent years begun to establish guidelines in order to minimize the risk of copycat attempts.

The role of the media in instructing audiences in the appropriate ways of dealing with death is the focus of Chapter 7. This approach, which sees journalism as providing a commemorative discourse in order to allow audiences to deal with their grief at the time of high-profile death while at the same time reaffirming journalistic authority, is firmly grounded in a cultural approach to the study of journalism. Walter (2006) believes that the media has taken over the role which medicine and religion had previously played in reaffirming social ties and repairing the social fabric after a disaster. Noting this increased prominence of the news media as a kind of facilitator in the grieving process, there have been a number of recent studies which have examined the media coverage of death as a form of memory construction. These studies view journalists as cultural producers who are part of interpretive communities which employ cultural narratives to manufacture news. Zelizer's (1992) influential work on the assassination of John F. Kennedy has led to a burgeoning amount of literature on the role played by the media in the creation of collective memory. Within this field, particular attention has been paid to news coverage of the deaths of famous personalities, leading to the notion of commemorative journalism.

Looking towards the future, Chapter 8 focuses on mass media representations in an age when new technologies have become entrenched in both journalistic processes for gathering news as well as in the accessibility of information about death. While the impact of new technologies on the presentation and reception of death online is heavily underresearched, the chapter discusses and critiques the small amount of literature that exists in this field, and presents a number of case studies to highlight important points. The ever-increasing popularity of the Internet means that death is even more visible in the public sphere than it had previously been. The availability of graphic photos as well as video footage is having an impact on the level of gory details that audiences are able to see, such as the execution of Saddam Hussein or the beheadings of journalists Daniel Pearl and Nicholas Berg. This in turn has an impact on mainstream media, which can link to these sites, albeit often with relevant warnings. Additionally, the growing popularity of social networking sites such as Myspace and Facebook, as well as personal blogs, are increasingly being used by journalists in order to provide background information on victims of violence. This practice brings with it an ethical conundrum of whether it is acceptable to use private images posted in a public space. Furthermore, there now exist a number of online funeral and grieving sites, through which people are using the mass medium of the Internet to report deaths and grieve for the dead.

The conclusion, which is presented in Chapter 9, provides a synthesis of the arguments discussed in the book and offers an outlook on areas of the field which still need further attention from scholars. The main argument here is that past research has tended to be disparate, conducted within individual paradigms and lacking holistic, inter-disciplinary and comparative approaches. To this end, the chapter suggests three main considerations to take into account when studying the representation of death in the news.

2
A History of News about Death

There are some common accusations about the way in which today's news media cover death and dying: death on television is portrayed in increasingly graphic ways, news programs are full of death and suffering, and death is being more and more sensationalized by the media. The list goes on in a similar vein. The general perception is that we live in a time of over-saturation of violent and graphic portrayals of death and dying. News broadcasts are ostensibly full of wars, crimes and disasters, creating an image that things have never been worse. And as news organizations are competing as never before for the attention of audiences, this supposedly leads to increasingly sensationalized news coverage, where the old motto 'when it bleeds it leads' rules.

While the news today certainly contains graphic and shocking displays of death and dying now and then, it is difficult to generalize about a perceived increase without comparative examples. So before we make sweeping assertions and argue that things have never been this bad before, we first need to look at what it has actually been like. Too often, normative statements are made with insufficient context, and it is necessary that we examine how death and dying has been on public display in the past, before making any meaningful comparisons. As this chapter demonstrates, the display of death and dying in the public sphere – and particularly in the news – has a checkered history. There have been times when blood and gore were quite prevalent in public discourse, while at other times they may have been hidden, or – as Mellor and Shilling (1993) have famously argued – sequestered. In fact, the extent to which death is present or absent in public discourse has been part of a major debate among scholars in the history and sociology of death and dying.

We therefore need to be very careful not to make any simplistic assertions about the nature and visibility of death in the news media. Rather, the coverage of death in the news needs to be seen in context. The context, that is, of the society and age in which these representations circulate. In his influential book *The Power of News*, Michael Schudson (1995, p. 203) has argued against the 'retrospective wishful thinking' that has occurred from time to time when scholars have argued about the existence of a golden age of journalism. News media are a reflection of the society they operate in, and as such it is important to examine wider societal developments and situate the representation of death in news against this background.

For instance, it is impossible to talk about only one discourse of death in the news. As this book demonstrates, the coverage of death and dying in the news – and the resulting scholarly approaches – are much too complex to be able to reduce death in the news to one paradigm. This is because death itself cannot be tackled from a reductionist perspective. In fact, the sociologist Glennys Howarth argues that death is immensely complex and cannot even be reduced to a basic distinction between public and private presence. 'It appears in both spheres, in expected and unexpected forms, natural and unnatural, to the willing and to the reluctant' (Howarth, 2007, p. 35). It is important to heed Howarth's warning when embarking on any analysis of how death is covered in the news; and this will certainly be the case when examining how death has been portrayed over the centuries. Quite often, the context (frequently a political one) is important in our understanding of, for example, why coverage was quite graphic in reporting during the Vietnam War, as compared to the near absence of any kind of death in the reporting of the first Gulf War. A comparison between these two wars alone should put to rest any undifferentiated view that the coverage of death has become consistently more graphic.

Before embarking on a historical overview of the coverage of death in the news, however, we first need to look at broader sociological developments. The next section sketches an outline of existing studies into the sociology of death and dying, in order to shed some light on how societies have dealt with the end of life throughout history.

The history of death and dying in society

At the crux of the issue of the (mass) mediation of death and dying is an argument over whether death is present or absent in public discourse, in particular in the news media. Researchers argue that the way in which death is portrayed in the media gives us clues as to how society views and experiences death. Up until the last two decades of the twentieth century, the prevailing view among scholars was that death had become absent from public discourse, and moved into the private realm, becoming somewhat of a taboo. This claim had been popularized by the French historian Philippe Aries (1974), who famously argued that death was forbidden in modern society.

In his seminal work which tracks how Western attitudes to death have changed over the past two millennia, Aries develops four periods through which we can analyze the history of death: the era of 'tame death', 'death of the self', 'death of the other' and 'invisible death'. Aries argues that for the first millennium, 'tame death' was characterized by an unspoken acceptance of the end of life, and people believed in an afterlife (or what Kellehear (2007) calls the 'otherworld'), which was connected with the earthly life. Yet around the turn of the first millennium, an era of 'death of the self' began, which was to last until the eighteenth century. Here, Aries sees a progressive emergence of people wanting to play an active role in their own death and in the process they individualized the experience of dying. The one controlling authority over death here was religion, or the church. In fact, as Howarth (2007, p. 20) notes, 'life, particularly for the poor masses, was made sense of in the context of death: poverty, misery and injustice were compensated by rewards in heaven and the promise of eternal joy'.

However, as Aries points out, the rise of secularization in the sixteenth and seventeenth centuries changed all that, and coupled with advances in the sciences, particularly medicine, death became a social problem to be controlled. Thus, Aries argues, death became more and more removed to the private sphere. Now it was the small family that was at the center of the experience of death, and a variety of cult-like practices emerged. During Victorian times, people kept the memory of their loved ones through *memento mori* such as paintings, photographs, death masks and busts of the deceased (see, for example, Ruby, 1995; Jalland, 1999). Visits to graves were also quite common, as was children's literature on death, which served the purpose of both scaring children into obedience and reducing the fear of death. In a way that many in the West would probably consider 'creepy' nowadays, people regularly took staged photos of their dead children – some in their caskets, others with surviving siblings at their side – and hung them in their homes or sent them to friends and relatives (Burns, 1990). Displays of grief in public were also quite frequent, although the 40-year period of Queen Victoria's public grief for Prince Albert probably still needs to be considered as excessive even in those times (Jalland, 1999). The Victorian era has often been held up as the high point of the public display of death, and is seen as the starting point of death becoming a more and more private affair.

During the 1920s, death was removed from the home to hospitals and nursing homes, and quickly disappeared from public view, leading Aries to call this period the time of the 'invisible death'. Religious and social rituals declined in importance, and it became more and more difficult for individuals to deal with their dying, as well as for the bereaved to deal with their grief. The removal of death and dying to the medical sphere thus resulted in the culture of a denial of death, according to Aries.

In his history of dying across the millennia, Kellehear (2007) also points out that dying (and the subsequent biological death) in the hunter-gatherer period was very much a community affair, which became progressively more private as humans began to live in permanent settlements. Dying became something shared with only the small family and a few friends, rather than the entire community. Even later, during what Kellehear calls the Cosmopolitan Age, dying has come to be an entirely individual and privatized affair. Importantly, however, he also points to a contrary development to the privatization of the dying experience. While dying became more privatized from the previous communal experience, the determination of dying has gradually become based less on personally observed criteria and more publicly controlled through murky institutional standards. This evolution became necessary as individual experiences of dying became more privatized. This meant that fewer people knew what dying was like and most, therefore, relied on the expertise of outsiders. Progressively, then, recognition of dying moved from individuals to nursing homes and governments. This, Kellehear (2007, p. 254) argues, has made the process of dying also a much more political affair: 'Every form of dying throughout human history has exhibited important political and moral dimensions. We now live in a time when these dimensions emerge at the forefront of their sociological influence on dying, even determining its very definition and who is eligible for its bestowal.'

The shift away from public bereavement to death and dying becoming a more private affair was also identified by Gorer (1965), who argued that natural death was excluded from public discourse. In his seminal article 'The Pornography of Death', Gorer argued that there had been a reversal of attitudes to sex and death since the nineteenth century, leading to death becoming the new taboo. 'Whereas copulation has become more and more "mentionable", particularly in the Anglo-Saxon societies, death has become more and more "unmentionable" *as a natural process*' (Gorer, 1965, p. 195; emphasis in original). However, Gorer (1965, p. 197) also noted that while natural death had become 'smothered in prudery', violent death was being increasingly displayed to mass audiences. This, he argued, had led to so-called 'death-denying' societies in the West.

This view of a 'sequestration of death', or 'removal of death from the public to the private realm' was also supported by Giddens (1991), as well as Mellor and Shilling (1993). Mellor and Shilling argue that the processes of secularization and privatization that have occurred in modern society have actually left many people alone in their quest for values that can guide them through life. While death may have been as unpleasant as it is nowadays, 'the encompassing religious orders assured both the terminally ill and the bereaved that death was "meaningful"'' (Mellor and Shilling, 1993, p. 415). Yet, the advent of Protestantism began to change attitudes to death, progressively instilling a fear of death over the past century. Arguably then, one could postulate that perhaps predominantly Protestant countries may be less inclined to show death than countries where Catholicism is the dominant religion, perhaps because Protestant countries tend to be more secularized. Staudt (2009a) finds it curious that America saw death increasingly repressed in the public sphere between the 1920s and 1960s, at the same time as Americans were becoming more secular. Since the 1960s, she argues, death has increasingly moved back into the publish sphere, while society has experienced an increase in religious matters. Some anecdotal evidence actually exists to support this claim, with scholars reporting that news media from catholic countries such as Spain and Italy, as well as much of South America, tend to show more graphic images of death than the media of Northern European and North American countries (see, for example, Paschalidis, 1999; Castanos and Muñoz, 2005; Seaton, 2005). However, very little empirical research has been undertaken so far to verify this claim, and, as Staudt (2009a) points out, such cross-cultural conclusions may be very difficult to prove scientifically.

Part of the argument for the sequestration of death has been the fact that most people are much less often confronted with death in the modern age than they may have been as recent as one or two hundred years ago. Back then, the average life experience was much lower and the child morbidity rate much higher. Death, until really not that long ago, was a common occurrence, and more people noticed the process of dying as groups of people lived closer together. However, with the advent of secularization, death began to be seen as something that could be avoided. This was later coupled with medical advances which enabled people to live longer than they would have previously. Simpson (1972) notes that death became something that was somebody's fault, as if death could always be prevented as long as one had enough money and the medical team worked hard enough. All these developments, according to the theses by Aries and others, led to the banishment of death and dying, as well as bereavement, to the private sphere.

In more recent times, however, a majority of scholars argue that death is moving back into public discourse, or perhaps that it was never as forbidden or removed as some have claimed. One of the strongest advocates of this view, British sociologist Tony Walter (1991, 1994), argues that social scientists are reconsidering the dominant preconceptions of the role of death in modern society. Walter (1996) identifies three dominant discourses through which death and dying have been seen over the course of the past centuries. In traditional societies, death was seen through the dominant prism of religion. Here, death was accepted and people lived with it, coping through prayer. In modern societies, medicine became the dominant discourse – death became something to be controlled and was avoided in conversation. Walter then identifies a third stage, that of the postmodern society of the mid to late twentieth century until now. Here, psychology has become the dominant discourse for dealing with death. There is greater emphasis on the individual, a return to 'living with dying' and people are expressing their feelings to cope with death. Walter (2006) notes that, in the reporting of disasters, the media, for example, are playing an increasingly important role in this expression of feelings. He argues that, following such disasters, media reaffirm social ties and repair the social fabric. In that regard, media take on parts of the role that medicine has played in the past. Bradbury (1999, p. 1) agrees with Walter when she argues that 'with the close of the modern era the privatization and sequestration of death that had become the mantra of social scientists has slowly been eroded by a new openness.'

Staudt (2009a) sees the beginning of this increased death awareness in the famous book *On Death and Dying* by Elisabeth Kübler-Ross (1973), which was first published in 1969. The book has been credited with opening up the public discussion of a topic which had previously been quite repressed. Since that time, Staudt argues, death has progressively moved further back into the public realm, and this has included the discussion of death in the news media. She argues that while death may still be hidden or invisible in some instances, movements to the contrary are now so strong that surely we can assume to have entered an entirely new era of how society deals with death. 'Instead of looking away, we are now trying to figure out techniques for observing death safely and with some level of comfort' (Staudt, 2009a, p. 3).

In a study of UK newspaper coverage of death, Walter *et al.* (1995, p. 583) also strongly refute Aries' (1974) claim that 'death no longer makes a sign'. In fact, they argue that death is by no means absent from public discourse but rather present in a variety of forms in the mass media. Walter *et al.* (1995, p. 582) note that 'a smaller proportion of the population of contemporary Western societies dies in any one day than in any society at any time in the history of humankind, yet through the news media death is now extremely visible'. However, they concede that only a minority of deaths is actually reported in the news. Furthermore, the stories that are reported concentrate on the deaths of public figures or the public deaths of private individuals. 'The deaths boldly headlined and portrayed by the news media are extraordinary deaths.... They are also types of death which, unlike the majority of deaths, typically occur in a public place' (Walter *et al.*, 1995, p. 594). Adding support to Walter's observations in regard to the presence of death in public discourse, Glennys Howarth (2007, p. 35) notes that 'whilst there is no doubting the privatization of many aspects of dying and grief, it may be that in their quest to uncover hidden death, social theorists have neglected to acknowledge the more public face of death'. Howarth also identifies the importance of avoiding simplistic divisions and dichotomies, as there is of course no such thing as one Western culture. In fact, pointing to social and cultural diversity in the West, Howarth (2007, p. 39) argues that 'denial of death might more properly be identified as a neglect of marginal experiences and practices surrounding death and dying'. This general debate about the presence or absence of death in public discourse serves as a useful background when examining in detail some of the ways in which the news media has reported on death through the ages. Contrary to the perception that the display of death in the news is a recent phenomenon, the remainder of this chapter will demonstrate that journalists have regarded death as an important topic ever since the first periodicals appeared.

Pre-journalistic representations of death and dying

While Johannes Gutenberg's invention of the movable type printing press in the mid-fifteenth century is generally credited with making the birth of the newspaper industry possible, interest in news has existed for as long as humans have inhabited the planet. News has always been of central concern to any society, be they pre-literate hunter-gatherers trying find out where the buffalo are grazing, or modern mediatized societies wanting to know what their celebrities have been up to. The types of news we desire differ quite markedly, and while some news are important for our lives in a very practical context, others are driven by our general curiosity in the fortunes of other people. But whatever the reason, humankind has always had a great 'hunger for awareness' (Stephens, 2007, p. 12).

Because death plays a central – if at times hidden – role in our social existence, news about death has been a significant component of any news delivery system. So for the earliest representations of death, we need to look much further than the birth of the newspaper. Accounts of death and wars have been important at all times, and Pheidippides' famous run from Marathon to Athens to report a Greek victory over the Persian army in 490 BC is a relevant part of this history. Interestingly, too, the fact that Pheidippides, according to legend, died shortly after having delivered the news, plays a central role in this story, as his death from exhaustion makes his efforts all the more dramatic.

However, news of death would have played a vital part even in pre-literate societies because of the impact death can have on disrupting the social order. While they were not used to inform about death in the sense that we understand news in the modern age, some of the earliest known representations of human life in the cave art of Stone Age people contained depictions of dead people (Kellehear, 2007). Borg (1991) believes that one of the earliest representations of human death as it happens (as opposed to those showing mythic heroes who were already dead) were displayed by sculptors in the Pergamon in the second century BC to illustrate the defeat and death of the Gauls. Focusing on the political role that such representations of death always play, Jean Seaton (2005) argues that it is significant that these first representations were of defeated enemies rather than the deaths of the victors. Indeed it is a tradition that finds expression in modern-day news reporting of wars, which rarely shows 'our dead', but treats 'their dead' more liberally.

In her seminal treatise on the historical development of news about violence, Seaton (2005) sees striking similarities between the violence on display in the Roman Games and that in modern news stories, particularly when viewed in terms of spectator demand. She argues that the Games played an integral part at the height of the Roman Empire, rather than contributing to its decline. In fact, she claims, the Roman Games and modern news media are similar arenas where politics are played out. Seaton believes the Christian martyrs, because of their decision to die willingly rather than be frightened by death, challenged the existing

order in the arena. 'Through their exploitation of the meaning of the
dominant entertainment the Christian martyrs unequivocally won the
struggle for control of public opinion' (Seaton, 2005, p. 71). This, she
says, is comparable to today's use of a variety of political interests, particularly suicide attacks, which manipulate the shared conventions of
the news.

Reports of death were also invariably a component of the early
newssheets which existed in Rome. The *acta diurnal populi Romani*, written by hand and displayed in public places, contained official news,
mostly featuring government announcements, official ceremonies and,
as one might expect, news of births, deaths and marriages. Giffard (1975,
p. 107) notes that the *acta* was also full of accounts of wars, as well as
'earthquakes, eclipses, famines and prodigies'. Later, the chronicles even
included news of crimes and divorce, and strayed increasingly into news
about social life and, as Stephens (2007, p. 57) reports, a large number of
human interest stories: 'Pliny the Elder attributes to the *acta*... the story
of the execution of a man whose dog simply would not leave his dead
master's side, even going so far as to follow his master's corpse into the
Tiber River in an effort to keep it afloat'.

In an interesting comparison to today's objections to the news media's
emphasis on gossip and entertainment, Stephens (2007) points out that
such complaints existed even during Roman times, notably by states-
men like Cicero, who objected vehemently to being sent too much
'tittle-tattle', such as reports of gladiators, burglaries and adjourned tri-
als. These kinds of perceptions, thus, have a long history, and 'people
have been following such stories, and high-minded people like Cicero
have been complaining about them, for millennia' (Stephens, 2007,
p. 55). In addition, Roman mosaics provide some striking examples of
the extent of gruesome imagery that existed of death. While it would
be hard to argue that those mosaics had any standing as documentary evidence comparable to modern photography, they are nevertheless
illustrations of the level of violence in that society. Seaton (2005,
p. 74), for example, reports that 'Roman mosaics abound with images
of detached or about-to-be detached body parts'.

An extension of this in historical terms and, as Seaton (2005) argues,
a further link to news representations today, is the development of
Christian imagery that has accompanied the rise of that faith. Seaton
makes the point that the representation of suffering has a long tradition in religion. She tells us that this viewing of 'others' real pain' is not
new, and in fact 'controlled brutality, designed for both an immediate
and a distant audience, played a central part in classical civilization', not

only in the way its representation shaped this suffering but also how it instructed audiences in their responses to it (Seaton, 2005, p. 84).

Accordingly, Seaton believes that the news media still display a number of religious elements, despite the fact they evolved out of secular ideas. She observes that many modern-day news photographs of mothers grieving for their children echo the *pietá* which developed in Europe in the fourteenth century (Schiller, 1971). The *pietá* (which is the Italian word for compassion) depicted the Virgin Mary cradling the lifeless body of Jesus in her arms, an image that was replicated numerous times over the centuries, and the most famous of which would have to be the sculpture La Pietá by Michelangelo, created in 1499. It would seem that in almost every natural disaster or war, some newspaper or TV outlet ends up depicting an image that resembles the *pietá*. Such pictures of mothers and fathers holding their dead children can often bring home the impact of a war or natural disaster. But they are also formulaic, in that they are repetitive and evoke certain emotions in us. This was the case in one particular photograph which emerged from the events of 11 September 2001. Taken by Shannon Stapleton from Reuters, it depicts the moment when rescue workers carry out the dead body of Father Mychael Judge, who had been killed in the lobby of the North Tower as the South Tower collapsed. Father Mychael's body is in a chair, his head tilted to the right, being carried out of the debris by five men, including two firefighters and a policeman. The image quickly became one of the most powerful photographs of the day, and has since been referred to by some as the 'American Pietá' (Prigge, 2006).

Seaton observes in her book that a crucial point which connects news to religious imagery is that both purport to show the truth. 'Christian imagery and the news share a relationship to truth. They do not merely represent reality: they also claim to be guarantors of the veracity of the events they depict. There may be elements of fantasy or imagination, and both are conventionalized, yet they claim a special relationship with the real' (Seaton, 2005, p. 92).

Death and dying in early newspapers

In around 1450, Johannes Gutenberg became the first to use a movable type printing press, an invention that would revolutionize the way news could be relayed. While the Chinese and Koreans had been experimenting with and using movable type, they had been restricted by the difficulties associated with the large number of characters of their languages. Gutenberg's press, in contrast, 'offered huge advantages of speed, convenience and quality of impression' (Stephens, 2007, p. 74). The resulting spread of printing presses around Europe, and the arrival of the first newsbooks, which were at first published in irregular intervals, opened up the transmission of news to ever growing audiences and increasing mass production. This new development obviously led to a lot of experimentation by publishers, who began to print news of all kinds of events.

Once more, death was a topic of considerable interest. Not only did the early English newsbooks report regularly about various European wars, but as Stephens (2007) highlights, they also focused to a large degree on subjects of human interest. He insists that when it came to graphic coverage of events, the newsbooks were in no way different from some of today's publications. 'Anyone who clings to the notion that today's sensationalism, as practiced by a supermarket tabloid, cable news show or even the most shameless journalist, is unprecedented could be set straight by viewing any of a number of 16th or 17th-century newsbooks' (Stephens, 2007, p. 100). In fact, sex and violence were the bread and butter of a number of newsbooks, and Stephens argues that the sixteenth and early seventeenth centuries seemed to exhibit a special desire for blood and gore.

To prove his point, Stephens (2007) cites a 1624 newsbook, entitled *The crying Murther: Contayning the cruell and most horrible Butcher of Mr. Trat*. Using language that one would be hard-pressed to find in today's media, the story is told of the murder of the curate of a Somerset church at the hands of three men and a woman. The murder apparently happened in the most gruesome of manners, and the description in the newsbook was no less so, explaining that the murderers 'did cut up his carcass, unbowel and quarter it; then did they burn his head and privy members, parboil his flesh and salt it up, that so the sudden stink and putrefaction being hindered, the murderers might the longer be free from [discovery]' (cited in Stephens, 2007, p. 100). This was followed by an explicit description of how Mr Trat's various body parts had been disposed of. Stephens argues that journalists have always had a fascination for sex and violence, and, as the public gobbled up these newsbooks, one could well argue that there exists a hunger in the public that desires such reports. In fact, Stephens (2007, p. 104) points out that the presence of this unprecedented amount of news about violence was not due to an increase in violence, but rather the new opportunities offered by the arrival of the printing press to distribute such news, which opened up new and larger audiences, 'whose appetite for sensation was, more or less, normal'. Speaking of 'new and larger audiences', however, we still need to remember who constituted these audiences. As Wiltenburg (2004) points out, it was in fact not the masses of lower classes, but the upper classes, the literate elites of society at the time, who were able to read newsbooks. Only when literacy levels in society at large were raised much later were newspapers able to reach the types of readers that ostensibly tabloid newspapers aim for in the modern age.

The developments in reporting on crime in England were quite similar to those in other European countries. In Germany, a number of printed non-periodical newsbooks and leaflets appeared in the early sixteenth century, usually reporting about a variety of events (Kunczik and Zipfel, 2005). One particular type of newsbook, the so-called *Newe Zeytung*, was very similar to the early newsbooks in England. Jürgen Wilke (1984) in fact has noted the importance that news of murders, brutality, executions, catastrophes and monstrosities played in these newsbooks. 'Quite a number were illustrated, and they amaze a modern-day observer with their at times meticulous, almost cinematic accounts of violence and atrocities' (Wilke, 1984, p. 244, my translation). In fact, wars, and the violence that came with them, seem to have been a major preoccupation of these newsbooks. Wilke (2005) notes that a study by Pfarr (1983) found three quarters of these *Newe Zeytungen* between 1512 and 1662 were predominantly about politics and the military, with a further four out of five political news stories concerned with war-related events.

And while photography was still hundreds of years away from being invented, woodcut images in some of these pamphlets often provided additional, and quite often extremely graphic, detail to the written accounts. The advantage of such images, of course, was the fact that even non-literate members of society were able to understand the stories that were being told (Wiltenburg, 2004). Publications were able to provide the appearance of blood through coloration, and some even provided diagrams of severed limbs – 'a sort of parts diagram showing the body reconstructed like a jigsaw puzzle' (Wiltenburg, 2004, p. 1390).

When newspapers were started in the new colonies in the Americas, death and violence were also high on the agenda for editors. Kitch and Hume (2008) point out that the first newspaper in North America, *Publick Occurrences Both Forreign and Domestick*, published in 1690, was filled with stories about death. The paper's owner, Benjamin Harris, had previously published the *Domestick Intelligence* newspaper in England, the first issue of which reported a story about a man hanging 'by the Arms in a Wood...with his Head and Hands cut off, and his Bowels pulled out' (cited in Stephens, 2007, p. 162). Add to that the story of poor Mr Trat, and one could certainly be forgiven for thinking that disemboweling was a popular pastime of murderers in those days. Other colonial newspapers were no different in their sensationalism, their pages replete with 'coverage of crime, disasters, accidents, sex scandals, monstrosities and executions' with at times extremely explicit descriptions (Copeland, 1997, p. 82).

Of course we need to question the veracity of such accounts. The stories of crimes were so full of gory details and hard-to-believe deeds that one might easily dismiss them as fiction. And, as Wiltenburg (2004) points out, their constant claims to truth make them perhaps even more questionable. However, it is equally important to remember that different standards of truth applied in those times. Here, Wiltenburg refers us to the work of Lennard Davis (1983) who argues that deeper moral truths were more important to tell than exact factual details which we understand as literal truth nowadays. Thus, whether the events that were reported in these early news accounts actually occurred in exactly the way described is perhaps not as important as the lessons they aimed to provide to their readers. In this way, we can see how newspapers even in those early days attempted to instruct readers in the ways in which they should respond to certain events in life. This 'instructive' function will resurface later in this book when we discuss the way in which news media provide their audiences with model ways of grieving for the dead.

The introduction of the penny press

The sensationalism that occurred in the early newsbooks only widened in the nineteenth century with the arrival of mass-circulation newspapers, which provided their readers with increasing amounts of images of death and destruction. Technological advances in printing, the arrival of machine-manufactured paper and, importantly, the invention of the steam engine, allowed newspapers to be produced much more cheaply and in a much better quality. In addition, literacy rates in the general public improved. All these factors enabled newspapers to quickly develop from providing (mostly political) information to the privileged few to reaching mass audiences. Stephens (2007) notes that, while the old Gutenberg-type presses had been able to produce around 125 copies per hour, in 1840 the *Sun* in New York City could be printed at a rate of 4000 copies per hour using a steam press. Only 11 years later, this increased to 18,000 copies per hour. Newspapers increasingly focused on the business aspect of their venture, in their effort to reach as many people as possible so as to attract more advertising. These newspapers could also be sold much more cheaply, with many early publications selling at just one penny, hence establishing the name 'penny press' in the middle of the nineteenth century. Here, a new form of popular journalism developed, aimed at working-class audiences, and one whose mix of crime and human interest stories was not unlike that provided in the early newsbooks centuries before (Stephens, 2007). The development of the penny press is relatively well-documented, and it is often seen as having laid the groundwork for modern newspapers (Thompson, 2004). In particular, the penny press distinguished itself by its dramatic focus on human interest stories, crime, war and disaster, providing many sensationalized accounts of these events. The arrival of the penny press is generally acknowledged as the beginning of sensationalism in the news media, but as we have seen throughout this chapter, human interest stories and sensationalized accounts have always been an integral component of news. Even Cicero was already complaining about such 'tittle-tattle'. The difference during the nineteenth century was that newspapers were now accessible for almost anyone. So while the sensationalism on display in the penny press may not have been new or all that different from the earliest newspapers (see also Nordin, 1979, on sensationalism in the early American press), it is the circulation seen in the days of the penny press that made the portrayal of death more ubiquitous in society.

Another remarkable development occurred at around the same time as the establishment of the penny press. The appearance of a number of illustrated magazines in Europe and the United States began to provide a large amount of visual coverage of all kinds of events. The nineteenth century not only made the production of newspapers cheaper and more efficient, but due to other technological improvements it was now also much easier to include images in these publications. Previously, very few people would have been exposed to much visual imagery. Up until the late eighteenth century, the reproduction of images was very costly and they could usually only be reproduced 400 to 500 times. However, at the turn of the century, vast improvements in wood-engraving and the invention of lithography, perfected over the ensuing decades, enabled printers to produce multitudes of images to a higher quality and with less cost (Burant, 1984). The illustrated press, while not able to compete with the cheap penny papers, placed a lot of emphasis on using elaborate images to report on events and it was popular with less literate segments of society. The images would originally consist only of artists' impressions replicated through woodcuts, which had become considerably cheaper during the nineteenth century. Towards the end of the century, the ability to reproduce photographs in newspapers and magazines would give the reporting on death and dying an entirely new perspective.

In her in-depth analysis of the French news weekly *L'Illustration*, Christina Staudt (2001) tracks how the magazine treated the subject over the course of the nineteenth century. Established in Paris in 1843, *L'Illustration* quickly established itself as a prominent magazine, and it distinguished itself through its lavish illustrations, at first made of woodcut and metal etchings, and later consisting of photographs. Staudt observes that during its early years, the magazine refrained largely from showing death in its pages, apparently testing its readers' sensibilities about what was acceptable to be shown. Over the years, however, and coupled with technological innovations as well as increased competition, *L'Illustration* 'increasingly allowed for a piercingly close and clear look at the dead' (Staudt, 2001, p. 362). Towards the 1890s, obituaries focused more and more on the actual death of a famous person, rather than their life. Quite contrary to obituaries in modern newspapers, the magazine published detailed, close-up photographs of the deceased on their deathbed. Further, while in the 1840s most photos of wars and disasters had concentrated on the general damage to buildings and the like, at the end of the nineteenth century, photos focused almost exclusively on the dead. The self-censorship which had been applied to photos of corpses earlier in the century was completely abolished, with the magazine offering 'a vast selection of deformed human remains and skeletal bodies for scrutiny by the reader' (Staudt, 2001, p. 285). The images of death were also regularly used to endorse certain political goals as well, such as patriotism and promoting a republican state with order and individual freedom. In fact, the display of death became so common that 'it is a rare issue of *L'Illustration* that does not contain at least one death-related image' (Staudt, 2001, p. 367).

In the United States and United Kingdom, the development was a slightly different one. Goldberg (1998) reports that the famous illustrated magazines such as *Harper's Weekly, Frank Leslie's Weekly* and the *Illustrated London News*, all established during the 1840s and 50s, covered murders and other crimes in quite considerable detail during their first two or three decades. Goldberg notes one particular story in *Frank Leslie's Illustrated Newspaper* from 1857, in which a Dr Burdell was viciously stabbed. A double-page spread in the newspaper included seven images with varying gory details, such as an image of the man's heart showing the injuries that were sustained, as well as an image of his face and the wounds it showed (Goldberg, 1998, p. 45). The *Illustrated London News* has also been shown to have contained, at times, quite explicit images of death (De Vries, 1967, 1973). And, much like Cicero was complaining during the times of the Roman *Acta*, the nineteenth century also saw objections to the sensational nature of news, which in turn are highly reminiscent of modern day arguments. In one such example, French poet Charles Baudelaire wrote in his journal in the early 1860s:

> It is impossible to glance through any newspaper, no matter what the day, the month or the year, without finding on every line the most frightful traces of human perversity.... Every newspaper, from the first line to the last, is nothing but a tissue of horrors. Wars, crimes, thefts, lecheries, tortures, the evil deeds of princes, of nations, of private individuals; an orgy of universal atrocity....
>
> (Cited in Sontag, 2002, p. 107)

Yet, around the 1870s and 80s, explicit images disappeared almost entirely from the pages of these illustrated magazines, while the stories themselves still presented quite graphic details at times. Goldberg (1998) has no certain explanation for this, other than the fact that at that time, the cheap tabloids began covering death in increasingly graphic detail. This ostensibly led to abstinence on the part of the illustrated press, which could not compete with the tabloids. Goldberg (1998, p. 42) notes that towards the last quarter of the nineteenth century, the illustrated papers 'disapproved mightily and vociferously of the explicit descriptions of violent crime in the cheap daily papers'. Nevertheless, reports of deaths were still quite graphic across the news media at the time. Seaton (2005) notes that war correspondents returning from the wars in the Balkans in the 1880s provided various detailed and vivid accounts of the massacres that took place there.

It is curious to note that this increase in the depiction of death in newspapers and magazines happens as the everyday experience of dying and death, the public death, was gradually being removed further into the private realm. Goldberg (1998) believes this is no coincidence. She argues that it is quite natural that, as fewer people had actual experiences with death, they searched for new ways to deal with their fears of dying. As a result, newspapers began simply to satisfy a desire for such images which existed in the general public. 'Even as death seemed to die and be properly buried, it sprang to life on the printed page and in various visual spectacles. Illustration moved in as death moved out' (Goldberg, 1998, p. 29). Of course at the same time, it was becoming much cheaper for newspapers to produce accounts and drawings of death, as well as, later on, photographs. We accept today that many people gain their knowledge of the world through the media; in fact one might say we live in a mediatized world. Using Goldberg's argument, the news media at the end of the nineteenth century started the long path towards becoming the main site for the public to gain knowledge about death in all its myriad forms. At the same time, news media increasingly told people what constituted 'good' and 'bad' deaths and how one should deal with them. As we have seen, early newsbooks took on this function as well, yet they arguably didn't have such a big influence at that early stage. Only with the arrival of newspapers printed for the masses during the nineteenth century did news begin to have a wider presence, particularly as the amount of primary experience people had with death declined.

When it came to sensationalism, the penny press was quickly superseded in the late nineteenth century in an even more drastic shift in the development of the mass media. The arrival of newspaper barons like Joseph Pulitzer and William Randolph Hearst in the United States, and Alfred Harmsworth (better known as Lord Northcliffe) in the United Kingdom also meant the dawn of a new era of journalism, usually referred to as 'new journalism' or 'yellow journalism'. Newspapers such as Pulitzer's *World*, Hearst's *San Francisco Examiner* and Northcliffe's *Daily Mail*, aimed to reach the wide masses courtesy of a low cover price and a mix of crusading politics, sensationalism, aggressive coverage and attention-grabbing campaigns (Stephens, 2007). The newspaper business once again expanded, leading to ever higher circulations that would soon reach more than one million on some days. More generally, the success of newspapers was now being supported by the emergence of one crucial component, without which we could hardly imagine newspapers today.

The arrival of photography

Photography had been invented as early as the 1820s, but it would take quite a few more decades until it became practical and relatively inexpensive to print photographs in newspapers. The earliest photographs appeared in newspapers around the 1880s, and while images had proliferated in the press by then in the form of engravings (which were often based on photographs) the impact was almost immediate. Above all, photography has one important advantage: Photographs claim to depict reality because they are action frozen in time. This makes them believable. Because they were produced by a camera, rather than an artist or engraver, they instantly assumed the mantle of being able to provide scientific evidence of an event. Andersen (1989) points out that this development occurred in line with a more general quest for scientific progress and emphasis on positivism. The camera, therefore, was 'viewed as the most accurate mechanism for revealing the physical world, the lens of the camera being considered more accurate than the lens of the human eye' (Andersen, 1989, p. 97).

There is obviously one great fallacy to this line of thinking. Cameras can only capture part of a scene, as restricted by the frame, and humans determine what gets to be in the frame. Thus, photographers are able to change and even distort reality, by focusing on one part of a scene but not another. And because early photographs needed long exposure times, only still scenes could be photographed, leading many a photographer to re-arrange the aftermath of destruction and death so as to make it more dramatic. Further, photographs are always displayed in a context, which can considerably change their meaning. While the implications of this will be dealt with later, I want to briefly outline here the impact that photography – and later the moving image –had on the development of the coverage of death in the news during the late nineteenth and early twentieth centuries.

Randell and Redmond (2008a) have drawn attention to the way in which photography quickly changed how death was displayed. They believe that photojournalism 'introduced a "reality" and an immediacy of representation that changed the image from one that was art-based, memorialized, and historical to one that was reality-based, democratic, personal, and everyday' (Randell and Redmond, 2008b, p. 2). We don't know when and where the first-ever photograph of a dead person was published, although it is likely, considering the tradition of publishing images of the dead during that time, that it wasn't a particularly extraordinary event. The earliest indication we have of photographs of death and destruction making it into newspapers actually stems from a time when photographs were still being transformed into wood engravings before they could be printed. Roger Fenton is generally identified as the first 'war photographer', having documented British military operations during the Crimean War in 1854 and 1855, but the first conflict to be photographed widely is one that happened only a few years later (Griffin, 1999).

During the American Civil War from 1861–65, photographers like Mathew Brady documented the horrors of the conflict in all their gruesome detail, and a number of photographs were published in newspapers such as *Harper's Weekly*. Others, such as Alexander Gardner and Timothy O'Sullivan also acted as chroniclers of the drama. Two of their most famous photos of that time show dead soldiers, even if the images' authenticity could be questioned in the sense that the bodies may have been slightly re-arranged for better dramatic value (Griffin, 1999). For the first time, readers were able to see more realistic depictions of how dreadful and cruel wars could be, when previously they had only been exposed to artistic presentations that inevitably glorified war. From now on, 'modern warfare was to be marked not only by mass armies and machines of mass destruction, but also by mass witnesses' (Paschalidis, 1999, p. 122).

Photographs of death have since appeared with some regularity. One other early documented example of death is the photograph of the execution of Ruth Snyder, which appeared in the New York tabloid *Daily News* in 1928. Snyder was sentenced to death by electric chair after her lover, Judd Gray, and she had been found guilty of murdering her husband. The case was classic tabloid fodder and the New York media was abuzz with salacious details of the proceedings. Even *The New York Times* reported the court proceedings daily on the front page, and above the fold (Ramey, 2004). Ramey has even compared the interest in the case with that shown to the OJ Simpson trial during the 1990s. With the court case finally over, Snyder was executed at Sing Sing Prison in New York State. The execution on 12 January 1928 was watched by 20 reporters, and one of them, photographer Tom Howard, snuck a miniature camera into the room and took a photo of Snyder at the exact moment of the execution. The image, which was slightly blurry as it captured the moment at which Snyder's body was twitching as a result of the electric shock, took up the entire front page of the *Daily News* the next day under the headline 'DEAD!' in large letters. The newspaper's circulation sky-rocketed as a result, reaching 1.5 million that day, at the time, the largest sale of any newspaper in American history (MacKellar, 2006).

But there have also been numerous instances where photos of death could have appeared in the news, and eventually did not. This has often been the case during wartime, when governments have imposed strict censorship – with perhaps Vietnam the exception. At the same time, a number of iconic war images do display death. One of the most famous war photographs of all time is the one taken by Robert Capa, which claims to show the moment a Republican soldier is shot during the Spanish Civil War in the late 1930s. The photo, usually referred to as the image of the 'Falling Soldier', or 'Death of a Republican Soldier', appeared in the French magazine *Vu*, and thereafter was published in *Paris-Soir*, *Life* and *Regards* (Brothers, 1997). The authenticity of the photo has been debated widely for some time, ever since Philip Knightley's (1975) original claims that it was staged. Most recently,

Spanish communications scholar José Manuel Susperregui has convincingly argued that the photo was actually taken some distance away from where the shooting had been claimed to have occurred, and in an area where no battles were taking place at the time (Rohter, 2009). While finding out the real story behind this iconic image is important in terms of Robert Capa's credibility of using photojournalism to provide documentary evidence, it is not the objective of this chapter. What is important is to acknowledge that photos of death began to become a relatively common occurrence in the press from the late nineteenth and early twentieth centuries.

As the mass media emerged as one of the most powerful pillars in Western society from the late nineteenth century onwards and people began to have less personal experience with death, they would be more and more frequently exposed to it first in newspapers and later in the electronic media, such as radio and especially through television. More recently still the Internet has provided an additional site for dealing with death. Many scholars argue that the display of death in the news media during the 1900s has proliferated to an extent that we are now saturated with images of horror and destruction like never before. As I will point out over the course of the next two chapters, this statement needs to be differentiated as the issue is quite complex. Certainly, however, the arrival of photography, and later television, made accounts of death and dying much more vivid. Goldberg (1998, p. 49) argues that 'many of the most famous news photographs of the century have to do with death', and, indeed, we can all easily recall seminal events in terms of the photographs which went around the world, from Capa's image of the Falling Soldier, the photos of the corpses in the Nazi concentration camps, Eddie Adams' iconic image of General Loan's execution of a Vietcong suspect, to footage of the assassination of John F. Kennedy and the subsequent shooting of Lee Harvey Oswald and, more recently, the hanging of Saddam Hussein that was filmed via a mobile phone and was widely available on the Internet. We will return to some of these images a little later in this book.

Conclusion

This chapter has demonstrated that representations of death have quite a long history. Humans have always recorded and commemorated deaths in their societies, so it is not particularly surprising that even the earliest accounts in writing dealt with the issue, such as the death notices and human interest stories in the Roman *Acta*. The early newspapers of the sixteenth and seventeenth centuries were no different, providing salacious reports from the depths of human nature. Gruesome murders were reported in harrowing detail, even though some sounded a little too outrageous to be considered true. Later still, as newspapers became much cheaper to produce during the nineteenth century and audiences expanded rapidly on the back of improved literacy rates, there were regular reports of death. Again, detailed images of death and dying – first as drawings, later as photographs – accompanied many such stories, continuing a tradition established over centuries previously. The development of the mass media during the twentieth century has led to an even larger amount of stories and images of the end of life. This has prompted a number of scholars to argue that death has never before been more present in the media.

At the same time, social historians have shown that death and dying became increasingly privatized in society at large during the twentieth century. While the death of a fellow human being was something most people had experienced in pre-settlement and even early settlement times, death progressively became a problem to be dealt with outside the home. Increasingly, people went to nursing homes and hospitals to die, and fewer and fewer people saw such processes occurring. Thus, many people did not know what death looked like, and the media began to fill the void. Yet, I would argue that it was not a case of the news media detecting this social need all of a sudden and fulfilling it. Rather, death had always been a hot topic in the news, even when attitudes to death were different. What did happen, however, was that such representations became more important to audiences who had lost touch with death. Sociologists even argue that the news, but also entertainment media, have taken over the role played by medicine and religion previously, and are now our primary way of experiencing death. As a result, we appear to be witnessing another shift in public attitudes to death during the early years of the twenty-first century. Staudt (2009b), for example, believes that we are leaving the age of the concealment of death and are entering a new phase of the recognition of death. She believes a September 2000 cover story in *Time* magazine is testament to that fact. The story, entitled 'Death in America', recounted the stories of dying Americans, complete with photographs. And indeed, if one looks at how death is dealt with on the Internet – the subject of a later chapter in this book – we can see that there seems to be a remarkable openness in talking about death and dealing with grief quite publicly. Yet, as Staudt acknowledges herself, mass death is still often concealed, frequently for political reasons, although I would argue also for economic, ethical and moral reasons, as journalists continually need to make judgment calls over what their audiences will find acceptable.

Looking at the evolution of news coverage of death throughout history thus gives us a much-needed perspective for analyzing how death and dying are represented in today's news media. For instance, some scholars believe that death has never been more present in the news. Similarly, many believe photographs of death are becoming ever more graphic in the detail they show. Yet, they rarely cite empirical evidence for such a claim. Death has been a topic in the news for centuries. As Seaton (2005, p. xix) has argued, modern news coverage of death is 'only the latest manifestation of the long history of the public representation of cruelty'. I would even argue that some of the early representations, such as those in the early newsbooks, were much more graphic in their detail than most of the reports we would see in today's news media. Largely, modern news coverage of death, while certainly prolific, has at the same time been hiding death, with very few Northern European and North American newspapers showing graphic images of death on a regular basis. So while death has perhaps become more public through its treatment and presence in the news, much of that coverage still tries to hide death. The reason that early representations were more graphic may lie with the fact that attitudes to death at the time were quite different, and death was perhaps more accepted. As death became more hidden in private, the actual representations, while overall certainly more numerous, have also tended to hide the actual moment of death as well. Journalists are members of the societies they live in, and therefore always hold and express to a certain degree the views and attitudes of the majority. In this way, they will be more likely to hold on to certain conventions in order to not upset their readers.

The following two chapters deal more closely with the way in which death is represented in the modern day news, from an overall perspective of the values placed on certain types of deaths and general textual representations, as well as from a visual perspective. This analysis demonstrates that the coverage of death in the news is complicated and varies over time and for certain events. Importantly, I will deal with some of the myths that have become established over time in relation to a perceived 'glut' of visible death in the news.

3
How News Media Place Values on Life

With the benefit of an historical context for the display of death in the news, I want to now examine in more detail some of the finer aspects of how the end of life is represented in today's media environment. I will focus here particularly on empirical evidence in terms of how prevalent death is, which deaths are accentuated in the news and, in the next chapter, how death is displayed through photographs. Interestingly, while death has substantial news value, and, as we have seen, has featured quite heavily in the news, very few studies have made death itself the center of attention. Mostly, studies have focused on deaths from violence, and have often been conducted within wider studies examining war reporting. Another focus has been on deaths from natural disasters, and how the locations of those disasters can have an impact on how prominent the reporting will be.

The vast majority of studies have been conducted from Western viewpoints and only examined how death is portrayed in Western news media. This has sometimes led to sweeping claims about how death is represented in the public sphere more generally, neglecting perhaps variations in terms of representations even within cultures (such as differences between tabloid and quality newspapers). Most importantly though, there have at times been implicit claims that death is displayed in the same way around the world. This, of course, is a dangerous assumption, and again we need to heed Howarth's (2007) warning that the debate about death in the public sphere needs to be treated in a differentiated fashion. We do know from anecdotal evidence that representations of death differ across cultures, yet no systematic comparative approach has been taken in this regard. Nevertheless, despite the varying contexts in which studies about death in the news have been conducted, when we put all those studies together, we arrive at a reasonably clear picture of how present death is in the news, which deaths are more likely to be covered, and the amount of graphic depictions we can expect in photographs.

The political economy of the media

Before we examine some of the more detailed studies into how death appears – and does not appear – in the news, it is necessary to briefly consider the context in which the news operates. Because of the importance of the concept of death for any society, and the resulting political repercussions which deaths can have particularly during wartime, a majority of scholars have examined these issues through a political economy context. In his seminal work on dying in the mass media, George Gerbner (1980) argued that portrayals of death and dying always served important symbolic functions of social typing and control. Thus, he argued, dominant social groups tended to be over-represented and over-endowed.

Seaton (2005) even believes that merely the fact that death is reported in the news gives it political relevance. Deaths therefore 'frequently represent conflicts of interpretation, the consequences of which are about the transfer of power' (Seaton, 2005, p. 211). Noys (2005) has also argued about the political importance of death more generally. The political economy approach to communication has long been a popular way of examining news content, and relations of power have been a focal point. As such then it is a more than adequate approach to examine how news media portray death, and many of the basic political economy arguments can be found to resonate in studies that have examined the coverage of death and dying.

Mosco (1996, p. 25) defined political economy as the study of 'the social relations, particularly the power relations, that mutually constitute the production, distribution and consumption' of communication, in a historical and cultural context. Political economy is thus concerned with ownership and control of the media, the strategies of corporate concentration and the links between media industries and capitalist structure in general (Sinclair, 2002). McQuail (2005) has noted that political economy theory has focused primarily on the relationship between the economic structure and dynamics of media industries and the ideological content of the media. Political economy views the media as part of the economic system and as closely connected to the political system. As a part of the economic system, the media is engaging in producing content and even audiences as a commodity. The result, then, is the increasing monopolization of the mass media, a loss of diversity and the reduction of less profitable operations such as investigative reporting (McQuail, 2005).

Yet, the political economy approach has also been criticized for placing too much emphasis on the production and distribution of content, while at the same time disregarding the meaning of this content. 'At its extremes, political economy does not dispute that media content under capitalism is ideological, but rather takes it for granted as obvious, unproblematical and transparent' (Sinclair, 2002, p. 27). Essentially, according to the political economy approach, the media act to reproduce the dominant ideology to the exclusion of those who lack the economic resources. Those who have the economic means will most likely not criticize the distribution of wealth and power, while those who do not have the economic means will not be able to publicize their dissent with the system for a lack of economic power (Murdock and Golding, 1977).

The relationship to the coverage of death in the news media should be clear. There always exist struggles over the meanings of death, and how these deaths are represented to audiences is part of this struggle. In their seminal work on the political economy of the media, Herman and Chomsky (1988) also noticed the importance death and dying play in the context of these battles for representation when they used a case study to compare US media coverage of the murder of a Polish priest with that of 100 religious murders in El Salvador and Guatemala. The details of the study are discussed later in the chapter, but suffice to say here that a large amount of the studies which investigated stories about death have done so from a political economy perspective. This short excursion into the basic concepts of the political economy of the media should suffice for now, but, due to the field's relevance, we will return to and elaborate on political and economic aspects of the representation of death again throughout the remainder of this book.

How people die in the news

A question that many researchers have asked themselves relates, on the most basic level, to how certain types of deaths are represented in news coverage. For example, a number of scholars have noted that some victims are simply seen as more worthy of our compassion than others. In his examination of killers and victims on US television programs, Gerbner (1980) argued that women and minorities were more likely to be represented as victims than others, as they were more marginalized.

This, he noted, had to do with the general power relations in society. Others have argued along similar lines. In her comprehensive examination of news reporting of death, Moeller (1999) stated that children and their mothers generally made for ideal victims. Höijer (2004) also notes that some victims are simply 'better' victims than others in narratives of death and destruction. She argues that adult men are usually not seen as worthy of compassion as they are typically not regarded as helpless or innocent. Elderly men, however, are considered weak and therefore more worthy of compassion. Such arguments are also supported in more empirical research. Sorenson *et al.* (1998) studied the news coverage of homicide in the *Los Angeles Times* and examined how well their findings compared to the epidemiology of homicide between 1990 and 1994. The news coverage did not correlate well at all with official homicide figures, as female, child or elderly victims were more likely to receive news coverage than others. This was also the case for those killed by a stranger and those who lived in wealthy neighborhoods. At the same time, Black or Hispanic victims and those with less than a high school education, as well as murders by firearm and murders where the victim knew the suspect well, were under-represented in the news.

If events contain any, or preferably a combination of these 'ideal victims', news coverage can elevate such events to a higher level, imbuing them with more relevance. Such an event, for example, took place on 1 September 2004, the first day of school after summer in the town of Beslan, in the southern Russian province of North Ossetia. On this day, a group of around 30 masked men took over the main school, holding well over 1000 people hostage in the process. The hostages included children, parents and grandparents as well as teachers. During the initial takeover of the school by what turned out to be people fighting in the name of Chechen independence, a small number of people were killed. The hostage situation continued for two days, until large explosions occurred in the gym of the school, where most of the hostages were held. In the resulting confusion more than 330 people were killed, including around 170 children and 30 kidnappers. The event triggered saturation coverage in the world's media, highlighting the importance the lives of children have in our world. As a case study of Beslan has shown, newspapers placed strong emphasis on the fact that children were involved, and developed a number of narratives around the issue (Hanusch, 2008b). The fact that the vast majority of photographs of children showed them being either carried by adults or with adults by their side also emphasized the vulnerability and helplessness of children. Similarly, stories focused almost exclusively on the children, while disregarding much news about the other dead involved. Thus, children were given the place of supreme importance here, in line with the notion that 'disasters involving the multiple deaths of children are used to reaffirm core values about the importance of children's lives, specific to late modern circumstances of extreme longevity and low infant mortality' (Seale, 1998, p. 125).

The value that is attached to some types of people may not be the same everywhere. Höijer warns we need to see the representation of death in the news in its relevant social context, for example, when it comes to issues of gender. 'That the ideal victim is a cultural construction becomes apparent if we consider historical and cultural variations in the victim status of women. Women who are assaulted by men are not always seen as victims, in some cultures not at all' (Höijer, 2004, p. 517). In a general context of social structures, it is not very surprising to find that some deaths are considered more important, or that some people are deemed more worthy of our attention. In their look at the anthropology of death, Palgi and Abramovitch (1984) noted that power structures in traditional societies had always meant that the death of a chief or a man of high standing had much wider-ranging consequences than the death of a stranger or slave. It is thus not extraordinary to see the deaths of powerful members of a society reported on in much more detail and with much more sensitivity than the deaths of ordinary people.

We have seen earlier that much of our experience of death in modern times has come through the media. But the types of death we are confronted with in the news are also the more unusual ones, despite their relative statistical insignificance. When we look at the news, it would seem that hardly anyone dies of natural causes these days, and that the world is full of murders, catastrophes and accidents. In other words, the deaths that are visible in the news are the unusual deaths. The reason for this lies of course in the nature of news, which often actively aims to provide reports of things out of the ordinary. So it is not surprising that content analyses of the causes of death in news reporting found a heavy reliance on violent death. In a study of US newspapers, as well as news and general interest magazines, Frost *et al.* (1997, p. 843) found that 'for most causes of and risk factors for death, there was a substantial disproportion between the amount of text devoted to the cause and the actual number of deaths attributable to the cause'. Among the causes of death that were most under-represented were tobacco use, as well as cerebrovascular and heart diseases. On the other hand, illicit use of drugs, death from car accidents, toxic agents and homicide were largely over-represented. Indeed, many more people die of natural causes every day than are killed violently, in accidents or disasters. In the United States, almost 50 per cent of people who died during 2006 did so because of two leading causes: heart diseases (including heart attacks) and cancer (Heron *et al.*, 2009). Yet only 5 per cent were killed in accidents, 1.4 per cent committed suicide and 0.8 per cent died as the result of a homicide. In other words, 34 times as many people die of diseases of the heart than are murdered. The situation is similar in many other Western countries.

In an examination of which causes of death were most prominent in two regional US newspapers, Combs and Slovic (1979) found that homicides, natural disasters and accidents were overemphasized in comparison to deaths caused by disasters, which were underemphasized. They also were not very surprised by this result, and cited as a major reason the fact such stories about violence generally provided more interesting and exciting news stories. Yet, a further reason was that violent death was likely a source of societal vulnerability about which people needed to be informed, while diseases 'may be less newsworthy because they are much more common, and inevitable, and because they most often take only a single life' (Combs and Slovic, 1979, p. 843).

A later study of the coverage of death in the foreign news sections of Australian and German newspapers found a similar reliance on violent death (Hanusch, 2008a). Violent death, including reports of bombings, suicide attacks and wars, accounted for almost 70 per cent of all stories about death, 12 per cent focused on fatal accidents and almost 7 per cent reported on deaths in natural disasters. In contrast, just over 7 per cent of stories focused on death as a result of natural causes, and not even 1 per cent of stories reported deaths from diseases. On the topic of deaths from diseases, Williams (1992) noted that in relation to the AIDS epidemic, US newspapers initially did not report the disease in much detail. Only when a public figure with whom journalists and the public could relate was affected, in this case actor Rock Hudson, did the coverage become more in depth. 'It changed the perception from a disease of Them to a disease of Us' (Williams, 1992, p. 10). This identification with victims is an important component of news coverage of death, as journalists are constantly aiming to enable their audiences to relate to events in stories.

A further type of death – suicide – has received some attention in the scholarly literature, even though it has been mostly approached from a media effects point of view, and will therefore be dealt with in more detail later. Suffice to say here that suicides are a particularly sensitive topic for the news media, who are often encouraged to avoid them completely or report only very sparingly, for fear of inspiring copycat attempts. In fact, Pirkis *et al.* (2007) found that only 1 per cent of suicides were reported in Australia. When the media do report on suicide, they have been found to partly reflect official reality (Pirkis *et al.*, 2002), but also to overemphasize some kinds of suicide (Pirkis *et al.*, 2007). In their study of Australian news reporting of suicide and mental health and illness in 2000, Pirkis *et al.* (2002) found 3762 news items on suicide alone, a surprisingly large number, although it was spread over quite a number of news organizations and types of media. The majority of these items were broadcast on radio, arguably a more fleeting medium than newspapers or television. In terms of the demographic groups which appeared most frequently, Pirkis *et al.* found that men and young people were prominent, as well as psychiatric patients, people in custody and indigenous people. While they acknowledged that particularly young males, but also psychiatric patients were indeed at higher risk of suicide than other demographic groups, they also noted that there were cases in which the news media representations did not coincide with official reality. For example, the primary focus in the news was on completed suicide as opposed to attempted suicide, even though the rate of attempted suicide is much higher in reality. Suicides by older people and women also tended to be over-reported, as were suicides using unusual methods (Pirkis *et al.*, 2007).

Others have found similar tendencies in news reporting of suicides (Michel *et al.*, 1995). The purpose of Pirkis *et al.*'s (2002) study was to raise awareness in the news media about the coverage of suicide. A follow up examination in 2008 actually found that Australian news organizations were rarely reporting the issue, 'unless there are compelling news values that promote the story onto the news agenda; namely the status of the person, the location of the death, the unusual or bizarre nature of the death, or the editorial decision that publishing the story is in the public interest' (Blood *et al.*, 2008). Such findings have been replicated elsewhere, for example in Scotland, where suicides were more likely to be reported if they occurred in a public place, involved a celebrity, were achieved by violent means, and involved males (Coyle and MacWhannell, 2002).

The values news media attach to foreign deaths

Identification with victims has been shown to be an immensely important consideration in journalists' decision-making about which deaths to report, and the way in which they will report them. Among journalists, there exist a number of – albeit tongue-in-cheek – formulas to identify how much deaths are worth when they occur abroad. In the United States, the formula goes something like this: 'One dead fireman in Brooklyn is worth five English bobbies, who are worth 50 Arabs, who are worth 500 Africans' (cited in Moeller, 1999, p. 22). It is somewhat similar in Australia, where a former foreign news editor stated this rule: 'One Australian is worth five Americans, 20 Italians, 50 Japanese, 100 Russians, 500 Indians and 1000 Africans' (Romei, 2004, p. 5). Of course these are only theoretical constructs and journalists do not sit at their desks with calculator in hand to decide which stories appear in the newspaper or news bulletin. They should further be understood as somewhat self-deprecating humor, because often journalists are only too aware of how difficult it is to choose some stories over others, and that this implies decisions about the values of people's lives.

At the same time, however, there is also a kernel of truth in these formulas. What they indicate is that we do possess certain parameters in our heads about the extent to which we can identify, and therefore perhaps also sympathize, with the misfortune of others. It is not, as Walter *et al.* (1995) point out, that audiences necessarily take particular pleasure in the pain of others, but it is about how people can identify with a story, be it because they have an affinity with the location or the nationality of victims. Therefore, there is a stronger interest component, something Walter *et al.* (1995, p. 587) call the 'it could have happened to me' factor. But the result of this, they argue, is often a de-personalization of distant victims, and a greater likelihood that graphic images may be shown. 'After the Armenian earthquake or during an African famine there might be accounts of a general state of shock, but not column after column about personal shock; there might be one representative personal story, but not story after story' (Walter *et al.*, 1995, p. 586). American journalist Walter Mossberg underlines the importance of location in deciding which deaths to cover:

> Is it a place Americans know about? Travel to? Have relatives in? Have business in? Is the military going there? You're not going to get on page one with something about Bangladesh nearly as much as you do with something about some country where your readers have some kind of connection . . . .
>
> (Cited in Moeller, 1999, p. 21)

At the same time, domestic deaths often evoke a heightened level of sensibility, so as not to upset readers or viewers who may have personally known the victims. For example, interviews with journalists have shown that they are extremely careful in this regard when covering domestic news of death (Hanusch, 2008b). Carruthers (2000, p. 277) also noted that the dead during 'one of "our wars" ' were also less likely to be represented in photographs, whereas it was more acceptable to show 'their dead'. Altheide (2003) argues that this process of othering defines people as outsiders, a process in which a dominant social group defines an inferior group. These minorities are thus under-represented in the media, which means 'lower numbers, less usefulness, fewer opportunities, more victimization ("or criminalization"), more restricted scope of action, more stereotyped roles, diminished life chances' (Gerbner, 1980, pp. 65–66). Seaton believes this kind of coverage mainly reinforces everything that is good about the society which receives the news, while portraying the reported society as one of social disorder. 'However weary, dirty, bloodstained, muddy, sweaty the observed society may be, reporters strive to appear clean, tidy and orderly' (Seaton, 2005, p. 217).

And, as Altheide shows in his analysis of how the victims of the 11 September 2001 attacks in the United States were portrayed, this can happen within one country, not just across borders. Comparing how September 11 victims were represented in the media with the portrayal of victims from other attacks, for example the Oklahoma City bombing in 1995, Altheide argues that the former were elevated to a more revered status, while the latter appeared somewhat less worthy. Hume's (2003) examination of the so-called 'Portraits of Grief' published in the *New York Times* following September 11 supports the view that these were 'special' victims. This is further indication of how political struggles over meaning appropriate news representations, as it would be hard to argue against the much higher political importance of the September 11 attacks.

Again, if we look at the political economy of the news process, the fact that victims who are 'like us' are preferred over the lives of people we have little in common with is not particularly surprising. Journalists work with their audience in mind, and it is a common belief that people are interested in the lives of people who are like them. That is, of course, a somewhat ethnocentric attitude, and even some journalists believe it is not the right one to take. Stephen Romei (2004), a former foreign news editor at *The Australian*, criticized it heavily, and said he believed the location of the event should be the least important issue. As unfair as it may seem, is it simply in human nature to feel more for those we can relate to? Moeller (1999, p. 22) seems to believe it is inevitable, when she says that 'we tend to care most about those closest to us, most like us. We care about those with whom we identify.'

Empirical evidence does support the tongue-in-cheek formulas presented earlier. A study of the coverage of death in a Scottish tabloid newspaper found that one of the main criteria for subjects' selection was their nationality, in that death stories from the United States and Western Europe were most likely to be reported in the paper (Meech, 1992). In an attempt to quantify the coverage of death from abroad, and perhaps come up with a formula to rival the tongue-in-cheek ones by journalists, Burdach (1988) studied a southern German tabloid newspaper's coverage of accidental death over a six-month period in 1972. Burdach measured the distances of each event to the newspaper's headquarters in Munich, and analyzed how many deaths had to occur at a certain distance in order to reach the minimum space of 10 cm^2 for a tabloid news story. His results showed that accidents at a distance of 10,000 km would need to show at least 39 deaths, those at 1000 km at least 6.5 deaths and those at a distance of 100 km only 1.1 deaths in order to qualify for a story.

Unfortunately, such an analysis proves overly simplistic when scrutinized. Geographical distance is indeed a factor in the process of deciding what makes news, as shown in a study by Singer *et al.* (1991), who concluded that geographic location influenced the space and time given to natural disasters in the press. But it is only one factor. Other links between countries, as Walter Mossberg's comments indicated earlier, surely play an important role, too. There are a large variety of countries at a distance of 10,000 km away from Munich, and they would surely not all be equal in terms of journalists' attention. One could be certain that a bus accident with, say, 10 deaths, would be much more likely to be reported if it happened in the United States than if the same kind of accident occurred in India or somewhere in Africa. By measuring geographic distance only, important political, economic and cultural links between countries are ignored, even though these may account for differences in coverage more frequently.

In an attempt to include a more differentiated approach to examining how natural disasters make the news, Adams (1986) analyzed US TV coverage between 1972 and 1985 and came up with a number of different factors. Dominant factors included the number of US tourists who visited a particular area, the number of estimated disaster deaths at an early stage, as well as the distance from New York City. Other measurable factors included the affected country's gross national product, political and economic ties with the United States, the number of

US citizens who have family ties with the affected country, as well as the proportion of leading journalists with the same ethnicity as the affected country. As part of Adams' analysis, we can also see what extensive influence a significant death toll can have. This is particularly important if an event happens in an area which is perceived as being prone to certain kinds of disasters. For example, an Australian journalist has been quoted as saying: 'You just get a bit immune to the buses going over cliffs in China and India, ferries going down in the Philippines or Bangladesh' (Hanusch, 2008a, p. 349). But at the same time, journalists admitted that if such an event had a large magnitude, especially in terms of an extraordinarily high death toll, it would move back into the center of attention.

It was arguably that combination of tourist numbers and the unprecedented size of the death toll which propelled the 2004 Boxing Day tsunami in South and Southeast Asia into the global media spotlight. While few serious academic studies have been undertaken into the global media response to the tsunami yet, a look at European, Australian and US news stories in the immediate aftermath, but also in the longer-term, appeared to concentrate mainly on the well-known tourist regions of Thailand and Sri Lanka (Hanusch, 2010). Because many Westerners had either visited the affected areas themselves, knew friends who had been there or were familiar with them through glossy tourism advertisements, the tsunami arguably affected them more than if it had only affected locals in, say Bangladesh or other flooding-prone areas.

Viewing death in the news through a political economy approach

As alluded to previously, the political economy approach has been a popular way to examine the reasons for why some deaths are reported while others do not rate a mention in the news at all. We have seen that the status of a person, their age and gender, are all important factors, particularly when the deaths have occurred in the news organization's home country. Another important factor is the cause of death, that is, whether it is the result of violence, an accident, a disaster, a disease or whether it is a natural death. But when it comes to deaths from abroad, explanations provided by political economy scholars have dominated the discussion. One reason lies in the fact that international news in general has been predominantly examined from a political economy perspective.

At the heart of those studies has been a concern about perceived imbalances in the international news flows. In a seminal study of news values – criteria which journalists employ to determine if an event will make the news – Norwegian researchers Johan Galtung and Mari Holmboe Ruge (1965) had argued that distance and lack of political and economic links were significant factors in some countries (particularly African and Latin American nations) receiving very little attention in the news. And if they did, it would usually only be because of major negative events, such as disasters and wars with a large toll, creating an image that these countries were bereft with problems. While Galtung and Ruge's study has been criticized on methodological grounds and some of the news values have been updated or redefined (see, for example, Schulz, 1976; Harcup and O'Neill, 2001; Koponen, 2003), their work has influenced a large number of follow-up studies, which have largely confirmed some of the main arguments. Tsang *et al.* (1988) noted that between 1970 and 1986 alone, at least 150 research papers were published which examined the flow of international news.

The two major worldwide studies into international news flows, conducted under the aegis of the International Association for Media and Communication Research (IAMCR) and UNESCO, found that geographic proximity, as well as political and economic factors, dominated news decisions. The first study, conducted in 1979 and covering 29 countries, found that events in a country's immediate geographic region dominated the news (Sreberny-Mohammadi *et al.*, 1984). But there was also an imbalance in the amount devoted to developed countries as opposed to developing countries. In news about developing countries, bad news made up a significantly larger number of news items, and the emphasis was on political crises and wars. There also existed an imbalance of news flow, with the Third World receiving far more news about the First World than vice-versa. In a follow-up study in 1995, researchers confirmed many of the main findings in terms of geographic regionalism, and political and economic linkages (Stevenson, 1997).

The argument over the imbalance of news flows and the marginalization of developing countries in a world news system that was dominated by Western political and economic interests even reached some of the highest policy levels at one stage. During the 1960s and 70s, a movement by developing countries argued for a New World Information and Communication Order (NWICO) in a number of international forums, most notably UNESCO, in an attempt to wrest some of the control of international communication flows from developed countries. Developing countries wanted to be able to report stories using their own journalists rather than having to rely on the Western-dominated news agencies. They also wanted to cover stories that would be of higher relevance to the developing world. In essence, they felt the need to balance all those negative stories about wars and disasters with more positive coverage (Hachten, 1999). Western opponents, however, argued it was merely an attempt to politicize international news, as, in their view, the NWICO sacrificed press freedom for the sake of beneficial reporting of a country. While discussions were increasingly intense for some time, leading the United States, Great Britain, Singapore and a few others to leave UNESCO, there was never any real resolution of the debate (Hachten, 1999).

Nevertheless, against the background of these disputes, a number of media scholars began to develop arguments around cultural and media imperialism, which critiqued the media within a framework of imbalance between the developed and developing countries (see, for example, Schiller, 1969). It was the marginalization of other countries, and particularly the framing of countries and actors whose political ideologies did not agree with those of the United States that were at the heart of Herman and Chomsky's (1988) argument in their seminal study *Manufacturing Consent*. Herman and Chomsky saw the media as reflecting dominant political interests and as important agents in propagating dominant ideologies. Their study is of particular interest here because of its examination of deaths in those countries of the periphery, which are often marginalized and under-represented in the news. It shows that through the media's news coverage, some people could be deemed as more worthy than others. At the same time, such coverage tells us who not to care about, thus affecting our potential levels of compassion for victims. We will examine issues around notions of compassion more closely later, but it is already important here to speculate about such audience reactions because of the fundamental role the audience plays in the news process.

Herman and Chomsky compared the coverage of the murder of a Polish priest with that of 100 religious murders, including those of some high-ranking church members as well as four US nuns, in El Salvador and Guatemala, across four US mainstream media outlets: the *New York Times*, *Time* magazine, *Newsweek* and CBS News. They found that the murder of the Polish priest, Jerzy Popieluszko, was both quantitatively and qualitatively more intensely covered than all the other cases taken together. This type of coverage, Herman and Chomsky argued, created two categories of victims. So-called 'worthy victims' were people who were abused in enemy states, as Poland at that time was part of the Soviet bloc. On the other hand, people who were abused by the United States, or one of its allies, were portrayed as 'unworthy victims'. Indeed, they found that coverage of worthy victims' deaths was much more comprehensive, including gory details and expressions of outrage and demands for justice. On the other hand, victims who were regarded as unworthy were given scant attention in the news and descriptions were less detailed. In line with some of the formulas presented earlier, Herman and Chomsky also employed an analysis of the number of articles per death and claimed that the worth of the Polish priest was between 137 and 179 times that of one of the victims in El Salvador and Guatemala. Or, in other words, 'a priest murdered in Latin America is worth less than a hundredth of a priest murdered in Poland' (Herman and Chomsky, 1988, p. 39).

In a more recent study that bears some similarities to Herman and Chomsky's effort, Christensen (2004) examined the coverage which a number of political murders received in the United States and the United Kingdom at the dawn of the new millennium. The study analyzed the deaths of Serbian Prime Minister Zoran Djindjic, Democratic Republic of Congo President Laurent Kabila, Swedish Foreign Minister Anna Lindh and Dutch Politician Pim Fortuyn, who had all been killed by assassins in politically-motivated murders. Sampling four quality newspapers from each of the two countries, Christensen found that roughly two-thirds of UK newspaper stories dealt with the Fortuyn and Lindh killings, while one-third dealt with those of the other two. In US newspapers, however, the trend was reversed, with 34 per cent of stories focusing on Fortuyn and Lindh and 66 per cent on Djindjic and Kabila. Christensen argued that the relatively heavy coverage of the Fortuyn and Lindh killings in the UK supported the assertion made by previous studies that Western media tended to marginalize events in culturally and politically non-proximate regions.

As for the US newspapers, Christensen believed that US foreign policy interests in the Congo and Serbia could be held mainly responsible for the high level of coverage given to the deaths there. But he was surprised that in the United Kingdom the killings of two national leaders in Djindjic and Kabila were overshadowed by the deaths of a foreign minister and an un-elected head of a then-minority political party. He suggested that it wasn't always the geo-political importance of a victim which was decisive, but that cultural and physical geography could play a more significant role. In addition, Christensen noted that political assassinations were quite unusual for such peaceful countries as Sweden and the Netherlands, and the killings therefore 'did not fit with stereotypical images of Swedish and Dutch societies' (Christensen, 2004, p. 36). On the other hand, political and social upheaval had been framed as the order of the day in Serbia and the Congo, and killings were therefore not so surprising.

This notion of cultural distance and a generally more complex decision-making process was extended in a comparative study of Australian and German quality newspaper coverage of foreign deaths, which employed a newly-developed holistic framework that could take account of a variety of cultural factors for analyzing death in the news (Hanusch, 2008b). In particular, the study criticized political economy of potentially limiting the analysis too much, and neglecting the influences which other factors, such as cultural values, could play in the decision-making process. Examining closely the kind of language used in stories about deaths from abroad, the study was able to identify a number of cultural factors at play (Hanusch, 2008d). Interviews with journalists further reinforced the notion that the process was incredibly complex. Thus, political or economic factors were but one part of the bigger picture.

A further way in which death appears regularly in the news is actually outside its prominence in the day-to-day news coverage. Newspapers in English-speaking countries in particular have a long tradition of honoring their dead through retrospectives about their lives. Who is remembered by way of such obituaries and how this is done can also give us clues to the values that are seen as important in a society.

Placing values on death through obituaries

Much of our knowledge about the study of obituaries is owed to the work of Nigel Starck (2005, 2006, 2007, 2008a, 2008b), who has extensively traced the history and modern practice of obituaries in the United States, United Kingdom and Australia. The earliest obituary, according to Starck (2006, pp. 3–5), was published on 2 July 1622 in an English newsbook, and recounted the life and death of Captain Andrew Shilling, who was a member of the East India Company. Obituaries soon became quite popular, growing in popularity in eighteenth century newspapers in Britain, before the practice was exported to America and Australia. During the nineteenth century, obituaries became ever more elaborate, before they hit a wall somewhat and were neglected between the 1920s and 80s. Since the 1980s, however, scholars have identified a remarkable return of the genre's popularity, attributed widely to developments in the United Kingdom. There, the establishment of *The Independent* and its new brand of obituaries, as well as the appointment of a new obituaries editor at the *Daily Telegraph*, revolutionized the practice (Fowler, 2007, pp. 6–7). More recently, the resurgence of the obituary in the United States and the United Kingdom has even led some US newspapers to allow ordinary people to write paid obituaries in an attempt to halt sliding revenues (Starck, 2008b). Whereas before the 1980s, newspapers gave relatively little space to obituaries, they are now a regular feature, to which newspapers like the *Guardian*, for example, devote at least two or three pages a day (Starck, 2008a). Originally, obituaries have tended to commemorate the lives of the powerful members of society. On some occasions, such as recent terrorist attacks, ordinary people's lives have also been given attention. Only four days after September 11, the *New York Times* began a series of obituaries on those who died in the World Trade Center collapse. The series was highly successful with readers and ran as a regular feature until 31 December 2001, during which time it had featured more than 1800 portraits in total (Scott, 2001). Similarly, when 202 people died in a terrorist bomb attack on the Indonesian island of Bali, including 88 Australians, *The Australian* newspaper published a series of obituaries under the banner 'Lives Cut Short' (Josephi *et al.*, 2007).

Just as much as news stories about death have been accused of bias, so have obituaries received attention from critical scholars. The idea behind this has been to examine which kinds of people newspapers consider newsworthy and thus important enough to have their lives commemorated through an obituary. If we look at the empirical evidence, similar trends to those in general news coverage emerge. For one, men are highly more likely to be featured in obituaries, as a number of quantitative analyses have found. In an early study, Kastenbaum *et al.* (1977) found that only 20 per cent of *New York Times* and 19 per cent of *Boston Globe* obituaries focused on women, a trend that was confirmed in Ball and Jonnes' (2000) extensive analysis of the *New York Times* spanning six years. Ball and Jonnes noted a very similar figure of 17 per cent for *The Times*, while Moremen and Cradduck's (1998/1999) comparative analysis of US quality newspapers even put it at only 12 per cent. In that study, other newspapers were found to have given women slightly more space, although they were still strongly under-represented. The *Los Angeles Times* devoted 19 per cent, the *Miami Herald* 24 per cent and the *Chicago Tribune* 29 per cent (Moremen and Cradduck, 1998/1999). In the United Kingdom, the figures are equally poor for women. In an analysis of obituaries in the *Guardian* during June 1995, Bytheway and Johnson (1996) found that

only 18 per cent were written about women. Starck's (2008a) comparative analysis of quality newspapers in the United Kingdom identified
similar figures, ranging from a low of 13 per cent for *The Times*, to
15 per cent in both the *Independent* and the *Daily Telegraph*, to a 'high'
of 19 per cent in the *Guardian*. Interestingly, Starck notes that the
Guardian's infrequent, reader-solicited obituary section called 'Other
Lives' actually devoted much more space (39 per cent of obituaries) to
women. Starck (2004) has also found a neglect of female achievements
in the Australian news media during a study he conducted for his PhD.
Melbourne newspapers *The Age* and *Herald Sun* fared only marginally
better than their UK counterparts, with women making up 24 and
23 per cent of obituaries, respectively. In the *Sydney Morning Herald*, this
figure rose to 28 per cent. On the other hand, there is an argument to be
made here that, as newspapers focus on elites, the gender bias depicted
in obituaries is merely a reflection of these societies which have been
historically male-dominated.

  While the biggest focus has tended to be on gender, studies of obituaries have found a number of other trends as well. As noted already, elites
are much more likely to be covered than ordinary people. Having a good
education seems to help here as well, as noted in Ball and Jonnes' (2000)
New York Times study and confirmed in Starck's (2008a) analysis of UK
newspapers. Performing artists, politicians, members of the military and
professionals tend to be among the most visible in obituaries. Fowler's
(2007) quantitative analysis of obituaries in UK newspapers (*The Times*,
Guardian, Independent, Daily Telegraph), as well as *Le Monde* and the *New
York Times*, has also demonstrated this dominance of the upper classes.
Within such a range of newspapers, however, there are important differences as well. As Fowler (2007, p. 132) notes, *The Times* and *Daily
Telegraph* tend to focus more on the aristocracy, while the other papers
focus on people without titles.

  There are aspects of ethnicity as well. Fowler notes that, not surprisingly, the vast majority of obituaries – around 70 per cent in UK
newspapers – are about citizens of the newspaper's country of origin.
Outside of their home country, however, newspapers tend to heavily
focus on people from similar cultural backgrounds. So, for example, US
citizens feature heavily in UK newspapers, whereas citizens of Asia, the
Middle East and Third World countries only make up between 12 and
7 per cent. However, that is only a relatively recent practice, as *The Times*
in 1948 and 1900 did not feature any people from colonized countries
or the Third World. Further, only the *Guardian* and *Le Monde* can be
deemed as outward-looking, according to Fowler (2007, p. 151). Those

two newspapers were also the only ones to give Blacks any meaningful coverage, at 9 and 8 per cent respectively, as opposed to only 4 per cent in the *New York Times*, for example. Hume (2000) has similarly noted that, over the course of American history, First Nations people have been very rarely profiled in obituaries, and during the twentieth century basically disappeared from their pages.

As we can see, then, much attention has been given to the way in which newspapers in the United States, United Kingdom and Australia pay tribute to their dead through obituaries. This practice of remembering the dead is not always replicated in other areas of the globe, however. While newspapers in the English-speaking world generally tend to commemorate the lives of famous people through stories written by journalists, this is not necessarily the case elsewhere around the world. In Iceland, for example, the vast majority of obituaries are actually written by ordinary people about ordinary people. Arnason *et al.* (2003) report that obituaries are a hugely popular pastime, with the biggest national newspaper *Morgunbladid* allocating up to 10 pages daily to accounts of Icelanders' lives and deaths. In a further interesting development, which Arnarson *et al.* attribute to a rise in spiritualism, many people can now have any number of obituaries written about them. In addition, many people even address the deceased directly in their obituaries. These obituaries are also generally not commissioned, and the authors do not have to pay any money for them to be published. Arnarson *et al.* note that around one-third of Icelanders are believed to read obituaries on a daily basis.

Some countries do not even generally use the obituary form to memorialize their dead. For example, Josephi *et al.* (2007) point out that there is no real obituary tradition in the German news media, perhaps with the exception of news magazine *Der Spiegel*. They believe that the main reason for this is a difference in legal and ethical constraints on the news media in the United States, United Kingdom and Australia on the one hand, and Germany on the other. While in English-speaking countries, people can generally not be defamed once they are dead, that is not the case in Germany. In addition, German ethical codes are quite explicit in their restrictions of how deaths can be reported, leaving very little room for any personalized stories, such as in the 'Portraits of Grief' or the 'Lives Cut Short' series.

This section has only examined the way in which obituaries tend to focus on certain types of people, but not others, in order to compare this to other news representations of death. But obituaries serve another important function in the way in which they portray 'ideal' lives to readers, thus instructing them, in a sense, on what is needed to lead a good life. In doing so, newspapers emphasize cultural values that readers are supposed to hold dear, a practice we see through much of what is usually referred to as 'commemorative journalism'. Because this is quite a wide-ranging area, it will be dealt with separately later.

Conclusion

This chapter has examined the way in which deaths are portrayed in the news today, pointing particularly to how certain lives appear to be valued over others, both in news coverage and in obituaries. One popular news value for journalists is 'the unexpected', or something out of the ordinary (Galtung and Ruge, 1965). It is for this reason that the more rare deaths, such as murders and accidents, are given significantly more coverage than those deaths that are relatively common, like those from heart disease. Further, murders and accidents usually cut people down in their prime, rather than at the end of a long and fulfilled live. They also generally involve the agency of other people, and therefore can be better placed in a journalistic narrative that looks for conflict.

Decisions about which deaths to include in the news are guided by wider cultural perceptions of whose lives are valued the most. Members of society who are deemed to be weak and defenseless, such as the elderly, women and children, tend to be over-represented, while adult men are often under-represented. Social status is also influential, as political, economic and cultural elites tend to be better known and are more powerful in society; therefore their deaths are more likely to be reported as well as remembered in obituaries.

Perhaps the largest amount of research on textual representations of death has been conducted on the values that are invariably placed on people's lives from abroad. The dominant finding in this area has been that the deaths of people who are like us are much more likely to be reported than deaths from countries with which our society has very little connection. As a result, most Western countries' newspapers place exceeding emphasis on deaths from other Western countries. Certainly there are cultural reasons for the imbalance of news reporting on death, but quite often the argument has been made also for political and economic reasons. In particular, Herman and Chomsky's (1988) work here has been influential. Other studies have confirmed the importance that geographic distance, political and economic links can play in determining whether a death makes the news. Of course, news organizations aim to present news that is relevant to their audiences, and as such will be more likely to cover places and people with which they may have an affinity. Arguments about simplistic mathematical formulas that are employed by journalists are obviously made in jest, even if the trends behind them are found in actual coverage. There is some truth to statements like 'one dead fireman in Brooklyn is worth five English bobbies, who are worth 50 Arabs, who are worth 500 Africans' (cited in Moeller, 1999, p. 22). But the process is more multifaceted, with a complex interplay of cultural, political and economic factors, as studies examining a variety of factors have shown. Thus, if foreign deaths include people who are like us, or they occur in countries with which we may have some affinity, be it even only through tourism, events are more likely to be reported. Unexpectedness again features here as a news value in that, surprising events are more likely to be reported than expected events. For example, if certain types of disasters or accidents happen again and again in a place, they may lose novelty value and therefore go unreported after some time. It was shown that fatal floods in Bangladesh, for example, have become such a common occurrence that many journalists do not see them as news anymore. The only thing that could return such events into the spotlight would be extraordinarily high death tolls.

We can see, then, that the basic news decisions about which fatal events to report are guided by political, economic and cultural influences. But this chapter has mainly looked at textual representations of death, and, in an increasingly visual age, the way in which death is portrayed through images is of growing significance. The next chapter therefore deals with the visual display of death in the news in more depth.

4
Visual Displays of Death

In an increasingly visual world, images of death have attracted considerable attention from scholars interested in how the end of life is displayed in the news. This is of course not surprising, as photographs and films have the ability to *show* us death, and to directly confront us with its reality. Written or spoken accounts can provide us with graphic details as well, and while they are often gruesome, seeing blood and gore for oneself is a lot more persuasive. We trust photographs and films simply because 'seeing is believing'. In fact, in today's world, as Susan Sontag (1977, p. 5) has argued, 'a photograph passes for incontrovertible proof that a given thing happened. The picture may distort; but there is always a presumption that something exists, or did exist, which is like what's in the picture'.

The arrival of photography in the nineteenth century allowed audiences to witness conflicts in ways they never could before. As a result, war and all its horror was now available to everyone: 'All those civilians, who were traditionally cut off from the direct perception of the war, were now able to be there, right in the front line, witnessing the bloody aftermath and carnage of the battlefield through the intrepid eye of the war photographer's camera' (Paschalidis, 1999, p. 122). Photographs, and later moving images, have come to stand in for reality, and while the veracity of textual accounts is often questioned, images are less so, despite the fact that it is relatively easy to manipulate their meaning. As a result of their ability to project reality, images, and particularly those that depict death and destruction, are seen as potentially powerful pieces of documentary evidence which are regularly used to make political points. This is because images rarely stand on their own. They are always woven into narratives, and most newspapers frame photographs in a certain way even by merely adding a caption or publishing them alongside news stories. One of the most important tenets of the practice of journalism is that it purports to tell stories that are true (Hartley, 1996), and the truth claims of images constitute a large part of that contention. Zelizer (1995) has traced the evolution of photojournalism to the 1930s and 40s – the time of the Spanish Civil War and World War II. She argues that photojournalists tried to establish their legitimacy by offering 'a "visual expansion" of journalistic practice, one that appears to increase the truthfulness of news and extends the adage that "the camera does not lie" to journalism's primary authority, the reporters' (Zelizer, 1995, p. 136). Journalism at the time was placing a lot of emphasis on its role of providing objective reports, and it was this aspect that photojournalists were encouraged to stress in their work as well. Yet, as Zelizer points out, photos are rarely published on their own, and are thus always supported by the written word, giving them more legitimacy, but also framing them in a certain way (see also Entman, 1991). This information around the photographs is incredibly important, as a caption can change the meaning considerably. Susan Sontag (2003, p. 10) reports that at the beginning of the conflict in the Balkans, 'the same photographs of children killed in the shelling of a village were passed around at both Serb and Croat propaganda briefings. Alter the caption, and the children's death could be used and reused.'

Brothers (1997) also argues that photographs are always published in a context of the cultural circumstances at the time, and therefore exist rarely in isolation or without meaning. As the next section will discuss, photographs are seen as having a denotative level – what they physically represent – and a connotative level – the meanings attached to that representation. While these always exist in some combination, this chapter will deal primarily with the denotative level, in order to examine just how much death is shown in the news, and in what way. I will also draw on some discussions about their meaning, but a later chapter will deal in more detail with the effects and potential meanings of such reporting on death. Primarily, this chapter is concerned with examining claims that the news media are publishing evermore graphic images of death, that there is an excess of blood and gore in the news. As we will see, there is considerable evidence to suggest otherwise.

Semiology and the analysis of photographs

Before we look more closely at the representation of death in photographs, it is important to briefly examine some theoretical background. Photography, when invented in the mid-nineteenth century and used in newspapers a few decades later, came to be known as providing accurate depictions of reality. After all, a machine – the camera – took the photos, and there was therefore no possibility of manipulating photographs. As such, photos are often seen as pieces of documentary evidence. The argument is that, quite simply, 'pictures don't lie'. And, of course, on a simplistic level, this argument is not wrong. What is depicted in a photograph is indeed what has actually happened. Robert Capa's 'Falling Soldier', discussed earlier, actually did fall, there is little doubt about it. But photographs can only ever show a part of the reality they capture, restricted by the size of the frame. We do not see a shooter so how can we know there was even anyone there? What may or may not happen around the camera is not seen in the photo. Similarly, photos always require an interpretation. The point of discussion in the case of Capa's photograph has been whether it actually depicts what its caption states: That it features a Republican soldier at the moment of death at Cerro Muriano in Spain. All it can really prove, however, is that a soldier fell. The site is not clearly identified, and it has actually been argued that the photo was taken near the town of Espejo, where, at the time the photo was presumably taken, no fighting occurred (Rohter, 2009). As a result, it would appear the photo may have been staged, dramatically altering its claim as a piece of documentary evidence, a claim that is central to the practice of journalism. Many of the photographs from other early wars were at least partly staged, for a variety of reasons, though mostly to dramatize the scene they depicted (see, for example, Griffin, 1999). And in more recent times, of course, the possibilities of digital technology have enabled photographers and editors to digitally alter images, in effect changing the depiction of reality as well.

The analysis of photographs therefore needs to examine such images not only on the superficial level of what they depict, but also the interpretations that an image can lead to. A particularly popular theoretical framework for the analysis of photographs has been the concept of semiology and its application in the work of French philosopher and linguist Roland Barthes (1967, 1972, 1977, 1981). Barthes built on the theory of semiology for analyzing language, which had been pioneered by Swiss linguist Ferdinand de Saussure (1983) in the 1916 work *Course in General Linguistics*, a collection of his notes published by de Saussure's students three years after his death. De Saussure argued that language operated through signs, which consisted of a signifier (the sound or image of a word) and a signified (the concept evoked by the signifier). Thus, the word 'ox' is a sign composed of the signifier (its appearance, that is, the physical letters o and x) and the mental concept (oxness) that one has of the type of animal. The mental concept depends on one's cultural surroundings. An Indian farmer, for example, would likely have a very different mental concept of an ox compared to that of an English person (Fiske, 1990). Importantly, there is no direct relationship between the signifier and the signified. It is entirely arbitrary, as there are no physical connections between the two.

Barthes (1967, p. 9) further argued that semiology aimed to take in any system of signs, including 'images, gestures, musical sounds, objects, and complex associations of all of these, which form the content of ritual, convention or public entertainment: these constitute, if not languages, at least systems of signification'. De Saussure had concentrated particularly on the denotative level of signs, which refers to their literal meanings. Dictionaries are good examples of signs operating on a denotative level. They present the basic, simple meanings of words. Barthes, however, was more interested in the connotative aspect of signs. Connotation refers to the meaning that members of a certain society or culture may extract from a word. A picture of ice may have quite different connotations for an Arctic Inuit, for example, compared to those it would have for someone living in the Sahara. A rose can be prickly as well as a symbol for love, and so on.

In his seminal work *Mythologies*, Barthes (1972) then introduced a second order of signs, that of myth. He noted that on this higher level, signs can again become signifiers in themselves, and are then *not* arbitrarily related to a signified, but that this happens quite on purpose. Barthes uses the numerous essays collected in *Mythologies* to prove his point by way of examining a number of contemporary French myths. Looking at the photo of a young black soldier wearing a French uniform on the cover of the magazine *Paris Match*, Barthes argues that on its own and taken out of context the photograph does not tell us much. However, if taken together with its signifieds, such as a different ethnicity, the military and notions of Frenchness, the photo continues a myth of imperial devotion and success. Returning to an example raised earlier, we can also see how modern news photographs can invoke myths when they resemble the *pietá* (Seaton, 2005). Arguably, such images invoke myths related to Christian values and compassion. We will return to the concept of myth in more depth later when discussing the way in which journalism commemorates death. For now, however, I want to focus more on the denotative level of photographs, in order to review the literature on what Western audiences are exposed to in news images of death and dying. The meanings of texts and images of death and dying are extremely important, and will, therefore, be dealt with in a separate chapter.

The presence and absence of graphic images of death

A perennial debate in the field of research on news images of death has been how present such images actually are. As we have seen, such a discussion is closely linked with the general debate about death in the public sphere. Many scholars have argued that photographs of death are becoming ever more visible in the news, and that especially graphic photos of human suffering seem to be everywhere (Sontag, 1977; Neuman, 1996; Moeller, 1999; Carruthers, 2000). However, at least in most Western countries, news organizations have a number of explicit rules which govern the publication of images of death. As others point out, many photos of death and dying actually never make it into the news, largely due to ethical restrictions and considerations of taste and public sensibilities. Taylor (1998, p. 193) believes that the press is 'careful to write more detail than it cares to show' and Campbell (2004, p. 55) argues that 'we have witnessed a disappearance of the dead in contemporary coverage'. Fraser (1992) notes that, while media bosses want ever more gruesome and detailed pictures of people dying, at the same time they filter out what they feel viewers should not see, thus 'cleaning up' events to make them acceptable to the public. In the British tabloid press, known to be very sensational, there even existed a taboo on graphic images of death and dying, resulting in very few such images being printed (Meech, 1992).

It is curious then, that very few quantitative assessments have been made of how the news media report death visually. Most scholars have restricted themselves to case studies of particular events where graphic photos were shown. Rarely, however, has a representative sample been investigated. The evidence from such studies demonstrates that death, and particularly graphic death, is indeed very seldom shown in Western newspapers. Jessica Fishman (2001) undertook a systematic analysis of the coverage of death in the *New York Times*, *Washington Post*, *New York Post* and *Philadelphia Daily News* and found that, while reports of death were common, very rarely did they show corpses. This finding has been reproduced in other contexts as well. Singletary and Lamb (1984) examined news values in award-winning photographs and found that 81 per cent were either about accidents, disasters, crime or violence. Of that percentage, around one-quarter showed personal injury or death, but only 2.7 per cent showed graphic details such as blood (Singletary and

Lamb, 1984, p. 105). However, as the authors noted, the sample was limited to award-winners, not the daily newspaper coverage, which might reflect different trends. Nevertheless, a study of German and Australian quality newspapers showed that the vast majority of photos running alongside stories about foreign death showed the deceased when still alive, or only scenes of general destruction devoid of corpses (Hanusch, 2008a). Dead bodies were only shown in 4.5 per cent of photographs, while blood was visible in a mere 1.7 per cent of images.

Even graphic death does appear from time to time in the news. As Taylor (1998, p. 79) argues, 'displays of the body in the press are a matter of changing custom. At different times the tendency may be towards seeing more of the body or towards restraint.' Some events may produce more graphic shots than others and newspapers' own internal guidelines may also differ, even within countries. Unfortunately, few comparative studies have been undertaken. A study by Westminster University year three undergraduate students, reported in Seaton (2005), showed an interesting trend in the British press, with an apparent increase over 20 years. The study examined the front pages of quality newspapers *The Times*, the *Daily Telegraph* and *The Guardian* for three months each in 1980, 1990 and 2000. In 1980, photos with blood appeared only twice, while in 1990 there were 11 and by 2000 there were 'nearly two dozen pictures with blood – including several top-fold pictures (the key image intended to attract purchasers) of people lying dead in great pools of blood' (Seaton, 2005, p. 19). In another comparative analysis, Fishman (2001) was able to show that, contrary to popular belief, tabloid newspapers showed less death than their 'quality' counterparts. While the tabloid newspapers generally avoided showing death altogether, a large proportion of graphic photos in the quality press were from abroad, bringing to mind the arguments related to a political economy of the coverage of death discussed earlier. The study of German and Australian newspapers (Hanusch, 2008a) also displayed differences within as well as across countries. In Australia, *The Australian* newspaper was considerably more likely to show graphic photos than the *Sydney Morning Herald*, while in Germany both the *Frankfurt Allgemeine Zeitung* and the *Süddeutsche Zeitung* showed very few such images altogether. In fact, the German newspapers showed only two of the total of 18 photos of corpses on display across all four newspapers over two months.

On the basis of arguments about the value of lives from abroad, discussed earlier, a few scholars have examined whether the textual representations are replicated in the visual coverage of death. Here, the evidence is relatively clear. While newspapers show very little actual death, when they do, the dead are more likely to be from abroad, and even more likely to be from distant cultural backgrounds. For example, Campbell (2004) has argued that if dead bodies do occur in the media, it is mostly the ones that belong to people from distant places. Examining the use of news pictures in *Time* and *Newsweek*, Tsang (1984) found that violence was more likely to be shown when from abroad, with 31 per cent of *Time*'s and 25 per cent of *Newsweek*'s foreign pictures portraying violence. This compared to only 12 per cent of *Time*'s and 13 per cent of *Newsweek*'s US pictures in the same category. Tsang (1984) also found that for culturally distant regions, such as Asia, the proportion of violent-oriented photographs was high, while for both Eastern and Western Europe, non-violent photos dominated. An analysis of Australian news coverage of foreign deaths and interviews with journalists appears to support such a view, while interviews with German journalists, on the other hand, indicated that distance may not always result in more graphic images. When asked whether he would publish a photograph of a famous dead Indian bandit with a bullet hole in his skull, a German foreign editor said: 'You really have to say he had significance for the region, and he may have been someone who had been pronounced dead a number of times but then never was. For us it would have no significance, I wouldn't publish such a photo because it's not interesting' (in Hanusch, 2008c).

Such differences point to larger variation between cultures, to which I have alluded previously, and the lack of research into this issue has been hampering our understanding of how news media cover death. The vast majority of scholars have only been concerned with Western news coverage, while neglecting large parts of the rest of the world to inform how Western coverage may be different or similar. This is, of course, a general problem in journalism and mass communications research, which has been dominated by Anglo-Saxon perspectives and is therefore not particularly surprising. However, based on the anecdotal evidence, research into how other countries' news media deal with death could broaden our perspective of the Western media as well. We have seen that within Western Protestant contexts, there exist some differences already, such as between general attitudes of journalists and actual news coverage in Germany and Australia. Similarly, Petley (2003) related an important anecdote by a British journalist about the aftermath of a mortar bomb landing in a Sarajevo street. A news agency camera crew had filmed the aftermath of the bombing, and journalists from various countries went about using part of the footage for their reports.

It was instructive to see how the reporters from different countries, and different television traditions, dealt with the pictures. The Italians used almost all of them: the brains, the intestines, the gutter literally running with blood in the rain. The French used the gutter and the bodies. The Americans used the gutter. We used none of these things: just the covered bodies being put into the ambulances, the empty pram, the abandoned shoes....

(Cited in Petley, 2003, p. 73)

The apparent difference between the United States and the United Kingdom on the one hand, and Catholic countries on the other has been noted by others as well. Seaton (2005, p. 128) reports that Catholic European and South American broadcasters apparently showed far more explicit footage of the events of 9/11 than their northern counterparts. Castanos and Muñoz (2005) believe a reason for this difference may lie in the different religious orientations, with Catholic countries having a different relationship with graphic death. Comparing Spanish and American visual culture, they argue that Protestant traditions are responsible for the 'antivisualist coverage of pain' that is so dominant in US media, while the Catholic roots with images of a bleeding Jesus on the cross may well be at the heart of Spanish newspapers' readiness to show more graphic images of death (Castanos and Muñoz, 2005, p. 6). Arab news channels such as Al Jazeera are also usually seen as being prepared to show more graphic images than American or Northern European channels, even though this is not necessarily always the case. For example, when US contractors were killed and their burnt bodies strung up on a bridge in the Iraqi city of Fallujah in 2004, Al Jazeera decided not to show the images, apparently because of a previous backlash in the United States when it had shown dead American soldiers (Robertson, 2004). Nevertheless, a spokesman for the station has said that its audience 'actually expects us to show them blood, because they realize that war kills ... If we were not to show it, we would be accused by our viewers ... of perhaps hiding the truth or trying to sanitize the war' (quoted in Sharkey, 2004, p. 18).

Other cursory examinations from around the world show that also the Thai vernacular press appears to show gory images of accidents and murders quite regularly, as do a number of South American newspapers. Many scholars argue that the visual coverage of events says much about the cultural circumstances in which it is portrayed (see, for example, Moeller, 1989; Brothers, 1997). Similarly, I have argued before that cultural value systems can influence differences in the reporting on death (Hanusch, 2008c). As a result, one could make the argument that a culture that is more death-accepting, or has a more open relationship with death, could also be more accepting of graphic coverage. In Mexico, an entire industry and national myth has developed around the Day of the Dead, with displays of skeletons that many in the West may find macabre (Lomnitz, 2005). Could there be a link between the resulting relationship with death and that country's newspapers quite regular display of death, sometimes in its most raw version? The answer is that we don't know yet, as we have very little hard evidence as to how the coverage of death differs, both across cultures as well as within, and – most importantly – why the differences may exist. This lack of research leaves us with a serious gap in our knowledge, and there is clearly still much work to be done here.

The political economy of images of death

As mentioned briefly earlier, photos always have political implications as well, and perhaps none more so than photographs of war. Therefore, this section deals with the way in which death has been covered visually in the news media of the United States and the United Kingdom. This is important because it demonstrates how government restrictions, but also self-censorship, may impact on whether graphic death is shown. Herman and Chomsky's (1988) influential work has provided a useful background against which to view the history of war photography, particularly during the twentieth and early twenty-first centuries. Their Propaganda Model sees five filters through which the news media decide which news to publish and how, which can lead to self-censorship. The five filters are: ownership of the medium, funding sources, sourcing of news, Flak and anti-ideology. Firstly, Herman and Chomsky argue that news media are (particularly in the United States) predominantly private corporations which are often part of larger conglomerates. As they need to protect their financial interests, this can lead to some information that may be damaging to the corporation being left out of the news. Secondly, these corporations rely on funding from advertisers, a source of income they do not want to upset for fear of losing it.

Sourcing refers to the processes which news media use to gather news. Herman and Chomsky argue that news audiences are demanding a constant flow of news, and news organizations as a result require access to reliable sources for such news. Consequently, they focus much of their attention on the loci of power, and constantly access comment and information from government and major businesses. This dependence, however, often leads news organizations to solidarity with these sources in order to guarantee further access, resulting in a tendency to reinforce the views and values of the dominant class in society. Similarly, government and large businesses may threaten media businesses with the withdrawal of certain rights, such as TV licenses, advertising or through legal threats, a practice Herman and Chomsky refer to as Flak. Finally, news media replicate the dominant ideology, rather than seriously challenging it. Before the end of the Cold War, this ideology was strongly anti-communist, and was repeatedly invoked by government to discourage the news media from criticizing attacks on communists. Since the fall of communism, Herman (1996) argues, the emphasis on anti-communism has been replaced by an emphasis on the 'miracle of the market'. While the Propaganda Model has come under attack from a number of scholars, and is often described as not much more than a conspiracy theory that takes an overly deterministic view of media behavior (Klaehn, 2002, p. 147), it nevertheless makes a forceful argument about the way in which the news media effectively censor themselves.

This background about the propaganda model and the political economy of news is important if we examine the way in which news images of war have been analyzed by a number of scholars. In times of war, governments need to maintain the support of their citizens through controlling the information they receive. The news media, in its ideal version of the fourth estate and a check on those in power, presents a potential challenge to governments by reporting events and displaying images that are counter to the government's own narrative of the war effort. Governments often try to limit the information coming out of war zones by imposing censorship or only granting news organizations limited access. Yet, as this section demonstrates, they rarely need to, as the news media throughout history have by and large supported national war efforts – with or without censorship. Particularly in relation to showing war casualties, news media err on the side of caution so as not to endanger the war effort on one hand, but also so as not to upset their audiences.

Images of death in wartime

Earlier, we examined the way death has been portrayed in the news throughout history, against the background of larger societal developments. Interestingly, an increase in images of death, first engraved woodcuttings and later photographs, appeared to coincide with the end of life becoming increasingly taboo in society. As photographs appeared in newspapers and magazines on a more regular basis, audiences began experiencing death, and particularly death from wars, in an arguably more realistic fashion. As I have pointed out, the American Civil War was the first war to be photographed on a continuous basis, but many people never got to see the photos as they were mostly hung in galleries or appeared in picture books. As World War I raged, the US government applied strict censorship, thus resulting in practically no photos of American losses in the news media. During the Spanish Civil War from 1936–39, however, war photography came of age. Brothers (1997, p. 2) notes that this conflict was indeed 'the first war to be extensively and freely photographed for a mass audience, and it marks the establishment of modern war photography as we know it'. Sontag (2003, p. 21) similarly cites it as 'the first war to be witnessed ("covered") in the modern sense: by a corps of professional photographers at the lines of military engagement and in the towns under bombardment, whose work was immediately seen in newspapers and magazines in Spain and abroad'. Photos of the dead were of course a part of it, none more famous than Capa's 'Falling Soldier'.

During World War II, the US government imposed strict censorship on any photos of fallen American soldiers, until, in 1943, President Roosevelt decided that his people needed to see a less-sanitized side of the war, in order to understand the gravity of the situation. Consequently, newspapers, magazines and newsreels started to include images of death on a regular basis, with one of the first appearing in *Life* magazine in September 1943. The photo, spread across the entire page, showed the bodies of three US soldiers at the edge of the surf on a beach in New Guinea, and the accompanying story asked: 'Why print this picture, anyway, of three American boys dead upon an alien shore? Is it to hurt people? To be morbid? Those are not the reasons. The reason is that words are never enough' (in Rainey, 2005). Subsequently, as the full horrors of the Nazi concentration camps became known towards the end of the war, newspapers, magazines and newsreels published an unprecedented amount of graphic images of the unthinkable horror. As Barbie Zelizer (1998) has pointed out in her much-acclaimed book about the holocaust, photos of the Nazi atrocities streamed back to the United States and the United Kingdom, where the vast majority were published immediately.

> Turning out roll after roll of black-and-white film, photographers relentlessly depicted the worst of Nazism in stark, naturalistic representations of horror: bodies turned at odd angles to each other, charred skulls, ovens full of ashes, shocked German civilians alongside massive scenes of human carnage. Within days of photographers'

arrival in the camps, the wires were flooded with scenes of explicit and gruesome snapshots of horror, the likes of which had never before been presented on the pages of the US and British popular press....

(Zelizer, 1998, p. 89)

By the time the conflict in Vietnam erupted, war photographers were used to capturing anything and everything before them, leading to what has been widely regarded as saturation coverage of dead bodies in the news media at the time. Furthermore, photos were for the first time complemented by television, and Vietnam was the first important war to be beamed into American and European living rooms. Audiences were all of a sudden able to join American troops in the jungles of Indochina, witnessing the horrors of war in moving images from the safety of their living rooms. The Vietnam War generated a number of iconic images that to this day shape our modern understanding of it. Who could forget the image by AP photographer Nick Ut, which showed a group of distressed Vietnamese villagers running towards the camera, including a naked nine-year-old girl with burns to her back from a napalm attack. Or the photograph of the Saigon police chief General Loan executing a Vietcong prisoner during the Tet Offensive, right in front of Eddie Adams' camera? The unprecedented media coverage, particularly through television, is still widely held responsible for turning the American public against the war. Indeed, as Daniel Hallin (1986, pp. 105–106) has pointed out, this view 'is accepted so widely across the American political spectrum that it probably comes as close as anything to being conventional wisdom about a war that still splits the American public'.

But the view that Vietnam was a watershed in the representation of graphic images of death, or even that press coverage could be held responsible for the lost war, has been criticized as a misperception that does not hold up against closer scrutiny. Both Hallin (1986) and Hammond (1989, 1998) dispute the view that graphic images from Vietnam swayed public opinion against the war, arguing that it is not based in much evidence. Hallin contends that the news coverage only started to turn against the war when there was already opposition to it at the elite level and audiences were beginning to turn against the war as well. Hammond notes that an analysis of US evening television newscasts between August 1965 and August 1970 found that only 76 of 2300 reports 'showed anything approaching true violence – heavy fighting, incoming small arms and artillery fire, killed and wounded within view'

(1989, p. 316). When bodies were shown on television, there were clear distinctions between American dead and Vietnamese dead. Cook (2001, p. 204) examined US network news coverage between 1965 and 1971, and found that, especially during the heaviest years of fighting between 1967 and 1969, 'television news coverage treated American and Vietnamese bodies differently, often using North Vietnamese dead in representational structures which sought to manufacture consent for the US war effort'. Cook argues that news stories showed very little concern for dead North Vietnamese, while treating American casualties with the utmost of care. In fact, as Hallin (1986, p. 130) points out, networks had quite explicit guidelines 'not to show film of identifiable American casualties, unless their relatives had been notified by the Defense Department'. As a result, Cook (2001, p. 206) notes that, 'when shown, American casualties were carefully framed and filmed', while 'Vietnamese bodies regularly were shown bleeding, wounded and dead'. Taylor (1998, p. 22) argues that it was only the different climate during the Tet Offensive that allowed the General Loan photo to be published. He notes that in 1962, when the war was still small and support for it strong, a very similar photo was universally rejected by editors, and only published in a small and obscure magazine.

Nevertheless, the popular wisdom, particularly in the US government following the Vietnam experience, was that the unfettered access granted to the news media then should never happen again. As a result, more recent wars have been much more tightly controlled, leading to perhaps even less images of dead US and UK soldiers in their respective media. Wary of the press from the Vietnam War, the UK government instituted so-called 'media pools' during the Falkland War in 1982, a practice that was also adopted in the 1983 US-led invasion of Grenada. These pools were used in order to keep as much control over reporters as possible, as the military conducted tours for them, thus deciding what they would be able to see. During the War in the Persian Gulf in 1991, this process was so complete that very few unauthorized images came out. As the historian Philip Taylor (1992, p. 268) points out in his account of the media performance at the time, despite the multitude of media organizations present, the images and accounts of the conflict were basically the same, as they all relied on information provided by the military: 'It was monopoly in the guise of pluralism'. As a result, the reports from the Gulf were supportive of the US-led efforts, and mostly uncritical reflections of the official line, not least because media owners saw it as being in their own interest (Kellner, 1992). Media coverage was dominated by images from smart bombs hitting their targets (despite the fact that many more missed), and very little footage from the ground was available. As a result, audiences saw a much more restricted picture of the war than they had previously. John Taylor (1998) points out that very few images of dead and wounded were visible, giving the appearance of a clean war. 'Video-tapes that showed Iraqis dying were withheld from television until after the war. Gun cameras on Apache helicopters filmed close-up the killing of individual soldiers, though viewing them was restricted to the military' (Taylor, 1998, p. 162).

Griffin and Lee conducted a visual content analysis of 1104 war-related pictures in *Time*, *Newsweek* and *US News & World Report* during 'Operation Desert Storm', and found that only 27 photos, or 2 per cent of the total, included wounded or killed American soldiers. However, almost all of them were 'either flag-draped coffins in US home-town funeral ceremonies or portraits taken of soldiers prior to deployment in the Middle East' (Griffin and Lee, 1995, p. 819). They were also struck by the small number of Iraqi casualties, especially as so many more Iraqis had died. Yet, only six photos – half a per cent – showed dead Iraqis. This fact, Griffin and Lee (1995, p. 820) argue, 'lends support to the charge made by many commentators that the US media cooperated with the military to eschew images of bloodshed and present the American public with a "clean war" ', a point backed up in Taylor's (1998) analysis of photographs from the same conflict. Describing the UK newspaper coverage of the war, he argues that incidents of mass killing, which did take place, 'either disappeared from – or, more strictly, never fully entered – the mainstream media' (Taylor, 1998, p. 180).

As an example of how photos were self-censored, Taylor cites the case of the attack by US forces on a large convoy of Iraqi vehicles on retreat from Kuwait during the last days of the war. An estimated 400–2000 people apparently died that day at Mutlah Gap on the road to Basra, leaving a long line of charred vehicles and corpses on the road. Taylor notes that it took three days for the first films and photographs of the incident to come out, and even then the coverage was muted and uncritical of the allied forces. Graphic images began appearing only after the censorship was lifted, but even then they were often not shown. The only really graphic shot came from photographer Kenneth Jarecke and appeared only in the Sunday *Observer*. It shows the charred and virtually unrecognizable head of an Iraqi soldier leaning through the trashed windscreen of his vehicle. But, while this image 'dispelled the air of unreality about a war with almost no pictorial evidence of death' (Taylor, 1998, p. 181), it did not get a run in any other UK newspaper for some days, and for even longer in the United States. It was almost used in *Life* magazine, but its managing editor withdrew it at the last minute 'in deference to children' (McCabe, 1991, p. 24).

Similarly, the reporting of the events of 11 September 2001, were distinguished by the absence of photos of the dead. Staudt (2009b) reports that the first issue of *Time* magazine after the collapse of the Twin Towers was devoid of bodies, excepting perhaps the image of the 'Falling Man', which showed people jumping to their death before the collapse of the towers. The magazine's editors 'deliberately and on principle chose to avoid pictures of fatalities in the special issues' (Staudt, 2009b, p. 161). Even the images of people jumping to their death were discussed at length, and while one was published, the editors later regretted this and did not include it in *Time*'s 2001 commemorative edition. Staudt does note, however, that later issues of the magazine would include more photos of the dead, albeit still a relatively small number. While in the United States the coverage of terrorism that affects US citizens has only arrived relatively recently, the media in the United Kingdom has a long history of reporting the conflict in Northern Ireland. Taylor (1991) has written about this coverage, noting among other things that while the reporting of fatal bombings was extensive, the appearance of dead bodies was still a relatively rare event. Most of the time, if bodies were visible in photographs, they were either concealed to hide their faces, or taken from a distance. Even in the bombing of a Pan Am airliner over the Scottish town of Lockerbie, 'no pictures matched the language of the writers, who did not baulk at describing people in states of reduction, from "shattered bodies" to "mangled remains" to "scraps of flesh"' (Taylor, 1991, p. 160). Taylor argues that overall, despite some of the colorful language, the coverage was still conventional and did not report much of the horrific detail.

Early evidence from the wars in Iraq and Afghanistan suggest that death is still relatively invisible in the US media, despite arguably less restrictive regulations with the arrival of 'embedded' journalists and a number of unilateral reporters present inside Iraq. News organizations, particularly in the United States, have been accused of being too uncritical in the lead-up to the Iraq War (Mitchell, 2008), and their performance during the conflict also suggests somewhat of a cheerleading role for their country. Despite the significant death toll in Iraq, a content analysis of front pages of the *New York Times* and *San Francisco Chronicle* in March–December 2003 and January 2006–March 2007 found that only 3 per cent of all front page photographs during that time dealt with the human cost of war (Roth *et al.*, 2008). However, the majority of these dealt with death only symbolically, such as through a photo of the deceased next to a grieving family member, or the severed head of a children's doll in an Iraqi marketplace after a bomb explosion. Only 35 of the 774 war photos in total (4.5 per cent) showed actual death, and only in six of those was a face visible. Again, we can see that photos of 'our' dead, even – or perhaps especially – in wartime, are very rarely shown, as there were only five actual American corpses shown, as opposed to 27 Iraqis. In an analysis of war photographs published in the *Chicago Tribune*, *Los Angeles Times* and *New York Times*, King and Lester (2005) found that only 5 per cent of images published in a one-week timeframe showed bloodied combatants, while a mere 1.1 per cent showed deceased soldiers. Interestingly, these numbers were very much the same as they found in an analysis of the newspapers' reporting of the Gulf War some 12 years earlier.

An examination of death and injury on ABC, CNN and Fox News newscasts in the first month of the war showed that 15 per cent depicted death or injury (Aday, 2005), while a study of photos in the *New York Times* and the *Guardian* found 6.8 per cent overall focused on death (Fahmy and Kim, 2008). In a comparative study of US television news, newspapers, news magazines and online news sites, Silcock *et al.* (2008) found that only 10 per cent of stories showed death or injury, although they did not differentiate further between such depictions to examine the number of photos of death. However, they found that of all the images shown on television, 15.1 per cent related to injury or death (equal to that found by Aday, 2005), compared to 9.1 per cent of all war-related newspaper photos and 8 per cent of photos in news magazines. On the Internet, the number was only 2.1 per cent of all stories, although one reason for the small number may lie in problems in data collection rather than stricter self-censorship online (Silcock *et al.*, 2008, p. 46).

Despite the relative lack of graphic images, governments have been worried about adverse reactions to media coverage of war deaths in other ways. During the Gulf War in 1991, the Bush Sr. Administration was so worried that it placed a ban on photographs of caskets carrying killed American soldiers arriving back home at Dover Air Force Base – ostensibly out of respect for the grieving families. It took 18 years until the policy was eased by the Obama administration in February 2009. Now, next-of-kin are asked if they would like the news media to record the arrival and transfer to the Air Force mortuary. Early indications are that two-thirds of families agree to have the media on hand (McIntyre, 2009), demonstrating a desire for their loss to be broadcast to the nation.

Photos, as Barthes (1977) and many others have argued, always exist in a context, and have a number of meanings attached to them. Quite often, particularly in war, these meanings are political, and as a result deaths are treated with much sensitivity. Even the enemies' deaths are subjected to scrutiny before publication, for fear of bringing 'our' troops into disregard. The obvious reason for the strict information management during the Gulf War was that if no dead were visible, it meant no one was killed. Of course, graphic images can also be used to highlight the plight of distant people and to spur governments into action, or at least to arouse compassion. Konstantinidou (2007) notes that the Greek newspaper *Apogevmatini* aimed to do just that in its quite graphic coverage of dead mothers and children during the Iraq War. Having discussed the hierarchy of death in terms of age and gender, we know that women and children's deaths are more likely to be reported, particularly if they died violently. They can easily be used for political purposes, to cry out that innocent people are being killed and the government should do something about it, as was the case in Bosnia and Kosovo in the 1990s. In such cases, of course, graphic images are always more likely to be used, in order to drive home the point to audiences. Seaton (2005, p. 224) notes that during the Kosovo conflict, 'there was an official relaxation of the rules that govern what is permissible, because shocking atrocities were the reason for the military intervention. Clearly, much depends on the purposes of the journalism: sometimes it must not be permitted to disturb; at other times the more disturbing the better'.

Judgment calls between these extremes can be quite difficult. When the former Chief of Staff of the African National Congress, Chris Hani, was assassinated in South Africa in 1993, most South African newspapers refused to print one particularly graphic shot showing Hani's head with blood surrounding it. However, the Johannesburg *City Press* did print it on the front page, partly to arouse the country's emotions. The paper's news editor said the photo was 'about the goriest we could find. I'm not into gore but I believed, everyone believed, that we needed to shock the nation a bit and deliver the story to them as blatantly, as raw, as it was, and this was the best we could do' (quoted in O'Dowd, 1996, p. 3). The photographer who took the photo also wanted it to be a piece of documentary evidence, and it was crucial that the face was visible so people would see it really was Hani. Rather than receiving many complaints, the newspaper found itself swamped with requests for copies of the photo, as Hani's supporters used it to commemorate him.

News organizations' production standards

While in war, official censorship as well as political purposes may have an impact on whether graphic images are published, there are also more banal reasons involved, particularly when it comes to domestic death. Foremost here are decisions on matters of taste and decency in news reporting, particularly in the United States and Europe. A lot of the time, newspapers shy away so much from publishing gory images because of a consideration for the feelings of their audiences. This relates to an interesting paradox: While gruesome and sensational stories are often believed to increase audience numbers, many readers and viewers are at the same time repulsed by graphic images. Many of the most famous images of death were first preceded by long editorial discussions about the appropriateness of publication and later often subject to extensive debates in reader or viewer feedback. The news media's squeamishness when it comes to graphic images can be well understood against the background of the earlier discussion of the history of death in Western societies. Death, at least until relatively recently, progressively moved into the private realm, with most people very rarely exposed to death and dying. Western society aimed to hide death, and the careful depiction in images is part of this tradition. And even though we have little hard evidence in terms of an increase in the presence of graphic death in the media, perhaps the fact that a number of scholars believe it to be so is in line with a more open view of death in recent years.

One of the more well-known considerations among journalists when confronted with graphic images of death and dying is what is sometimes referred to as the 'Breakfast Test' for newspapers and the 'Dinner Test' for television (Peterson and Spratt, 2005, p. 14). Journalists believe that most of their readers or viewers access their news while eating, and who would want to see anything upsetting during a meal? Similarly, children may often be present at those times, so the issue of the protection of minors comes into the equation as well. Taylor believes that it is not so much about ethics and morality rather than a matter of morals and taste. He argues that 'the balance the papers try to strike is between the right to know (which is connected with the right to see) and the right to be shielded from too much reality' (Taylor, 1998, p. 70). In their analysis of the way in which US newspapers published disturbing photos from the events of 9/11, Kratzer and Kratzer (2003) found that newsroom debates centered mainly around possible reader responses, privacy of the victims and whether the photographs could adequately communicate the story. Distance played a role even in this event, with one editor from

an Eastern newspaper saying that if they had been on the West Co
in the Midwest they would have published the disturbing photos. 'In
fact that it might have been one of our readers jumping to their death,
falling to their death, is what kept us from running it' (quoted in Kratzer
and Kratzer, 2003, p. 44).

When Pennsylvania state treasurer Robert 'Budd' Dwyer committed
suicide in 1987 by shooting himself in the mouth live in front of TV
cameras at a news conference, editors throughout the state were faced
with a difficult decision. How should they treat this event of obvious significance, but which also consisted of extremely graphic footage? Only
three out of 20 stations throughout the state showed the suicide in their
noon news cast, while only one carried it in the evening, complete with
a warning for viewers and a discussion with mental health experts afterwards (Parsons and Smith, 1988). It should be said that stations only
showed Dwyer pulling the trigger and slumping to the ground, but not
the pictures of him sitting on the ground with blood streaming out of
his mouth. The main reason not to run the footage was obviously that
it was too graphic and contravened matters of taste. Parsons and Smith
(1988, p. 89) quote one news director as saying: 'We want good video
but we want the video for its news value. We're not looking to shock
people'.

There are quite a number of ethical guidelines restricting the visual
depiction of death in Western societies, and often the topic is covered
under a sub-heading relating to issues of taste, as well as privacy and
coverage of conflict. Ethics are an important part of journalists' value
systems, even if they don't always apply these rules. Some newspaper
and, especially, broadcasting codes have quite explicit restrictions on the
coverage of death and graphic images. The BBC's editorial guidelines,
for example, are quite detailed in the way they regulate the coverage of
graphic death.

We will always need to consider carefully the editorial justification for
portraying graphic material of human suffering and distress. There
are almost no circumstances in which it is justified to show executions and very few circumstances in which it is justified to broadcast
other scenes in which people are being killed. It is always important
to respect the privacy and dignity of the dead. We should never show
them gratuitously. We should also avoid the gratuitous use of close
ups of faces and serious injuries or other violent material....

(BBC, 2005, p. 54)

Most broadcast organizations in Northern Europe and North America have similar guidelines, even if not always in such detail. Similarly, many newspapers and national press councils have their own guidelines that cover the reporting of death. In Australia, the Press Council's guidelines instruct journalists to 'have regard for the sensibilities of their readers, particularly when the material, such as photographs, could reasonably be expected to cause offence. Public interest should be the criterion and, on occasion, explained editorially' (Australian Press Council, 2003). While the actual clauses are relatively broad, the Council's executive director Jack R. Herman (2002) reported how the Council had argued that the publication of scenes from overseas events, which identified individuals, was more acceptable:

> The Council has adopted a general approach that there is a difference between photographs of the unidentified victims of foreign carnage and a front-page picture of a body in a local community where the victim is well known. (...) It is a matter of balancing the use that can be made of a picture that might be considered offensive against the public interest in having the matter brought to attention....
>
> (Australian Press Council, cited in Herman, 2002)

In Germany, the *Pressekodex*, which provides ethical guidelines for journalists, goes even further in its restriction on the coverage of death, dealing with the issue in a number of its clauses. For example, Clause 10 states that written or visual publications which could offend moral or religious sensibilities are not allowed. Clause 11 deals with the sensational depiction of violence and brutality. According to sub-clause 11.1, a depiction is inappropriately sensational when the person is disparaged down to an object, a bare instrument. Further, sub-clause 11.3 states that the reporting of accidents and disasters is restricted by respect for the suffering of victims and the feelings of relatives. Those affected by the event should as a rule not become victims a second time through the nature of the reporting (Deutscher Presserat, 2005).

An analysis of 35 journalism ethics codes in the United States which addressed images found that while there was considerable mention of digital manipulation and staging of photos, only nine codes (26 per cent) addressed images of tragedy and violence (Keith *et al.*, 2006). All of the codes encourage positive discussion of graphic images of death, although there are some minor differences in attitudes. Most importantly, Keith *et al.* (2006) argued that because only so few codes actually provide written guidelines on the topic, it is more important in future research to focus on identifying and examining unwritten guidelines, which invariably exist in every newsroom.

As I pointed out earlier, the depiction of death in the news media differs depending on the context, between countries and even within countries. In a study of German and Australian newspapers' coverage of death in foreign news, some important differences between the two countries were identified (Hanusch, 2008a). However, at least in Australia, there were also considerable differences between the two newspapers analyzed. While *The Australian* showed quite a few photographs of death, the *Sydney Morning Herald* showed considerably less. A reason appears to lie with individual management at the newspapers and the personal beliefs of editors and managers. While a number of journalists at the *Sydney Morning Herald* noted that their editor did not like to publish photos of death, at *The Australian*, an editor remarked that he thought newspapers should show even more:

> You could make the point that newspapers go against public interest by not almost every day showing graphic photos of car accidents. You have a responsibility to show (that) a kid gets in a car, he goes out for a drive, this is the result of it; here it is. To send a message: 'you guys have to be really careful because this is what can happen to you'. And the pictures can powerfully bring that home ....
>
> (Cited in Hanusch, 2007, p. 35)

Sometimes, showing too much can also have consequences for individual journalists. Fishman (2003, p. 56) reports that a photojournalist who covered the death of Bill Cosby's son Ennis was eventually fired for photographing the dead body from too close a distance. In her study of photojournalists' decision-making in relation to graphic images, she also found that the less of a body we see, the more acceptable it is to publish the photo. However, political contexts can also shape different ethical decisions about similar photographs. For example, Fahmy (2005) found that photojournalists believed it was more politically sensitive to print graphic images of the Afghan War than of 9/11.

The need for most North American and Northern European newspapers to present their audiences with relatively sanitized images can also lead to another ethical conundrum – the digital altering of images. Most ethical guidelines expressly forbid digital manipulation, and journalists can often get around it by cropping a photograph or cutting shots in half. This was a method British channel Sky News used in a photograph of one of the tsunami dead in 2004, in order to spare her modesty (Pollard, 2005). However, from time to time, the issue of digital alteration comes up. Following the Madrid train bombings in March 2004, newspaper editors were presented with one particularly powerful shot of the carnage, but unfortunately the photo contained what is believed to be a severed femur in the bottom left hand corner. The photo would end up on many of the world's front pages, but it wasn't the same image everywhere. In fact, most American newspapers believed the bloody limb was too distasteful for their readers, and decided to crop the photo. *Time* Magazine didn't, but strategically placed type over the offending body part. One notable exception was the *Washington Post*, which ran the full photo in color on the front page. The picture editor at the *Post*, Michael duCille later said: 'My argument when I have a picture like this that has some excruciating, gut-wrenching emotion, is incredibly gory, devastating, and is hard on the eye – I apply a scale that compares the news event, the situation, look for the overriding reason to present such a situation to the viewing public' (cited in Irby, 2004). In the United Kingdom, however, the situation was quite different. Here, the *Daily Telegraph*, *Sun*, *Daily Mail* and *The Times* digitally removed the body part so that readers would only see a pile of rocks. The *Guardian*, on the other hand, chose to grey out the body part to make it less bloody. Irby (2004) quotes Bob Bodman, the picture editor at the *Daily Telegraph*, as saying:

> It was a fantastic photograph, the carnage of the bombing was amazing. The limb in the foreground was distracting, and I did not want to crop the image. It is not a huge problem for us to remove hands and things from the picture to clean them up ... if you don't change the context. We try not to show body parts.

Examples such as these show that, contrary to popular opinion, journalists do discuss, often at some length, the pros and cons of publishing certain graphic photographs. Rather than presenting readers and viewers with the full smorgasbord of gruesome images before them, they actually choose quite carefully, and are often quite conservative about what they show. At other times, and in different contexts, however, there may be a bigger willingness to show death in all its horrifying detail, at least for a short time. Much, of course, also depends on the public's willingness and preparedness to see gory images, an issue we will discuss later, along with the effect such images may have on the public.

Conclusion

A number of studies critical of the news media have complained about a perceived increase in images of death and dying in the late twentieth century and early twenty-first century. When we examine the empirical evidence, however, a slightly different picture emerges. Death, it would seem, is still largely hidden from our newspapers and television screens. This chapter has traced the visual depiction of death through the ages, and found images that were at least as and sometimes even more graphic. Empirical data also show that only a very small percentage of photographs actually depict death – at least in North America and Northern Europe. This appears to be the case across television, magazines and newspapers, and across popular and quality news. Similarly, even during times of war, images of death are relatively rare, particularly so if they are 'our' dead. Nevertheless, the level of graphic images does appear to fluctuate, and can differ between different news media, and particularly from event to event, depending also on the political circumstances at the time. As we have seen in Taylor's (1998) discussion of the General Loan photo, a similar image had been rejected some years previously, when the political context was different. As the studies of war photos have demonstrated, political and economic factors have often played a role in this regard.

The situation in relation to the general level of graphic images appears to be different in other parts of the world. This might well be due to a difference in religious values, as well as other cultural circumstances and approaches to death. It seems likely that journalism's squeamishness today is an expression of the general death anxiety that has existed in the West during the twentieth century. Journalists take into consideration the feelings of their audiences, and these, for some time, have apparently been against seeing images that are too graphic. As we have seen, Western attitudes to death appear to be changing towards a more public debate around death and dying, and death as a subject is certainly quite present in the news today – just perhaps not so much in photographs. Maybe images are the last frontier in that regard, and with time and an ongoing increase in death awareness in society, photographs will tend to be more explicit. There is little comparative data available over time periods, however, to support any such claims as yet. What does seem clear is that economic imperatives do not seem to play such a large part, at least in the way some have argued. Often, it is believed that it is the need to sell papers that is responsible for sensationalized photos, but this is only true to a certain extent. In fact, economic imperatives often work against publishing photos that are too gory, as journalists fear losing readers and advertisers.

In debates around images of death, there often appears to be a lot of conjecture and arguments are frequently based on anecdotal observations. For example, journalists at an Associated Press managing editors and photo managers conference believed that American newspapers were now more likely to publish graphic images than they were before 9/11 (Alford, 2004). On the other hand, Zelizer (2004) believes that American newspapers are actually less likely to show graphic images since the experience of that fateful day. Without empirical data, we simply don't know who is right. It may be that both sides are, as it could depend on whose dead we are talking about. Obviously, what is needed is a more representative look at how news media cover death and dying across time. The majority of studies discussed in this chapter have looked mainly at case studies, rather than taking a long-term approach to examining general news content over a certain timeframe. Similarly, we know very little – in empirical terms – about how the coverage in the West differs to that elsewhere around the world. Anecdotal evidence abounds about graphic coverage in the Arab World, Latin America and Southeast Asia in particular. Comparing practices in those parts of the world could potentially give the West a new perspective on the coverage of death and dying.

As pointed out in the introduction to this chapter, I was here mainly concerned with the denotative level of images of the end of life. A more detailed analysis of connotative aspects, and particularly audience reactions to images of death, will come later. But first, the following chapter will deal with an often forgotten aspect: the impact that reporting on death can have on journalists themselves.

5
The Impact of Covering Traumatic Assignments

An overwhelming majority of the literature discussed so far has painted a rather bleak picture of how the news media deal with death and dying. Some of these arguments include that journalists are ostensibly only interested in showing ever more graphic deaths in a pursuit of ratings. A tendency in such studies has been the portrayal of journalists as emotionless, almost robotic figures whose only purpose of existence is to select ever more graphic photos and videos to titillate audiences. Quite often such scholarship has allowed for only a very limited degree of agency on the part of journalists. Yet, the effect that the coverage of death has on news workers has often been neglected, despite the emergence of a very vibrant field of study into how doing their work may lead to serious post-traumatic stress disorder in journalists.

The chapter on representations of death in the news discussed the various tongue-in-cheek formulas that journalists supposedly employ in selecting certain types of death. Yet very few studies actually went further to examine in more detail the process journalists go through to arrive at their decision. This chapter will therefore briefly review the influences on journalists' decisions, before examining the limited amount of studies that have actually interviewed journalists about this process.

Following this discussion, we move the focus slightly to examine what impact the gathering and reporting of fatal news has on journalists. In the Anglo-American ideology of journalism, news workers are supposed to be objective bystanders, who merely report on the news and do not take part in it. As such, journalists are supposed to be unaffected by the news, regardless of how traumatic it may be. Showing emotion has, in this male-dominated profession, long been seen as a sign of weakness, and the common way to deal with covering a particularly gruesome accident was to go to the pub for a debrief with a few stiff drinks.

However, as this chapter shows, there now exists quite significant evidence on the impact that covering traumatic events has on journalists. Such scholarship argues that journalists need to be seen as akin to other trauma workers, such as police officers and emergency personnel, and that there is an urgent need for increased training in this area.

Influences on journalistic decision-making

Before we examine some of the influences on journalists' decisions about whether to cover death in a certain way, it is necessary to look at what we know about journalistic decision-making in general. How and why journalists make certain decisions has been one of the most widely asked questions by journalism scholars. In this research tradition, journalists have generally been viewed as gatekeepers, as they have the power to decide whether a news item makes it 'past the gate' and ends up in the news. In what is widely regarded as the first study of the decision-making processes in a news organization, David Manning White (1950) traced the editorial decisions of a wire service editor at a mid-Western newspaper in the United States, whom he called Mr Gates. On the basis of the editor's judgments, and reasons he gave for discarding certain news stories, White argued that gatekeeping was an essentially subjective and highly individualistic process, putting individual world views at the forefront of the decision-making. However, through the vast number of studies conducted since White's seminal work, gatekeeping has come to be seen as much more complex with a variety of levels of influence. It is now widely acknowledged that seeing influences as operating on purely the individual level is too simplistic, and that higher, more opaque levels exist, such as the unwritten rules of news organizations, the ideology of journalism and even cultural world views within the journalist's country of origin. The most influential theory revolves around five levels: the individual level, the routines and practices level, the organizational level, the extra-media level and finally the social system or ideological level (Shoemaker and Reese, 1996). McQuail (2005) also arrives at five levels, ranging from individual/role, organization, medium/industry/institution to society and international levels. Other models range across only four levels but are very similar, such as Donsbach's (2003) individual, professional, institutional and societal levels, or Weischenberg's (1992) onion model, which accounts for a role context on the individual level, through to a functional, structural and overarching norms context. Other scholars have developed broadly similar models (Ettema *et al.*, 1987; Esser, 1998; Whitney *et al.*, 2004; Preston, 2009). Most recently, the German journalism scholar Thomas Hanitzsch (2009) has synthesized these various approaches, and proposed a three-step model of individual, organizational and media systems' influences, constituted by five levels.

The individual level includes journalists' personal and professional backgrounds and orientations, as well as their specific roles and occupational characteristics within the news organization. Professionalized decision-making processes, such as the use of news values, presentation formats and writing styles make up the level of media routines. A broader, yet no less important, influence comes from the organizational level, which includes newsroom influences, editorial decision-making and advertising considerations. Media structures constitute a further level, which refers to economic imperatives of the news organization. The systemic level refers to the social, cultural and ideological contexts within which journalists work, and includes political and legal conditions of journalism. However, this level also includes notions of a nation's culture and social contexts – Shoemaker and Reese (1996) include these in their ideological level – and it is here that influences can be most difficult to detect.

In the context of how journalists make decisions in regard to news about death and dying, we can see that influences can also come from a variety of the above levels. For example, I have argued earlier that community attitudes toward death in Victorian Britain were quite different from those during the middle of the twentieth century, when Western society aimed to hide death. As community attitudes may arguably have been changing again toward more acceptance of death at the end of the twentieth century, journalists may be becoming more open to showing death. In a similar vein, there is reason to believe that cultural differences in attitudes to death may affect the extent to which death is shown in the news, as evidenced by the comparisons between news media from Catholic and Protestant countries discussed earlier.

On yet another level, political economy influences may impact on whether journalists decide to select stories from certain places only if a significant number of people have died. Tabloids are often perceived as more sensationalist in their coverage of death, pointing to individual newsroom influences on the organizational level, despite Fishman's (2001) finding that US tabloids were actually more reluctant than elite newspapers to show graphic death. Similarly, ethical frameworks exercise an important influence on how death is reported in the news. On the individual level, journalists' personal views also affect whether or not they will cover death in certain ways. For example, individual journalists may at times transgress newsroom policy when they have the opportunity (Hanusch, 2008b).

Yet, despite the considerable evidence on journalists around the world (see Weaver, 1998), very few studies have actually attempted to make journalists' attitudes to reporting death the focus of enquiry. Where they do exist, such studies have usually employed in-depth interviews with working journalists in order to find out some of the motivations and influences involved in how death is eventually displayed in the news. One of the common points of interest has been related to the tongue-in-cheek formulas journalists employ when deciding on whether or not to cover deaths from abroad. Proximity is thus an immensely important criterion that makes death newsworthy. If people who are like us die, they are simply seen as more important for readers to know about – an issue which, of course, is at the heart of journalism as it aims to provide news that is relevant to audiences. In short, journalists' decisions are influenced by considerations relating to cultural and geographic proximity, frequency of similar events, political-economic aspects, audience sensibilities, interests of the news organization, their own views and those of their superiors (Hanusch, 2008b).

Most importantly, journalists think very carefully about the ways in which they report death. This is particularly the case when displaying death visually – here, many journalists are acutely aware of their audiences' sensibilities. Peterson and Spratt (2005) have criticized existing gatekeeping studies for neglecting to study more deeply personal – and even traumatic – influences in deciding what news is. In their in-depth interviews with US print and television picture editors, they found that journalists often use their own emotional reactions to images, their personal sense of ethics and the specific policies of their employer when making decisions about photographs. One rule that is employed by newspaper editors the world over is the so-called 'Breakfast Test'. A number of studies have found that newspaper journalists often ask themselves the question of 'Would I want to read this over breakfast?' before deciding whether to publish a graphic photograph (O'Brien, 1993; Moeller, 1999; Hanusch, 2008b). In the television business, a similar rule is applied in the 'Dinner Test' for early evening news broadcasts (Peterson and Spratt, 2005). And while the test may not usually govern final decisions over whether to use a graphic photo or not, as editors interviewed by O'Brien (1993) acknowledged, it nevertheless influences decisions to a degree. Even in the use of language, some journalists exercise extreme caution, admitting to contemplating even the use of minor words so as not to sensationalize death unnecessarily. For example, journalists from both Germany and Australia acknowledged that they tended to use standard terms such as 'died' to describe the death of a person, rather than other variants, such as 'deceased' (Hanusch, 2008d).

The way in which this repeated exposure to deaths, accidents and disasters may affect news workers has been little researched until recently. As the following sections will outline, journalists are not the emotionless and sensationalist voyeurs they have been made out to be by some commentators, but rather can be deeply affected by their work, even when they experience traumatic events only second-hand at the picture desk.

Journalism and trauma

Research into how the coverage of death and other traumatic events affects journalists has accelerated considerably over the past decade, driven mainly by the establishment in 1999 of the Dart Center for Journalism and Trauma at the University of Washington. The work of the center, and particularly the work of journalism professor Roger Simpson and psychologist Elana Newman, has, over only 10 years, considerably raised awareness of the potential effects that journalists' work can have on their mental health. The center is now housed at Columbia University in New York, with a research facility at the University of Tulsa, as well as offices in Europe and Australia.

Anecdotal evidence of how journalists' work could impact on them has existed for some time, even before the first empirical studies to capture the phenomenon began. In a study investigating anecdotal evidence of how journalists have dealt with trauma over the centuries, Fedler (2004) found that witnessing calamities was one of nine reasons that led to symptoms of post-traumatic stress, including nightmares, alcoholism, depression and anxiety.

One of the most well-known examples is the fate of South African photojournalist Kevin Carter, who in July 1994 committed suicide, only weeks after receiving a Pulitzer Prize for his photograph of a starving Sudanese child being stalked by a vulture. Carter had taken the photo during a trip to famine-ravished Southern Sudan in 1993, where he came across the emaciated little girl who had stopped to rest on her way to a feeding station. The photo had an immediate impact around the world after it first appeared in the *New York Times*, with many readers wanting to know what happened to the girl. According to his account, Carter had waited for the vulture to disappear, but later scared it away when it wouldn't leave. What happened to the girl in the photo, however, was never known. Having received the Pulitzer Prize for photojournalism the next year, Carter eventually succumbed to the mental anguish accumulated during a career of war photography, and he committed suicide at the age of 33. In his suicide note, Carter wrote of severe depression and being deeply troubled by what he had encountered as part of his work: 'I am haunted by the vivid memories of killings & corpses & anger & pains... of starving or wounded children, of trigger-happy madmen, often police, of killer executioners' (in Macleod, 1994).

Substance abuse has also been reported by journalists who have been exposed to traumatic events. Anthony Loyd (1999, 2007), an English war correspondent, has written extensively about his time covering wars in Bosnia, Chechnya, Sierra Leone, Afghanistan and Iraq. In his books, Loyd often refers to his heroin addiction as a way of dealing with the traumatic events he has witnessed. Interestingly, he says that while on assignment, he never craved the drug, whereas coming home led to an immediate desire for it. In his latest book, however, Loyd notes that he isn't drawn to heroin anymore, ostensibly because he has found other ways of dealing with his war experiences.

Similarly, when the highly respected Australian journalist Peter Lloyd was found in possession of the drug ice in Singapore in July 2008, it triggered revelations of the tremendous amount of traumatic incidents he had experienced. In an interview, Lloyd admitted to using the drug in an attempt to rid him of nightmares he had since covering events such as the 2002 terrorist bombings on the Indonesian island of Bali and a suicide bombing briefly after the homecoming of former Pakistani prime minister Benazir Bhutto. In one particularly haunting nightmare, an Australian man 'his head empty – Lloyd had seen its contents spill out when schoolgirls moved him out of the hospital mortuary – accuses the reporter of taking away his dignity in death by staring at him' (Cooke, 2008). Following his arrest and intensive face-to-face counseling, Lloyd was finally diagnosed with post-traumatic stress disorder, allowing him to make sense of the various symptoms he had been experiencing.

Lloyd had also covered the 2004 Boxing Day tsunami, one of the most deadly natural disasters in recent memory, and which attracted unprecedented media attention around the globe. Reporting on the tsunami was another Australian foreign correspondent, Kimina Lyall, who happened to be holidaying at a beach resort on a small Thai island when the disaster struck. Lyall, an experienced reporter who had also covered Australia's biggest massacre at Port Arthur in 1996, was at once directly affected by a news event as well as immediately going into reporting mode. She was later diagnosed with post-traumatic disorder, and left the news business altogether (Cooke, 2008).

There are plenty of other cases, and it is not always just reporting from the scene of a fatal event but often the follow-up that causes reporters to experience secondary trauma. Here, the 'death knock' has been described as having a lasting effect on many journalists, particularly if it is their first one. Death knocks mean having to talk to the families or friends of victims and ask them how they feel. They usually occur when 'a reporter and/or photographer has to approach a bereaved family or a friend following an unexpected and sudden death or serious injury. It is sometimes referred to as getting the "weeping widow" story' (Castle, 1999, p. 145). And despite the fact that unethical behavior involved in death knocks is often publicized, this does not mean that journalists are not emotionally affected by death knocks (Castle, 1999; Berrington and Jemphrey, 2003).

Yet, traditionally, journalism's ideological notions of objectivity and passivity on the part of the reporter have long banished talk within the profession of the toll that reporting on traumatic events takes on journalists. News workers are not supposed to get involved, they are merely there to observe, and, thus goes the argument, are able to compartmentalize what they see, not letting it affect them. As Coté and Simpson (2000, p. 43) put it, they are supposed to be able to 'channel raw emotions into one compartment of the mind without interfering with the tasks that have to be carried out in pursuit of a story'. In addition, they argue, as long as they acted professionally, they should not be affected: 'A steady focus on professional conduct at all stages of a reporting assignment protects the journalist' (Coté and Simpson, 2000, p. 43). Dworznik (2006) points out that often journalists may believe they are not allowed to have emotional pain or feel they are not supposed to be traumatized. Simpson and Boggs (1999) have also pointed to an unspoken law among journalists that requires them to completely detach themselves from an assignment and not let it interfere with their work.

To process a traumatic event often meant going to the pub to have a few beers to forget, and then move on. That such an assumption cannot be upheld is only slowly being realized among editors in the industry, aided by the substantial body of work that now exists in this area (Simpson and Coté, 2006). Journalistic notions of objectivity, problematic as they are in themselves anyway because journalists constantly need to make subjective decisions about what they decide to show us, also cannot shield reporters from being affected by what they see. While they may deal differently with their emotions, and some journalists do in fact claim they can compartmentalize what they see and not let it affect them, they often contradict themselves later, showing how they are affected after all, but perhaps in ways they may not recognize (Simpson and Coté, 2006).

Today, in no small part thanks to the work of the Dart Center, there is growing acceptance of the effect that covering traumatic events can have on journalists. In fact, many believe journalists need to be seen as similar to other first-response trauma workers, such as firefighters, police officers and other emergency workers.

Definitions of post-traumatic stress disorder

Before delving into the literature on journalism and trauma, it is necessary to take a brief look at the scientific reasoning behind such studies. Firstly, what do we actually mean by trauma? Coté and Simpson (2000) note that trauma can be defined in both medical and psychiatric terms. The first definition refers to serious or critical bodily injuries, which may be caused by violence or an accident. In psychiatric terms, however, trauma has a different meaning, and refers to emotionally painful, distressing or shocking wounds, the effects of which often last for a considerable period of time. Experiencing a traumatic event is quite a common occurrence for the general population, with studies suggesting that between 40 and 80 per cent of people experience a traumatic event in their lives. By far not all of these are affected by such an event for any considerable period of time, however.

While survivors of such violent events as wars, natural disasters and accidents would have undoubtedly suffered emotional stress through the ages, post-traumatic stress disorder (PTSD) was not diagnosed until 1980. According to the American Psychiatric Association's (2000) official definition, this type of mental disorder may exist if an individual's anxiety symptoms last for more than four weeks. Anxiety symptoms which last for less than four weeks and more than two days are generally classed under the term of Acute Stress Disorder. In order for PTSD to be present, an individual must have been exposed to a traumatic event, involving them personally experiencing, witnessing or confronting an event which involved actual or threatened death or serious injury. In addition, the person's response must have involved intense fear, helplessness or horror. There are three main symptom groups for PTSD as defined by the American Psychiatric Association (2000):

1. Intrusion: The individual must be constantly re-experiencing the event in at least one of these ways: through recurrent and intrusive distressing recollections of the event; recurrent distressing dreams of the event; acting or feeling as if the event was recurring; intense psychological distress when exposed to signs that resemble an aspect of the event; or physiological reactivity on exposure to such signs.
2. Avoidance: The individual must persistently avoid stimuli which are associated with the trauma, indicated by at least three criteria: efforts to avoid thoughts, feelings or conversations associated with the trauma; efforts to avoid activities, places or people that arouse recollections of the trauma; an inability to recall important aspects of the trauma; strongly diminished interest or participation in significant activities; feeling of detachment or estrangement from others; restricted ability to show affect; or a sense of a foreshortened future.
3. Arousal: The individual must display at least two persistent symptoms of increased arousal which were not presented before the trauma: a difficulty to fall or stay asleep; irritability or outbursts of anger; difficulty concentrating, hyper-vigilance; or an exaggerated startle response.

Depending on the duration of symptoms, PTSD may be acute (symptoms lasting less than three months) or chronic (symptoms lasting more than three months). If PTSD occurs more than six months after a traumatic event, psychiatrists talk of delayed onset PTSD. Some of the symptoms that sufferers from PTSD may experience include aggressive behavior, cynicism, depression, exhaustion, nightmares, flashbacks, sleeping difficulties, substance abuse, shame, physical pain, an inability to maintain relationships as well as social withdrawal.

A number of researchers have examined the prevalence of PTSD in the general population, although the majority of such studies have been conducted in the United States and Europe (Farhood *et al.*, 2006). One influential study, which surveyed almost 6000 people in the United States, found an average PTSD rate of 7.8 per cent (Kessler *et al.*, 1995). Men, despite being exposed to a higher number of traumatic events, appeared to develop PTSD less often than women, with the prevalence rate for men at 5 per cent, as opposed to 10.4 per cent for women. Breslau *et al.* (1998) arrived at a slightly higher lifetime prevalence of 9.2 per cent for the general population, with a rate of 13 per cent for women and 6.2 per cent for men. Interestingly, European studies have found much lower rates. In their study covering Belgium, France, Germany, Italy, the Netherlands and Spain, Alonso *et al.* (2004) found a rate of only 1.9 per cent overall (0.9 per cent for men and 2.9 per cent for women), while another study in Germany found rates of 1 per cent for men and 2.2 per cent for women aged 14–24 years (Perkonigg *et al.*, 2000). However, as Frans *et al.* (2005) have pointed out, the conditional risk of developing PTSD was the same for the US studies and Perkonigg *et al.*'s study, indicating a higher exposure to trauma in the United States. In their own study of PTSD lifetime prevalence in Sweden, Frans *et al.* (2005) found an overall rate of 5.6 per cent, and similar gender differences, with the rate for men at 3.6 per cent and for women at 7.4 per cent.

Yet, when we look at other countries around the world where people have been exposed to much more regular levels of violent events such as wars and natural disasters, we can see the rates of PTSD rise considerably. Farhood *et al.* (2006) found that almost all of the civilian participants of their study of the south of Lebanon had been exposed to a traumatic event, and the lifetime prevalence rate of the population was 29.3 per cent, again with significant difference between men (20.9 per cent) and women (36.6 per cent). A study of returned Kosovar refugees found a PTSD rate of 23.4 per cent two years after the events they had been exposed to (Eytan *et al.*, 2004), while de Jong *et al.* (2003) found rates of 15.8 per cent in Ethiopia, 17.8 per cent in Gaza, 28.4 per cent in Cambodia and a very high 37.4 per cent in Algeria.

As we can see, the evidence from psychiatric studies shows that a higher exposure to traumatic events also results in a higher prevalence of PTSD symptoms in the general population. This holds true when we look at specific professions in society. Here, people working in emergency services, the police as well as the military, are particularly prone to developing PTSD. A number of studies have demonstrated that emergency service workers and police officers are at significantly higher risk of developing PTSD than the general population. For example, Ozen and Sir (2004) found a PTSD rate of 25 per cent in search and rescue personnel two months after the May 2003 earthquake in Bingöl, Turkey. Chang *et al.* (2003) found that 21.4 per cent of firefighters who had attended a Taiwanese earthquake showed symptoms of PTSD, and Bennet *et al.* (2005) found a similar rate of 22 per cent for British ambulance workers. In their review, Newman *et al.* (2003) also note general estimates to be between 18 and 25 per cent for emergency workers. Another profession which suffers from elevated rates of PTSD is the military. According to the evidence, around 30.9 per cent of male and 26.9 per cent of female Vietnam veterans have had PTSD at some point in their life after the war (Kulka *et al.*, 1990). For the Gulf War, rates range from 8 to 16 per cent (Wolfe *et al.*, 1999), while 11 per cent of soldiers who had been on duty in the war in Afghanistan and 15–17 per cent of those who had been in Iraq during Operation Iraqi Freedom showed symptoms of PTSD (Hoge *et al.*, 2004).

In summary, then, we have strong scientific evidence to suggest that increased exposure to traumatic events leads to increased symptoms of post-traumatic stress disorder. Anyone who is exposed to a high number of traumatic events, be it because they live in a war-torn country or work in a profession which exposes them to many deaths and injuries, is more likely to suffer from PTSD than someone who has had few such experiences. In relation to the occupation of journalists, the link here is quite apparent. Disruptive and traumatic events such as wars, natural disasters, accidents or violence are the staple of the news media, and as a result many journalists will be exposed to them. Hence, Simpson and Coté (2006, p. 37) argue that 'journalists can suffer trauma simply by doing their work – by visiting scenes of destruction, and talking to, and photographing, people who have been injured or traumatized'.

The prevalence of PTSD in journalists

Historically, journalists' experience of trauma has been little documented in the scientific literature, with very few studies undertaken until closer to the turn of the millennium. Since the start of the mid-1990s, however, we have seen an exponential growth in studies of journalistic trauma, thanks in large part to the work of the Dart Center for Journalism and Trauma.

In the first study to examine the effects that traumatic events could have on news workers, Freinkel *et al.* (1994) surveyed journalists who had witnessed the execution of double murderer Robert Alton Harris at San Quentin State Prison on 21 April 1992. It was the first execution in California since 1976, and as a result attracted particular interest from the news media. Believing that witnessing the execution by cyanide gas would be psychologically traumatic for the 18 journalists present, Freinkel *et al.* conducted an acute stress reaction questionnaire with 15 of them some weeks after the event. They found that several journalists displayed a significant number of dissociative symptoms similar to people who had endured a natural disaster. The study demonstrated that 'merely witnessing violence may be sufficient to promote the development of dissociative, anxiety and other symptoms, even in the absence of physical risk' (Freinkel *et al.*, 1994, p. 1338).

In a further, more exploratory look at trauma symptoms in journalists, Simpson and Boggs (1999) surveyed 131 journalists from daily newspapers in Washington and Michigan, and found that many of them had experienced violence directly, with 86 per cent having personally covered a violent event. Of all the respondents, almost three-quarters had covered a fire, two-thirds a car crash and just over half had reported on a murder. Simpson and Boggs found that many journalists displayed psychological stress symptoms and generally were very similar to other emergency workers in their experiences of and emotional responses to traumatic events. Almost half of the respondents (46 per cent) said they had not been prepared at all for their first trauma assignment, with a further 26 per cent saying they had not been well prepared, demonstrating the general lack of trauma awareness in US newsrooms at the time. And while journalists had generally experienced a number of traumatic events, four out of 10 could still vividly remember their first trauma story. Simpson and Bogg's study also confirmed findings of the general PTSD literature in that increased exposure appeared to lead to higher rates of PTSD. This, they argued, increased even more if journalists had witnessed a particular type of traumatic event: the scenes of car crashes, which 'produced powerful images of injury and death, images that return unbidden to the awareness of the reporter' (Simpson and Boggs, 1999, p. 18).

As we can see, these early studies into the way in which the coverage of traumatic events such as death affects those reporting on them, showed similarities between journalists and other emergency response workers. However, as Newman *et al.* (2003) point out, both studies did not employ the stringent criteria for measuring PTSD and examined a relatively small sample. Further arguing that one needed to distinguish between photographers and reporters – as reporters might be able to deal with trauma better because they could use writing as a release – Newman *et al.* conducted what has become one of the more influential studies in the field. Their survey of 875 professional US news photographers revealed that almost all of them (98 per cent) had been exposed to a traumatic event. Again, automobile accidents, fire and murder were the most common events, with car crashes most likely to be ranked as the most stressful assignments to cover. Yet, despite such overwhelming exposure to trauma, rates of PTSD were comparatively low. Depending on the type of calculation, Newman *et al.* found that only 5.9–6.7 per cent of respondents met the criteria for the disorder. When we compare these figures to those of the general population presented earlier, we can see that photojournalists are not more likely to suffer from PTSD. Nevertheless, some factors were found to be related to a higher risk of PTSD, including the number of traumatic events covered, the dimensions of journalists' assignments, their personal history of trauma experience and the social support which journalists can call on.

Similarly low rates of work-related PTSD have also been found in a study of 866 US newspaper journalists, undertaken by Pyevich *et al.* (2003). While exposure to traumatic events was again very high for this group (96 per cent) and three-quarters reported some level of stress symptoms, only 4.3 per cent of respondents could be classified as displaying PTSD symptoms. However, other studies have found higher rates, although they were frequently based on relatively small sample sizes. In a study of 167 US print and TV journalists, Smith (2008) found a rate as high as 9.7 per cent, while Teegen and Grotwinkel (2001) found an even higher rate of PTSD prevalence. Their online survey of 61 journalists – mostly from the United States and Europe – revealed that 13 per cent of respondents had developed full PTSD, while a further 15 per cent suffered from partial PTSD. A study of South African journalists found that 16 of 50 respondents (32 per cent) displayed symptoms severe enough to be diagnosed with PTSD (Marais and Stuart, 2005). In Australia, a study of 57 print journalists found that those journalists who had reported on trauma during the three years leading up to the study displayed significantly more psychological symptoms than those who had not covered trauma (McMahon, 2001). As a result of their trauma assignments, journalists were more likely to suffer from depression, social dysfunction, anxiety and insomnia. While such symptoms would usually decrease over time, McMahon noted that more experienced journalists who had covered a number of traumatic events were more likely to suffer from intrusive thoughts and avoidant behaviors than younger colleagues. Younger journalists, on the other hand, were more prone to suffer from anxiety and insomnia related to traumatic events. For a significant number of trauma-reporting journalists, symptoms tended to last for some time. In particular, 43 per cent of journalists who reported depression symptoms at the time of covering the traumatic event also experienced these symptoms long-term (McMahon, 2001, p. 53).

Some interesting evidence exists in a domain of journalism where the job description is almost defined by death and destruction: war journalism. This area has been researched in quite considerable detail by the psychiatrist Anthony Feinstein, who has published two books on the topic (Feinstein, 2003, 2006) as well as numerous journal articles. Driven by the lack of psychological evidence about the emotional well-being of war journalists, Feinstein *et al.* (2002) went about examining the prevalence of trauma-related symptoms in 140 war journalists working for major news organizations CNN, BBC, Reuters, CBC, Associated Press, ITN as well as an organization representing freelance journalists. They also included a comparison group of 107 US journalists who had never covered war, to control for factors and stresses specific to the practice of journalism, and later conducted in-depth interviews with one of every five respondents in each group. They found that war journalists were significantly more prone to alcohol abuse, reporting two to three times the amount of alcohol intake in the comparison group. War journalists were also significantly more depressed and displayed more intrusion, avoidance and arousal symptoms, leading to much higher rates of PTSD. In total, Feinstein *et al.* found that 28.6 per cent of war journalists suffered from PTSD, and 21.4 per cent experienced major depression. These rates were four to five times higher than those in the general population, and twice as high as those in police officers. Subsequent in-depth interviews confirmed the view that war journalists were greatly affected by their symptoms of PTSD: 'Every war journalist with PTSD spoke of considerable social difficulties, such as an inability to adjust to life back in a civil society, a reluctance to mix with friends, troubled relationships, the use of alcohol as a hypnotic, and embarrassing startle responses that led to social avoidance' (Feinstein *et al.*, 2002, p. 1574).

In a later study of embedded and unilateral journalists in the Iraq War, Feinstein and Nicholson (2005) examined the psychological trauma symptoms of 85 journalists employed by US and UK news organizations. The prevalence of symptoms was somewhat lower than in Feinstein's first study, with 15 per cent suffering at least moderately distressing intrusive PTSD symptoms, while 7 per cent were moderately depressed. Feinstein and Nicholson argued it was possible these results were due to the fact that none of the surveyed journalists saw the beginning of the Iraq War as their most dangerous assignment.

Noting that the vast majority of studies in the field have tended to address different types of events in their sample, which may have led to more symptom variation, Weidmann *et al.* (2008) examined 61 German, Austrian and Swiss journalists who had covered the 2004 Boxing Day tsunami. The study revealed that journalists who reported on one of the largest natural disasters in recent memory repeatedly experienced a number of potentially traumatic situations. All interviewed journalists had frequently seen extremely destroyed areas, while almost

90 per cent at least once smelled intense odors of decay. Journalists were also frequently exposed to death, with 80 per cent watching dead bodies in close proximity at least once and half of them frequently. Further, 65 per cent had at some point been exposed to a large assemblage of dead bodies, again half of them frequently. However, eight months after the tsunami, when the study took place, only 6.6 per cent of respondents fulfilled the criteria for a PTSD diagnosis. Similarly, only 7 per cent showed symptoms of depression as a result of covering the aftermath of the tsunami.

Nevertheless, as strange as it may sound, the experience of post-traumatic stress disorder may also result in some positive responses. McMahon (2005) found that many journalists who suffered from PTSD at the same time experienced the positive response of Post Traumatic Growth (PTG). This means that journalists underwent a process of significant self-enhancement that made them feel as though their life was richer but at the same time more terrible (McMahon and McLellan, 2008). Interestingly, McMahon found that the existence of PTG and PTSD alongside one another was significantly more likely to occur in cases where the trauma was related to journalists' jobs, as opposed to personal traumas. This phenomenon, however, is as yet very little researched, and more work is required in order to validate the results.

Yet, while the research shows that journalists are exposed to large numbers of traumatic events in their work, and a significant minority develops symptoms of post-traumatic stress disorder as a result, what stands out is the fact that the vast majority appear to be able to cope reasonably well with the trauma they are exposed to. In order to find out more about the strategies that journalists use to deal with trauma, Dworznik (2006) conducted in-depth interviews with 26 US television reporters and photographers in order to examine their personal narratives about their experiences. She found that journalists tailored their personal stories about traumatic events they had witnessed in line with four motives: to clarify a sense of purpose, offer justification, maintain a feeling of efficacy and control, or to increase self-worth. Thus, Dworznik argues that even though many journalists may not admit to adverse emotional effects as a result of covering traumatic events, they nevertheless seem to employ individual ways of dealing with their experiences. Therefore, they cannot be simply seen as the emotionless robots they have sometimes been described as. 'The more traumatic or difficult the incident, the more motives the subjects seemed to employ in order to give a sense of meaning to that experience' (Dworznik, 2006, p. 550).

This demonstrates the need for de-briefing of journalists following traumatic experiences, in much the same way as emergency workers.

In a national survey of 400 US news people, Beam and Spratt (2009) tried to shed more light on the relationship between journalists' reactions to trauma and their job satisfaction. In further evidence that not all journalists are severely affected, they found that the experience of traumatic events did not seem to have any significant effect on their job satisfaction, morale or career commitment. This, they argue, indicates that 'journalists are a resilient group who enter the field understanding that reporting and editing may expose them to tragedy' (Beam and Spratt, 2009, p. 432). This is reinforced when we look at Feinstein *et al.*'s (2002) point regarding the finding that the percentage of war journalists who suffered PTSD symptoms is equal to or somewhat less than that of war veterans. However, Feinstein *et al.* argue that the important difference is that, generally, soldiers and police officers receive considerable training to deal with the trauma they encounter, while war journalists tend not to.

Beam and Spratt's (2009) study also suggests that newsroom training and awareness are a vital component in the mix. Journalists showed higher levels of job satisfaction and morale when they felt they were supported by management in dealing with emotional problems after covering traumatic events. This is in line with the research conducted by Weidmann *et al.* (2008) who found that journalists whose supervisors and colleagues showed a low degree of acknowledgment displayed more post-traumatic and depressive symptoms. As we can see, management and general newsroom awareness and support are crucial in helping journalists deal with tragic experiences. Yet, a significant number of journalists have declared that they were either not at all prepared or that preparations were highly insufficient.

Trauma training for journalists

Nevertheless, the increased awareness about the effects of traumatic experiences on journalists' mental well-being has led to the establishment of a number of educational institutions which aim to help provide journalists with strategies to deal with trauma. The Dart Center for Journalism and Trauma has already been mentioned, but other organizations such as the International News Safety Institute and the Committee to Protect Journalists have increasingly raised awareness about the issue. Even journalist organizations such as the Society of Professional

Journalists in the United States and, perhaps most importantly, individual newsrooms have started to provide briefings and counseling sessions for their staff (Beam and Spratt, 2009).

That awareness-building and training for dealing with trauma are extremely crucial has been demonstrated in the scientific literature at large. A study by Guo *et al.* (2004) demonstrated that non-professional volunteer rescue workers involved in the 1999 Chi-Chi earthquake in Taiwan suffered from significantly higher rates of PTSD than professional rescuers. While few studies have examined specifically what amount of trauma-related training journalists had received, anecdotal evidence suggests this number is small. Considering that most journalists are confronted with death or violence within their first five years on the job (Johnson, 1999), it would seem logical to include such training at an early stage.

Over the past decade or so, a number of training initiatives have sprung up around the globe, mostly associated in some way with the work of the Dart Center for Journalism and Trauma. Simpson and Coté (2006; Coté and Simpson, 2000) have published two editions of their book-length account of journalism and trauma, replete with journalists' own stories of how they dealt with their experiences, as well as a number of helpful tips aimed at journalists in the field. The Dart Center's website is a treasure trove of information, which presents case studies, online learning modules and a course syllabus for journalism and psychological trauma.

A number of journalism schools at universities, particularly those linked with the Dart Center, have also established trauma training for students, some as early as the mid-1990s. At the University of Washington, an advanced reporting course includes a two-week focus on the issue, while at Michigan State students are exposed to it in introductory courses. At Indiana University, students have written literature reviews on journalism and trauma (Dworznik and Grubb, 2007). While only few large-scale evaluations of such programs have been published, anecdotal evidence suggests that students find them very useful. Maxson (1999) noted that interviews with 41 graduates from the University of Washington revealed that within their first few years the vast majority had been exposed to traumatic incidents in their work, and 79 per cent described some emotional effects from them. While only 14 of respondents had undergone the journalism and trauma training, all stated that it was a potentially useful exercise.

In order to find out more about the ways in which journalism students deal with their first potentially traumatic assignment, Dworznik and Grubb (2007) conducted a quantitative survey of 84 advanced-level journalism students from a large Midwestern and a large Southern university, as well as the student section of the Society of Professional Journalists. In addition, five students who had reported on a death-penalty murder trial were interviewed in depth. Their results were revealing in that students who had covered the murder trial, and who had not received trauma-specific training, were surprised at how much they were affected emotionally and wished they had been better prepared. On the other hand, the survey showed most students were aware of potentially traumatic incidents they might encounter in their work, with little difference between students who had received trauma training and those who had not. Dworznik and Grubb (2007, p. 204) noted that it was possible students 'are either reluctant to admit to not being prepared, or actually believe they are prepared despite lacking any real experience on which to base this conclusion'.

Still, many journalists remain without training or counseling after traumatic events. In a recent study from New Zealand, Hollings (2005) found that of 13 journalists who had reported from the areas struck by the 2004 Boxing Day tsunami, eight said they had received no counseling on their return. There is obviously still some way to go for news organizations to more adequately deal with their employees' exposure to trauma.

Conclusion

This chapter has discussed a number of studies of the trauma symptoms that journalists display, as well as the risk factors that may predispose journalists to develop post-traumatic stress disorder. We have little reliable data about what percentage of journalists is really affected. Figures vary between 5.9 per cent of photojournalists who suffer from PTSD (Newman *et al.*, 2003) to 28.6 per cent in war journalists (Feinstein *et al.*, 2002). It does seem highly likely, not just based on the evidence but also on commonsense, that war journalists are at higher risk of developing severe trauma symptoms. Feinstein's (2003, 2006) studies interviewed reasonably representative samples of war journalists, and results for this sub-group of news workers appear quite reliable. Yet it is surprising to see that only 6.6 per cent of journalists who covered the tsunami, an event during which they were exposed to numerous potentially traumatic experiences, could be diagnosed as suffering from PTSD.

In a synthesis of the research into journalists and trauma, Smith and Newman (2009) noted a number of risk factors that could lead to a higher prevalence of PTSD. These included whether journalists had been exposed to war, a greater number of traumatic events (both in a personal and professional capacity) or to assignments that had a higher intensity. In terms of work experience and age, studies had found that younger journalists with less experience, but also older journalists with more exposure to traumatic events, were more likely to be affected. Personal attributes can also be factors, such as negative beliefs about oneself or others following trauma, negative emotions such as anger, and a difficulty with emotional expression.

A number of studies were forced to deal with the problem of their method and sample size, which may have had an effect on their results – an issue often noted in the literature itself. Some studies suffered from very low response rates and respondents were self-selected, potentially leading to skewed results as those who had experienced severe trauma may have been more likely to respond to the study (McMahon, 2001; Teegen and Grotwinkel, 2001). Further, many studies employed surveys to determine some of the symptoms, but an accurate diagnosis for PTSD cannot be made without interview (see Newman *et al.*, 2003). A further problem for the comparability of results between studies has been the fact that often different measurement tools were employed. Some studies have used the so-called Impact of Events Scale (IES) to determine the number of intrusive, avoidance and arousal symptoms, while others have used the PTSD Checklist. Newman *et al.* (2003) argue that the latter is a more stringent criterion for measuring the disorder, yet not all studies have since employed it. As a result of these various methodological limitations, there is still some confusion as to the real level of post-traumatic stress disorder in journalists, other than to say that a significant minority is affected by it.

The field of journalism and trauma is still very young and we know relatively little about the complicated ways in which traumatic events such as death affect journalists' decision-making as well as their emotional well-being. Yet, it is also a particularly vibrant field which has grown quite quickly over the past decade. We have seen that journalists are not emotionless and sensation-hungry human beings who simply run from one tragedy to another, completely detached from what is going on around them. To the contrary, journalists can be described as first responders in much the same way as emergency relief workers (Hight and Smyth, 2003). A number of journalists have undoubtedly suffered tremendously at times from the haunting scenes they have witnessed, regardless of whether they were actually diagnosed with PTSD or not. For some, the trauma has been so great that it led to substance abuse like alcoholism or drug-taking. For others, it even played a factor in them taking their own life. The stigma that has traditionally been attached to journalists who show emotions may well have played a part in them finding it difficult to deal with the nightmares, anxiety, shame and social withdrawal, all symptoms of the trauma they had experienced. But for a much larger number of others, life has gone on reasonably normally – for what reasons is not yet entirely clear.

6
Audience Responses to Death in the News

So far, this book has examined the processes of selection, production and transmission of news reports of death. As we have seen, there exists quite a variety of studies into the way in which the news media approach the issue. At the heart of many such studies, however, have been not only the actual messages, but also a concern over the meanings that audiences may extract from such reports. And while empirical research has shown that death is rarely displayed in graphic detail in the news, some have argued that there are too many such images, which are driven by the voyeuristic demands of the audience. The result, they believe, is an audience that cares less about others. This notion of compassion fatigue in Western society has been a topic of much debate as of late. The term compassion fatigue actually goes back to earlier notions of burnout among trauma workers, who experienced feelings of avoidance and other secondary stress symptoms as a result of their work (Figley, 1995). And while this concept has been applied to measure traumatic stress in news audiences, the term has also been adopted by media scholars. In a media studies context, compassion fatigue has come to be seen as a process of 'becoming so used to the spectacle of dreadful events, misery or suffering that we stop noticing them' (Tester, 2001, p. 13). Yet, while the origins of burnout lie in empirically measurable symptoms of stress, the debate over a media-induced compassion fatigue has been largely normative. This chapter will first review these normative debates among media scholars, before moving to a more evidence-based examination of what we know about audience attitudes to images of death and dying. This is followed by an examination of how the field of trauma studies has lately contributed to our understanding of the ways in which audiences experience news coverage of traumatic events. Finally, I pay special attention to the impact of suicide reports on news audiences.

As this chapter demonstrates, we actually know relatively little about audience attitudes to, and effects from, news coverage of death. The research in this area has been quite patchy, and arguments are often derived from studies which have looked at broader issues. I should also point out that we need to remember that audience attitudes are not always static and can change from time period to time period, and even across similar cultures. As Jean Seaton (2005, p. 290) notes, 'what contemporary audiences are prepared to watch and what they make of what they see are not the same as they used to be, and they will go on changing. At any point such values feel fundamental and even "natural", yet they shift with great rapidity.' Such an argument resonates, of course, with a point made earlier in relation to the history of the representation of death in the news and the wider sociological literature about our attitudes to death. I have argued that graphic depictions of death – both in words and images – have a long history that to some extent reflects audience attitudes to death.

The effect of media messages on audiences

How audiences react to news has been an important scholarly endeavor for quite some time, which has become even more relevant, and arguably more difficult, in today's media-saturated environment. Many of the studies discussed in the previous chapters were conducted with a concern for how stories would impact on society, even if they did not test for any effects. The study of media effects has a long and varied history, with the media at times regarded as all-powerful, and at other times as a more opaque influence. McQuail (2005) identifies four historical phases in media effects research which are useful in providing some basic theoretical background for the remainder of this chapter. The first phase, according to McQuail, extended from the beginning of the twentieth century until the 1930s. During this time, which included the introduction of radio and film to mass audiences, media were seen as pervading public life, and as all-powerful, as evidenced by their use for advertising and war propaganda. Media were thought to provide stimuli which resulted in a direct and predictable response from audiences. However, very little scientific investigation was undertaken to examine such arguments. As a result, the second phase, which lasted from the 1930s to the early 1960s, saw considerable efforts to empirically test the assumptions of the stimulus-response model. A much more complicated picture of media effects began to emerge; and McQuail notes that many researchers were somewhat disappointed by the small amount of evidence they could find to confirm previously-held assumptions. While media effects were indeed found, they were not as direct as expected. However, as McQuail points out, the notion of the media as having little effect never took hold for long, and it has since been challenged as a myth by others.

Instead, a third phase began in the 1960s, driven by the increasing pervasiveness of television in Western society and a renewed belief in powerful mass media. This time, however, the focus was not on direct effects, but rather 'a shift of attention towards long-term change, towards cognitions rather than attitude and affect, and towards collective phenomena such as climates of opinion, structures of belief, definitions of social reality, ideologies, cultural patterns and institutional forms of media provision' (McQuail, 2005, p. 460). The fourth phase, which began in the late 1970s and continues today, has seen a period of negotiated media influence. Now, a social constructivist view allows for powerful media, but also for powerful audiences. Social constructivism sees the news media as constructing images of reality in predictable and patterned ways, while audiences interact with the media content and construct their own social reality from it (McQuail, 2005, p. 461). The discussions earlier in relation to the ways in which images carry denotations and connotations also fit well here.

Carey (1989) has observed that one reason perceptions of media influence have changed over time may lie in the fact that other social transformations took place at those times. Indeed McQuail (2005) also argues that during times of crisis and war, perhaps mass media actually are more influential as audiences rely on them even more for information and governments, business and other elites try to use them to influence public opinion. This point is particularly relevant, as a considerable amount of research on the effect of news stories about death has tended to focus on war and disaster reporting. Before examining how scholars have examined the effect of such stories, however, we need to briefly examine another area in which news media may have an influence.

News media influences on government policy

An examination of the relationship between the mass media and government policy is essential when we examine how deaths, particularly during wars and natural disasters, may affect people. Researchers have paid a considerable amount of attention to the relationship between the mass media and foreign policy, with studies showing influence to be complex and going both ways. On one side, arguments have been made for the influence of mass media on foreign policy, also known as the 'CNN effect' (Strobel, 1996). However, other analysts have downplayed it and instead argued that the media work to mobilize support for the foreign policies of the government, something that Robinson (2001) termed the 'manufacturing consent' school of thought, derived from the influential book of the same name by Herman and Chomsky (1988).

In an in-depth study of the role of the media in British diplomacy, Cohen (1986) argued that its role was three-fold. Firstly, news media were sources of information to members of diplomatic missions; secondly, they were channels of communication among policymakers; and thirdly, they were means to shape opinions and gain support for policies from abroad and at home. Researchers have since argued there are also a number of cases in which news coverage influenced foreign policy. Strobel (1996) believes a good example of media influence on foreign policy is the CNN effect. He argues that CNN is able to influence foreign policy through its instantaneous coverage of breaking news events, which stimulate public opinion, which in turn demands instant responses from the government, thereby shaping foreign policy. But Strobel sees the media acting mainly as providers of information and whether government decision makers use the information or are used by it depends largely on the officials themselves.

The notion that the news media play a powerful role in influencing policy, particularly at times of war and human suffering, has entered the realm of folklore to the extent that many people now take it as given. However, a number of researchers have challenged this notion and also examined the reverse influence. Robinson's (2002) argument links closely to Herman and Chomsky's (1988) propaganda model, which argues that the media are subservient to and follow government agendas in the reporting of foreign news. He notes that this 'manufacturing consent' model emphasizes the ability of governments to influence journalists 'and the tendency of journalists to both self-censor and perceive events through the cultural and political prisms of their respective political and social elites' (Robinson, 2001, p. 525). Further, Robinson discerns two versions of the manufacturing consent paradigm: an executive and an elite version. The executive version (for example, Herman and Chomsky, 1988; Entman, 1991; Herman, 1993) emphasizes the extent to which media coverage conforms to the agendas of government officials, who are understood as members of the executive. The elite version revolves around the work of Hallin (1986) and Bennett

(1990). In his analysis of the US media's coverage of the Vietnam War, Hallin (1986) found the coverage only turned critical once some of the political elite in Washington had started to turn against the war. Bennett (1990) argued along the same lines, saying that when the media covered dissensus in policy, it was purely because of its responsibility to highlight these conflicts within the centers of power. Both Hallin and Bennett therefore leave room for the media to actually be critical of the executive, albeit only if disagreement over policy already exists (Robinson, 2002).

However, Robinson (2001, p. 529) argues that 'elite manufacturing consent theory tends to ignore the possibility that journalists might actually take sides [...] during elite debates over policy [...] and in doing so become active and powerful participants in a political debate'. Robinson notes the large amount of evidence which suggests that media coverage does play a role in creating policy, such as in the Vietnam War or in the lead-up to the US intervention in Somalia. He acknowledges that critical journalism is unlikely to occur when there is a consensus on policy, but suggests that media can influence policy when there is none in place or when dissensus exists.

The effect that news reports may or may not have on audiences as well as government policy is important to keep in mind for the following discussion of research into the way in which news reports of death may affect audiences. As in the debates over general media effects, we will see that research in this area is also characterized by disagreements over the degree of influence which news reports have. Firstly, I examine arguments in relation to news reports of human suffering in the modern media-saturated context, and how these supposedly lead to compassion fatigue among audiences. This discussion is largely based on theoretical explications and lacks comprehensive empirical approaches to support it. However, following this discussion, I examine evidence from the few empirical studies that exist, before reviewing slightly different arguments from a more scientific approach which is rooted in the study of trauma.

The compassion fatigue thesis

Earlier, some of Roland Barthes' ideas about semiology were discussed, in particular the way in which images have denotations and connotations. While addressing images in essays earlier in life, Barthes (1981), in his last work, concerns himself more in-depth with photography; and it is his work in *Camera Lucida*, as well as Susan Sontag's (1977)

On Photography, that has been influential for much of the recent visual analysis of death, particularly for ideas about how stereotyped images of suffering supposedly lead to compassion fatigue among audiences. Partly a very intimate account of his grief for his late mother, for whom he cared full-time during the final months of her life, Barthes here deals with the, at times quite personal, meanings we extract from photographs. As he was rummaging through old photographs of his mother, Barthes noticed how the vast majority of them did not touch him in any meaningful way, but only reminded him that she was dead. The images to him meant death, as they were taken at a time that had passed. One photo of her, at the age of five and physically unrecognizable to him, however, struck a chord with a grieving Barthes, for to him, it encapsulated her spirit. He thus developed the concepts of *studium* and *punctum*, which were two elements of a photograph. *Studium* refers to the intention of the photographer that appears in a photo, and allows interpretation against a common cultural or political background. News and war photographs, according to Barthes, display a lot of *studium* in that they are interpreted similarly by members of the same culture. *Punctum*, on the other hand, refers to unintentional details within a photograph that were not intended by the photographer and that are interpreted differently and in very personal ways by those looking at them. The photo of his mother at the age of five displayed such *punctum*, Barthes said. Thus, he criticizes the generic, the obvious in news photographs, arguing that they are portraying only one single message. He sees no *punctum* in such images, and while they can shock, they cannot actually disturb. 'These journalistic photographs are received (all at once), perceived. I glance through them, I don't recall them; no detail (in some corner) ever interrupts my reading: I am interested in them (as I am interested in the world), I do not love them' (Barthes, 1981, p. 41).

In relation to news photographs of death, then, we can use Barthes' work to argue that images that are too literal, rather than engaging audiences for a cause, have the potential to actually desensitize the reader, as there is nothing left for their imagination that could really draw them into a photo and more deeply contemplate its message. Audience reactions are important particularly at times of human suffering, as images, political as ever, are sometimes believed to be capable of influencing the populace into action.

Barthes' disappointment in news images is very similar to Susan Sontag's analysis in her collection of essays published in *On Photography*, another seminal work in the field published in 1977. Sontag also argues that photographs have a leveling effect and that they discourage the viewer from intervening, particularly in the case of images of human suffering. Sontag believes that photographs much more so than television have the potential to stir public emotions, simply because they freeze a moment in time and can be looked at again and again. She argues that photographs like the one of Kim Phuc, the South Vietnamese child sprayed by napalm running towards Nick Ut's camera, 'probably did more to increase public revulsion against the war than a hundred hours of televised barbarities' (Sontag, 1977, p. 18). Sontag admits that seeing photos of German concentration camps for the first time at the age of 12 had genuinely shocked her. But at the same time, the experience numbed her to the repeated viewing of images of atrocity.

> To suffer is one thing; another thing is living with the photographed images of suffering, which does not necessarily strengthen conscience and the ability to be compassionate. It can also corrupt them. Once one has seen such images, one has started down the road of seeing more – and more. Images transfix. Images anesthetize....
>
> (Sontag, 1977, p. 20)

Sontag believes that the glut of aestheticized photographs of suffering has actually made us less compassionate, less provoked by them. In fact, the first shock wears off with repeated viewing, she says. 'The vast catalogue of misery and injustice throughout the world has given everyone a certain familiarity with atrocity, making the horrible seem more ordinary – making it appear familiar, remote ("it's only a photograph"), inevitable' (Sontag, 1977, pp. 20–21). And there is support from a number of other scholars about images of suffering that adhere to certain norms which are repetitive. Zelizer (2002, 2004) argues that photography of war tends to be informed by and actually invokes previous photographs, in a sense using old and tried templates for new events. This, of course, is not only true for images, but for much news coverage of disasters that is formulaic (Lule, 2001). Additionally, Sontag argues that, in themselves photographs do not have the power to make us understand, and can therefore only ever remain a representation of a surface. Both Zelizer (1998) and Sontag (2003) believe that images do have the power to influence the public, but in order to do so, news media must act as a mobilizing agent by providing the necessary narratives around images.

Sontag and Barthes' arguments have inspired a long tradition of scholarly criticism of the visual news coverage of death. The formulaic coverage of atrocities, it is argued, does nothing to rouse audiences' empathy into action, but in fact leads to compassion fatigue. In her study of compassion fatigue, Moeller (1999) argues in much the same vein as Sontag, although her arguments extend across all news coverage, not just images. Moeller believes that journalism's formulaic treatment of foreign wars, disasters and diseases does much to contribute to compassion fatigue amongst Americans. 'A single child at risk commands our attention and prompts our action. But one child, and then another, and another, and another and on and on and on is too much. A crowd of people in danger is faceless. Numbers alone can numb. All those starving brown babies over the years blur together' (Moeller, 1999, p. 36).

However, in a forceful critique of the compassion fatigue argument, John Taylor (1998) renounces commonly-held views in this regard. He challenges Sontag's point that photographs in themselves cannot make us understand by pointing out that they always exist in some context.

> Documentary photographs in the press rarely stand alone. They are almost always accompanied by headlines, captions, and stories which guide readers in how to view them. The fate of photography depends not so much on the content of the image itself as on its placement, on the extent that it is moved from one setting to another, and the way it is used to narrate events, or to support newspaper stories.…
>
> (Taylor, 1998, p. 19)

Taylor does not believe in the argument that audiences now experience compassion fatigue because of the surfeit of photography that acts as an analgesic on passive audiences. Instead, he believes the phrase compassion fatigue makes an unsustainable claim: 'It hints at an earlier stage when compassion was intense but which has simply become spoiled by the abundance and voyeurism of media coverage' (Taylor, 1998, p. 19). The claims of compassion fatigue advocates cannot be supported when scrutinized, Taylor contends. He argues against the notion of a surfeit of photography, pointing out, much in line with evidence already discussed, that we actually see very few graphic images in the news. The reason, according to Taylor, lies in the 'ecology of images' that makes such photos relatively rare and costly. Secondly, he vehemently opposes the notion that photography is an analgesic, as though it only lulls its viewers into a position of security from which they can view the suffering of others. For support, he cites John Keane (1996) who has similarly argued that audiences do experience a number of reactions when seeing graphic images, such as moral revulsion, avoidance or a need to discuss them.

Taylor believes that laying the blame for compassion fatigue at the hands of photography is to forget that it is a human tendency to forget past instances of suffering. 'Forgetfulness is not the fault of photography but of those who choose not to respond to shameful incidents, or refuse to acknowledge their existence' (Taylor, 1998, p. 25). In his book, Taylor notes a number of ways in which war photography is a crucial element of democracy. Using examples from the Gulf War, Bosnia, Rwanda and other recent conflicts, he points out how rarely graphic images are actually seen in the news, before making the case that such images are still important, so as to avoid forgetting. He believes there are a number of possible reactions to seeing photographs of suffering, including pity and outrage, action, revulsion and indifference. Most of all, Taylor (1998, p. 194) argues that the power of the photograph may be somewhat limited 'but it is not therefore useless'. In fact, if such images exist and are circulated in the public sphere, then 'forgetting about them or refusing to see them becomes a deliberate choice, a conscious act of citizenship: then people are choosing ignorance over knowledge' (Taylor, 1998, p. 195). Taylor also demonstrates the effect that graphic news reporting of death can have on government, citing the example of California Senator Diane Feinstein, who said she eventually voted for the lifting of the weapons embargo in Bosnia due to the impact a photo of a woman hanging from a tree in Srebrenica made on her.

In another work critical of compassion fatigue thesis advocates, David Campbell (2004) argues that many of their arguments do not stand up to further examination. To support this claim, he points to the relatively small number of images of death and dying in the news, as well as the fact that millions of pounds in donations in the United Kingdom are evidence that public empathy 'is anything but exhausted' (Campbell, 2004, p. 61). Campbell further believes that the compassion fatigue critique also confuses unwillingness by governments to become involved in instances of human suffering overseas with a lack of public empathy. Nevertheless, he acknowledges that the generic quality of some photographs of suffering has the potential to diminish the horror of the event, but he also issues a call for more images to be seen, as not doing so would not further our understanding of others either. Campbell argues that there are three economies which govern the use of photos of death in the contemporary news media: the economy of indifference to others, the economy of 'taste and decency' and the economy of display, which refers to the way in which meaning is created through the use of surrounding text. Campbell (2004, p. 55) believes that an intersection of these three economies 'means we have witnessed a disappearance of the dead in contemporary coverage which restricts the possibility for an ethical politics exercising responsibility in the face of crimes against humanity'.

How important graphic images can be is demonstrated in the killing of James Byrd in 1998. Byrd, an African-American, had been dragged alive behind a pick-up truck by white supremacists until his body hit a culvert and his arm and head were severed. Rushdy (1999) laments the fact that no photos of the murder were available in the news, despite their graphic nature. He believes that such images have the potential to shock the public at large, and perhaps stir sections of the community into action. 'Why do we need to see the corpse? It is possible that pictures of graphic violence still have the power to make an impression' (Rushdy, 1999, p. 77).

Interestingly, Sontag herself later renounced some of the ways in which her original ideas about compassion fatigue had been taken further. In her 2003 book, *Regarding the Pain of Others*, Sontag (2003, p. 105) noted that at the time she wrote *On Photography* she believed that 'as much as they create sympathy...photographs shrivel sympathy'. However, she said, she was not so sure now. She still believed that the relentless showing of atrocity and suffering, particularly on television, inures audiences to the horrors of war and gives them an opportunity to remain or become indifferent. But at the same time, she thought that such images are still important, as only through them can wars become real for audiences. Sontag argued that demands to cut images of carnage back and work toward an ecology of images were misguided. In so much, she agreed with the case made by Taylor (1998), which sees the publication of graphic images as more important than the sensibilities of audiences.

> Let the atrocious images haunt us. Even if they are only tokens, and cannot possibly encompass most of the reality to which they refer, they still perform a vital function. The images say: This is what human beings are capable of doing – may volunteer to do, enthusiastically, self-righteously. Don't forget.
>
> (Sontag, 2003, p. 115)

That images are polysemic is also acknowledged by Sontag herself: 'Photographs may give rise to opposing responses. A call for peace. A cry for revenge. Or simply the bemused awareness, continually restocked by photographic information, that terrible things happen' (Sontag, 2003, p. 13). In fact, Sontag vehemently criticized what she described as the views of critics in the rich countries who have the luxury of merely being spectators, safe in the knowledge they are far removed from the suffering they are watching. But, she points out, 'There are hundreds of millions of television watchers who are far from inured to what they see on television. They do not have the luxury of patronizing reality' (Sontag, 2003, p. 111).

Cottle (2006) believes that it is not automatically the case that graphic images of death and suffering will actually produce anti-war sentiments or undermine the stomach for war, and that these instances are rather rare. But he also admits that such images are still useful and necessary, because they are 'potentially bearing witness to the suffering frequently caused in our name and which should never be rendered invisible on moral grounds of civility, taste or decency' (Cottle, 2006, p. 99).

There is a way of stirring audiences' emotions while at the same limiting graphic imagery as much as possible. In a recent, particularly valuable contribution to the scholarship of visual representations of death in the news, Zelizer (2010) has drawn attention to the fact that a popular way of depicting death in journalism has actually been by way of images where people are not technically dead yet. She notes that many images, which have usually been regarded as photos of death – such as the General Loan shooting, the death of Ruth Snyder, or the Lee Harvey Oswald shooting – actually need to be classified as 'about-to-die' images, because they show degrees of impending death, rather than completed death. Through a move to the subjunctive, from 'as is' to 'as if', such images, Zelizer argues, allow journalists to circumvent the rules on taste and decency, and sanitize images' visualization. Such images, which ask the viewer to fill in the details for themselves, are also able to elicit, comparable to Barthes' *punctum*, a multitude of emotional responses ranging across the entire spectrum. Certainly, Zelizer believes, such images may be more able to move the public; yet further support the argument that compassion fatigue is not inevitable.

The arguments of compassion fatigue advocates and those who deny that pictures are necessarily the cause are not so different from each other. Seeing formulaic images can certainly lead one to notice them less, or to see them as less real. What is important is that they are placed in context, and this seems to be at the heart of Sontag and Moeller's arguments. Sontag eventually admitted that such images are still impor-tant, but it seems she wondered about the way in which they were displayed and, as a result, used. In an analysis of images from the civil war in El Salvador and the ways in which they were used, Andersen (1989) believes that while they may have raised public awareness of the suffering, they did not actually create an outcry opposed to US involvement in the war. She notes that 'photographs of corpses lying in the street, and even piles of corpses, were published, but the accompanying articles and captions rarely included adequate explanations as to who had done the killing' (Andersen, 1989, p. 99). Thus, the importance of portraying suffering lies in the way in which images are explained and contextualized. Andersen believes that the photos could have had more of an effect on audiences had they been given this context. As Sontag later acknowledged, horrific images are still necessary, but it is the fact that they are so rarely portrayed in an adequate context which worries compassion fatigue advocates.

There is certainly a strong argument to be made for the importance of displaying graphic images of suffering in the news, even if they do not always lead to immediate action. As Taylor (1998) pointed out, there is a difference between public action and action by governments, and it does appear that compassion fatigue advocates have tended to confuse one with the other. Certainly, images can still shock and, if displayed carefully, will continue to do so, as Zelizer's (2010) examination of 'about-to-die' images shows. If we had no images from war-torn countries, would we be even remotely interested in those wars? Shocking images do still have the power to at least cause a small stir, as the following section demonstrates.

Evidence for audience reactions

John Keane (1996) strongly opposes the view that audiences are passive receivers of images of horror who are overwhelmed by their sheer amount. He believes that in fact there are a variety of responses to seeing such images. Such a thesis, he says,

> supposes that the audience comprises hapless and gullible idiots who are incapable of interpreting or reinterpreting images of violence, even those which are presented with explanations of their origins, causes and ethical implications, and that the audience is therefore at most capable of catharsis, or gross satisfaction in the misfortune of others. This assumption that audiences are stupid misanthropes flies in the face of considerable counterevidence that they sometimes experience moral revulsion at the violent images with which they are confronted . . . .
>
> (Keane, 1996, p. 179)

Tester (2001, p. 133) also argues that 'we might be bored and apathetic a lot of the time but, sometimes, something happens which stirs us out of stupor and inspires us to take part in events like telethons'. Such an approach is obviously more in line with recent research on the way audiences draw meaning from media texts, as it accepts that news stories are polysemic rather than all-powerful transmissions of messages that always have the same result. However, as noted by Walter *et al.* (1995) and Höijer (2004), there have been very few surveys of audience attitudes to seeing death in the news media.

Höijer (2004) has in fact conducted a small study of the audience in this regard. She criticizes approaches from critical media scholars who see the audience as passive spectators without compassion, and notes that Moeller (1999) 'almost takes it for granted that the American audience she discusses does not care about the human suffering it is fed with by the media' (Höijer, 2004, p. 528). Instead, she sees a need to actually examine how audiences react to and interpret news coverage of violence and suffering, and, based on surveys in Scandinavia, she identifies a two-sided effect. On the one hand, news reporting can actually lead to global compassion, while on the other, ignorance and compassion fatigue are also evident. Thus, a much more differentiated picture emerges that takes into account the varying meanings people draw from media coverage, and the reactions they have.

> We should not idealize the audience, believing that all we need to do in order to awake compassion and engagement is to expose people to pictures of humanitarian disasters. Neither should we believe the opposite, that the audience mainly turns away in cynicism and compassion fatigue, fed up with reports of expulsions, massacres, genocide, and terrorist and bomb attacks....
>
> (Höijer, 2004, p. 529)

And in fact, there are impressive examples of public compassion. Following the 2004 Boxing Day tsunami in the Indian Ocean, the unprecedented news coverage of death and destruction around the region resulted in a huge outpouring of donations from all around the world. Even as these lines are being written, donations are being sent to Haiti following the devastating January 2010 earthquake. An empirical study of 22 earthquakes around the world found that increased television news coverage was related to an increase in private donations (Simon, 1997). When US network news coverage was higher – mostly as a result of a higher death toll – private donations increased as well, but interestingly, government assistance and aid from outside the United States did not. These were more associated with the number of affected people, rather than just the dead.

At the same time, however, Kinnick *et al.* (1996) have also found that compassion fatigue as a result of news reporting does exist, at least in some of the 316 people they surveyed. In contrast to much of the normative literature discussed earlier, they used a more clinical definition of compassion fatigue as burnout and found a strong link between compassion fatigue and the mass media. For example, it appeared that social issues such as homelessness and AIDS were more likely to be at risk of compassion fatigue, while violent crime and child abuse resulted in lower levels of burnout. Kinnick *et al.* (1996) argued that the mass media contribute to compassion fatigue firstly by providing stories that serve as aversive stimuli which prompt avoidance and, secondly, by sending large numbers of negative messages which foster desensitization to social problems. Importantly, however, they could not make out a uniform type or even level of compassion fatigue among audiences. For those who were already negatively predisposed toward a social problem, pervasive media coverage only reinforced such notions and fostered desensitization. But for those respondents who were initially sympathetic to an issue, a number of outcomes were possible. Pervasive media coverage is thus able to foster a variety of reactions: (a) disinterest due to boredom; (b) frustration when it appears nothing can be done; (c) increased emotional sensitivity and empathy with victims; or (d) avoidance because of empathic distress, that is, compassion fatigue. Such findings link in with the wider literature on how people receive images, which is discussed in the next section.

Effects of graphic images

Due to its inherently visual nature, television has been at the forefront of the study into the ways in which images can have powerful effects. Kepplinger (1991) has noted that audiences are indeed much more likely to believe what they see, rather than what they hear or read. In addition, images have been found to be more capable than text to demand audiences' attention (Garcia and Stark, 1991; Lang, 2000), and also are more likely to be remembered by them (Graber, 1990; Kepplinger, 1991; Brosius, 1993; Nabi, 2003). Television news images are also deemed to be more likely to elicit emotional responses from audiences and, as a result, may be more capable of influencing public opinion.

Graber (1987, p. 76) believes that visual footage which accompanies television news stories will actually 'make audiences care about an issue and the people involved in it'. In particular, negative messages, such as news about death, are believed to generally receive more attention from viewers. However, when such items contain emotion as well, viewers are more likely to avoid such messages altogether (Lang *et al.*, 1995). Similarly, Newhagen (1998) found that viewers were much more likely to avoid images of disgust, such as graphic images of death, than images that evoked anger or fear. In turn, memory scores were also better for anger and fear, while images evoking disgust were remembered less often. Newhagen concluded that for news producers who wanted to achieve certain reactions from their viewers, it was much more appropriate to begin news items with images of anger, as subsequent information was memorized better. In much the same vein, an experiment with US college students found that while morbid scenes are most compelling for viewers of crime news, they frequently don't actually remember them (Artwick, 1996). Instead, faces of living people who were affected by crime were much more memorable, leading Artwick to suggest that such images should be included in crime news rather than graphic images.

Much of the evidence considered here, however, only concentrated on issues surrounding basic information processing like attention and the recall of news items, rather than investigating the ways in which such images may influence viewers. In fact, the belief in the media's powerful effects on public opinion and foreign policy has been long-established, and, until recently, was rarely challenged. Journalists themselves often think that their work can have powerful effects on the public (Fahmy and Wanta, 2007). However, as we have seen already in the discussion on graphic images during the Vietnam War, studies have found that such images were only published once audiences and some elites had already turned against the war, and were therefore more a reflection of public opinion rather than its driving force (Hallin, 1986; Taylor, 1998). Similarly, Perlmutter (1998) also found that such notions of the powerful media were more a construct of the political establishment itself than grounded in any empirical evidence. Despite rare empirical evidence to support the view of the powerful media, Domke *et al.* (2002) have argued that 'it is both one of the oldest and one of the most current assumptions of political theorists, elites and news pundits that vivid, striking images have a particularly strong impact on public opinion and, in turn, on the political behavior of individuals'. Yet, as some scholars have observed, this assumption has so far rarely been examined in any meaningful detail (Domke *et al.*, 2002; Spratt, 2005).

Some researchers have begun to challenge the dominant paradigm. For example, Perlmutter (1998) examines a number of images which have come to be perceived as 'icons of outrage'. He examines each in some detail for the impact the photograph had on government policy as well as public opinion. While he believes that some images are certainly able to influence public opinion and ultimately impact on foreign policy, there are many more cases in which this does not hold true, as evidenced in his study of students who had problems recognizing many so-called 'iconic' images. Rather, he concludes, people react to photographs of suffering in very complex and ultimately unpredictable ways (Perlmutter, 1998). Pfau *et al.* (2008) also note that the existing evidence for television news' capability to sway public opinion is quite equivocal. In relation to news about death, a study of students' attraction to morbid stories on television, in textual form as well as in photographs, yields interesting results. Bennett *et al.* (1992) expected to find that television stories would be regarded as more interesting by their respondents, but they were surprised to find that this was not the case. In fact, there was no significant difference in terms of attraction and aversion reactions between any of the three media they tested, prompting the authors to speculate that television may be unfairly singled out.

Domke *et al.* (2002) examined the influence that previously held views can have on the meanings which audiences extract from news photographs, by studying responses to the famous John Paul Filo photograph of a woman screaming over the body of a dead anti-war protester in the May 1970 Kent State University shootings. Rather than responding favorably to the anti-war movement, they actually found that audiences responded more favorably to those opposing the protesters, that is, the government. The reason for such an unusual result, they concluded, lies most likely in people's often-negative considerations about protesters: 'Clearly, the manner in which many issues are covered by news media – both in terms of news texts and photographs – is *not* purely cognitive *or* affective' (Domke *et al.*, 2002, p. 147; italics in original).

Further evidence to support the notion that a variety of meanings emanate from news photographs has come from audience perceptions of Joe Rosenthal's iconic 'Flag raising on Iwo Jima' image (Spratt *et al.*, 2005). The researchers compared views of the photo among college-age students before and after 9/11, and discovered some significant differences in the meanings they extracted from it. While mainstream print media had encoded the image 'with pro-American symbolism of national patriotism, unity, and victory' both before and after the events of 9/11, the image had 'renewed meaning for the young respondents, triggering associations with the new national tragedy and their negotiated perceptions of national identity' (Spratt *et al.*, 2005, pp. 118–119). Indeed, images of death may stay with viewers longer under certain conditions. A phone survey conducted two months after 9/11 found that those who had reacted to the events with the emotions of sorrow or shock tended to better remember the graphic images of people jumping from the towers as well as images of corpses. At the same time, such memories also increased their level of concern with terrorism (Fahmy *et al.*, 2006).

It is therefore quite likely that images, even graphic ones, can have at least some potential to stir public emotions, which in turn may or may not engender change in government policy. However, in particular, graphic images of death and dying may also have an adverse effect. For example, audiences mostly say they do not want to see close-up images of the dead and injured, and there appear to be some measurable negative effects of such coverage.

Audience attitudes to graphic images

A nationwide survey in Britain about audience attitudes to news coverage of the Gulf War found that the vast majority did not think it was acceptable for television news show close-ups of the dead or badly injured (Morrison, 1992). In fact, only just fewer than 10 per cent of people supported including such pictures. Most people were in favor of showing scenes from a distance, so the faces of the dead were not recognizable, or showing only scenes after the dead and badly injured had been removed. Similarly, a Pew Research Center report found that 70 per cent of Americans were appreciative of the US media for its restraint in showing graphic images of the remains of four US contractors who had been killed in the Iraqi city of Fallujah in March, 2004 (Silcock *et al.*, 2008, p. 37). Indeed, according to the report, only 7 per cent of those surveyed said they would support the use of more explicit images. Such statistics do lend some support to the squeamishness on the part of journalists in censoring many graphic images, at least when they are 'our dead'. In fact, rather than just matters of taste, they also may have a very basic economic background. If news media showed too much, they may run the risk of losing part of their audience.

Across cultures, however, such audience sentiments can vary. News organizations in other countries, like the pan-Arab news channel Al-Jazeera, often show a much larger amount of graphic images. During the

Iraq War, this coverage also received attention from US political elites, who identified it as sensationalist and responsible for stirring anti-US sentiment in the region. A pilot study of Al-Jazeera viewers' attitudes to the channel's coverage found an overwhelming support of the inclusion of graphic images. Almost nine out of 10 respondents supported the use of graphic visuals, both for the Iraq War as well as the Palestine/Israel conflict (Fahmy and Johnson, 2007). Mindful that their study had a number of limitations, such as self-selection of respondents and low Internet penetration in many Arab countries, Fahmy and Johnson nevertheless were able to demonstrate that at least a trend exists in a higher acceptance of graphic images in the Arab world than in the West.

However, even in the West people do increasingly choose to view graphic imagery as the Internet has opened up new opportunities in this area, a point that will be discussed in a later chapter. So why do people look at graphic imagery, despite often professing to not want to see it? Psychiatrist Frank Ochberg, an expert in trauma studies, believes it is a biological reality that we are interested in images of horror and terror. He says our usual response to such images is 'curiosity, interest, and even a certain amount of pleasure. That doesn't mean we're callous or corrupt or sadistic. It just means we're participating in a biological reality' (Ochberg, cited in Simpson and Coté, 2006, p. 147).

Seeing images of death and disasters may also have a very real impact on audiences in terms of the trauma such viewing may generate. We have already seen that journalists can invariably get affected by the traumatic events they report on, leading to post-traumatic stress disorder (PTSD). But of course, in a similar way, those who read about and view reports from traumatic events may also be affected by such news coverage. In the recent past, a number of studies have begun to look at the ways in which audiences can develop symptoms of traumatic stress.

Audiences and post-traumatic stress disorder

In light of the previous discussions about the perceived existence of a compassion fatigue among news audiences, it is important to acknowledge here that such approaches have rarely been conducted from a clinical perspective. As I have already pointed out, compassion fatigue originally refers to the way in which first responders to traumatic events experience emotional burnout and stress. This leads to secondary traumatic stress, which Figley (1995) puts on a par with PTSD. Therefore, this section focuses on the way in which the field of trauma studies has addressed the issue of compassion fatigue and PTSD of audiences.

It is important to remember that the more normative studies discussed earlier have tended to look at compassion fatigue more as a phenomenon that makes audiences care less about others, while trauma studies examine it in the light of the psychological impact on audiences themselves.

While experiencing traumatic events indirectly, for example through the media, may not have the same effect as direct exposure, researchers have nevertheless found some evidence to suggest that increased exposure to trauma may heighten acute and post traumatic stress disorders. In a review of existing literature, Cantrell (2005) notes that while such studies are certainly still in their infancy, early results suggest that adults and especially children seem to be affected by viewing media coverage of traumatic events. Two main traumatic events have received attention from researchers so far, with studies conducted after the Oklahoma City bombing in 1995 (Pfefferbaum *et al.*, 2001, 2003) and after 9/11 (Schuster *et al.*, 2001; Ahern *et al.*, 2002; Schlenger *et al.*, 2002) all lending support to the theory of a link between the amount of television viewing and symptoms of post-traumatic stress.

Such studies have found that, in the case of television viewers who had been directly exposed to trauma, the more they followed media coverage of the event, the more likely it was that they would develop symptoms of PTSD and depression, both in the immediate aftermath and long-term. For those who had not been directly exposed to an event, there was still a higher likelihood of developing symptoms of anxiety and distress the more they followed the media coverage (Cantrell, 2005).

The level of stress and anxiety that audiences have following traumatic events such as terrorist attacks appears to depend not only on the amount of images they see, but also the kinds of images. For example, Ahern *et al.* (2002) discovered that there was some connection between stress symptoms and the number of times New Yorkers viewed certain images of the 9/11 attacks, such as 'an airplane hitting the World Trade Center' and 'people falling or jumping from the towers of the World Trade Center'. The strongest correlation between image exposure and the prevalence of PTSD existed in the case of the images of people falling. However, respondents who were not directly affected by the events did not seem to be more likely to develop PTSD or depression. Similarly, a study two months after the events of 9/11 found that the level of television viewing as well as the number of graphic images seen correlated with clinically significant psychological distress symptoms (Schlenger *et al.*, 2002). On the other hand, Tucker *et al.* (2000) could not find a link between the amount of television viewing and increased symptoms of PTSD, in a study following the Oklahoma City bombing.

Most studies have given special attention to the way in which children and teenagers react to seeing traumatic events on television. For example, Pfefferbaum *et al.*'s (2001) study of 2000 middle-school students seven weeks after the Oklahoma City bombing discovered that those who had no direct exposure to the bombing were still more likely to exhibit post-traumatic stress symptoms the more they had watched television news footage related to the incident. Another study found that children who had watched the explosion of the space shuttle Challenger on television either live or shortly afterwards displayed traumatic symptoms in the short-term (Terr *et al.*, 1999). Blanchard *et al.* (2004) also found that television viewing of news images from 9/11 was a predictor of higher rates of post-traumatic stress in college students in some instances. Similarly, Ray and Malhi (2005) reported that teenagers in India were negatively affected by the events of 9/11 in a survey completed within three weeks of the event. Those who witnessed it on television were more fearful and shocked than the ones who read about it in the print media. Further, girls experienced more fear and sadness than boys, who experienced more anger. Similar links between exposure to news coverage and stress symptoms have also been identified in a number of other studies following the 9/11 attacks (see, for example, Schuster *et al.*, 2001; Fairbrother *et al.*, 2003).

As for the type of news medium with the most impact, the evidence is still equivocal. While Pfefferbaum *et al.* (2003) suggest that exposure to print media is more likely than television to lead to symptoms of post-traumatic stress in children, Ray and Malhi (2005) found that those adolescents who had watched the events of 9/11 on TV displayed more fear and shock than those who only read about them in print. In addition, Saylor *et al.* (2003) actually found that the Internet was a stronger predictor than either television or print media.

The evidence about the impact of viewing traumatic events in the news is still quite limited, and there is obviously a need for more research. One problem, for example, lies in a relative lack of inquiry into the content of the actual news coverage, beyond mere differences between graphic and non-graphic images. Similarly, as Cantrell (2005) points out, 'it is unknown if people who are more distressed choose to consume more disaster-related news, or if news of the disaster causes distress, or if there is some other causal mechanism'. Further, so far, most studies have concentrated on two high-profile events only, and there is a need to examine other cases and perhaps longer-term trends as well.

Nevertheless, there does seem to be some link, and as a result there has been a tendency to suggest that 'younger children, at least, do better if provided with some protection from the full intensity and repeated coverage by media of trauma and disaster' (Pine *et al.*, 2005, p. 1786). There is obviously a link here to journalists' decisions about whether to publish graphic images or to withhold them from public view. In fact, the evidence on post-traumatic stress in news audiences provides at least some support for journalists when censoring images for reasons of taste and decency.

Effects of news reporting of suicides

Another area of the news coverage of death that has received considerable attention from researchers is the reporting of suicide. Here, scholars have been particularly concerned with the way in which media reports of suicide may result in an increase in suicides in society. The study of suicide and the media was originally inspired by Johann Wolfgang von Goethe's (1989 [1774]) novel *The Sorrows of Young Werther*, which tells of a young man's love for an already-engaged woman. Werther, eventually realizing that he will never be able to be with the woman he loves, decides to take his own life by putting a gun to his head. An apparent spate in suicides around Europe following the book's publication was attributed to Goethe's work, leading the book to be banned in some places. The sociologist David Phillips (1974) coined the term 'Werther effect' two centuries later, when he examined the way in which media portrayals of suicide may lead to copycat attempts. Phillips examined front page stories of suicides in Britain and the United States between 1947 and 1968, and found that following 26 of the front page stories, suicide rates increased, particularly in the immediate area of publication. On seven occasions, however, suicide rates actually decreased. Subsequent research conducted by Phillips (1979, 1985), as well as a growing number of other scholars, has firmly entrenched the notion of imitative suicides caused by news reporting. Studies found not only that newspaper stories appeared to be linked to increases in suicide rates, but also that television news had at least some impact (Phillips and Carstensen, 1986, 1988; Kessler *et al.*, 1988). Interestingly however, the impact of television reports of suicide is less clear than that of newspapers, perhaps due to the more fleeting nature of television news and the resulting brief airtime given to stories. However, Gould (2001, p. 205) believes that while early studies of television's influence were more equivocal, 'recent studies support an imitative effect of television news reports on suicide'. Some studies have also found a corresponding decrease in suicide rates during times of newspaper strikes (Motto, 1967; Blumenthal and Bergner, 1973).

Reasons for suicide contagion are generally viewed according to social learning theory, which posits that there already exists a group of vulnerable individuals in society, who may, however, exhibit only latent suicide potential (Gould, 2001; Stack, 2005). Once news stories about suicides appear, it is believed that the inhibiting element in those individuals is reduced and they are more likely to commit suicide, often copying the type of suicide reported. In a review of 38 studies of non-fictional media portrayals of suicide, Gould (2001) finds a number of characteristics that appear to increase the risk of news reports leading to higher suicide rates. Firstly, it seems that story placement, size and intensity of reporting lead to higher imitation of suicides. Secondly, there is some evidence to suggest that suicides of celebrities, which presumably are much more publicized, also increase the number of copycat suicides (Wasserman, 1984; Stack, 1987, 1990). Thirdly, while research findings have been equivocal in terms of gender and age-related imitation, the evidence does appear to support the notion that individuals who are similar to those reported on may commit suicide, with generally younger people more susceptible to suicide contagion (Gould, 2001). Nationality may even matter, as evidenced in a study in Japan which found that non-Japanese suicides did not lead to an increase in suicide rates, while Japanese suicides did (Stack, 1996). Fourthly, in terms of environmental characteristics, Stack (2005) notes that research suggests that epochs before television showed less imitative suicides, due to the absence of an additive effect of intense coverage. Gould (2001, p. 200) believes her review of research into the phenomenon supports the view that 'the existence of suicide contagion no longer needs to be questioned'. Pirkis and Blood's (2001) review of 34 studies arrives at a similar conclusion, even confirming a number of indicators to suggest that the relationship is most likely causal.

Not content with merely narrative reviews of existing research, however, Stack (2005) has questioned assertions of clear links between suicide reports and imitative suicides by conducting a content analysis of 419 findings from 55 studies. He finds that, contrary to popular belief, 64.2 per cent of the findings actually report the absence of an imitative effect. He argues that the discrepancies in the research findings are mainly due to methodological differences. For example, aspects of story content have an influence on whether imitative effects can be found. In this way, 'findings based on entertainment and political celebrity stories were more than five times as likely to report imitative impacts than their counterparts' (Stack, 2005, p. 129). In addition, findings based on stories which contained strong negative definitions of suicide, that is, didn't glorify the topic, were 99 per cent less likely to find copycat suicides. Television reports also appeared to be 79 per cent less likely to result in imitated suicides than newspaper stories. Finally, Stack (2005) found that studies of the imitative impact on women were 4.89 times more likely than others to find an effect, while findings on young or middle-aged persons did not appear to find an increase in copycat attempts. This latter finding was surprising given the general consensus that teenagers are more at risk of imitative suicides, although Stack (2005) points out the basis for such beliefs was often based on atypical research designs.

It is important to note that the above studies focus only on non-fictional reporting. The research into the impact of fictional media portrayals of suicides is much more equivocal, with some studies finding an effect, and others finding no effect (Blood *et al.*, 2001; Gould, 2001). In this sense, we can assume with some confidence that, in general, suicide is more contagious when reported as a real life event, rather than in a movie.

Still, a number of scholars have been critical of sweeping claims that news reporting causes an increase in suicides. Blood *et al.* (2001) note that many of the existing studies take the stimulus-response view in relation to effects of the news media. As a result, such studies disregard entirely the possibility – widely acknowledged in modern audience research – that audiences actually draw various meanings from media texts, and are capable of resisting messages. In addition, they argue that studies generally have not explored the actual content of stories about suicide: 'Content is taken as a given and viewed as a stimulus. Little attempt is made to analyze the range of meanings available in media portrayals of suicide and related issues' (Blood *et al.*, 2001, p. 60). They further point out that researchers have paid little attention to the amount of news coverage which those who committed suicide had actually been exposed to, and there was also a lack of examination of long-term effects of news reporting of suicide. This lack of analysis would leave little room to provide useful guidelines for news media to follow, other than just curbing suicide stories *per se*.

Mostly, methodological issues have hampered the validity of some results. For example, Hittner (2005) re-examined Phillips (1974) and Phillips and Carstensen's (1986) studies, adjusting for what he regarded as a methodological error in their studies. He found that the Werther effect could not be supported in the 1970s study, and was only partially supported in the later study. Stack (2005) has also noted that some arguments can be misleading. He cites a study by Marzuk *et al.* (1994) which examined New York suicide rates following the publication of a suicide guide that recommended suicide by asphyxiation. Following publication, the suicide rate for this method increased remarkably (an incredible 313 per cent), but overall the rate of suicides did not. Hence, Stack believes that suicide reports may not actually lead to an increase in suicides at large, but those who would have committed suicide anyway copy the reported method. Sullivan (2007) is particularly critical of the existing research that claims to have proved a link between suicide in the news and actual increases in suicide. He believes that much of the research has left out other potential factors, and that there are too many methodological differences between the different studies, an issue that Stack (2005) has also critiqued. Therefore, rather than simply accepting assertions of narrative reviews of the existing literature (for example, Gould, 2001), Sullivan (2007, p. 157) believes that 'based on careful assessment of the presented evidence, skepticism about the link between publicity about suicides and imitation is warranted'.

Nevertheless, the perception among many today is that news reporting of suicides does have at least some impact on suicide rates. This has led many countries to adopt guidelines on the reporting of suicide in the media. A review of news media guidelines in Australia, New Zealand, the United States, Britain, Canada, Hong Kong and Sri Lanka, as well as those established by the World Health Organization, has found that all agree on a number of important points (Pirkis *et al.*, 2006). Despite having been set up at different levels, with varying input from journalists, all guidelines emphasize the need to

- avoid sensationalizing or glamorizing suicide, or giving it undue prominence
- avoid providing specific detail about the suicide
- recognize the importance of role models
- take the opportunity to educate the public
- provide help/support to vulnerable readers/viewers.

One problem associated with the varying levels of journalistic involvement in the development of guidelines is the potential clash with basic news values, such as conflict, human interest and unusualness. As a result, the extent to which such guidelines have been implemented by news organizations varies considerably (Blood *et al.*, 2007). Many journalists are still not aware of the guidelines, and there have been few studies to investigate the effect such guidelines have had. Blood *et al.* (2007) point out that Australian news media were still not always following the guidelines, with the method and location of suicide reported on a number of occasions. There is potential that guidelines, if implemented, can help reduce copycat suicides, with one study from Austria finding a reduction in the rate of suicides (Etzersdorfer and Sonneck, 1998). However, as Pirkis *et al.* (2007) note, such studies are few and far between, and there is obviously much more work needed to validate such results.

Conclusion

The literature on audience reactions to and effects of news coverage of death and dying is marked by a variety of approaches which as yet have not been able to convincingly address central issues. Arguments which assert that increasingly graphic representations of disasters necessarily lead to compassion fatigue among audiences are mostly based on normative assessments rarely grounded in empirical evidence. The normative theory of compassion fatigue as advocated by Moeller (1999) is based on a stimulus-response model of communication. It assumes that there already exists a certain level of compassion that is progressively eroded by constant exposure to emotional images and stereotyped disaster coverage. But who is to say that people have not always been less affected by people in distant places? It would therefore seem much more likely that certain photos are perhaps unable to arouse more compassion, rather than saying they lead to fatigue. Secondly, the compassion fatigue thesis assumes that all viewers will be affected in the same way, rather than acknowledging that audiences are constituted of a variety of people who will have varying responses. As Kinnick *et al.*'s (1996) study found, some people may certainly experience compassion fatigue, but there will also be others who may feel empowered to act. The fact that disasters such as the tsunami in the Indian Ocean in 2004 and the 2010 earthquake in Haiti resulted in enormous amounts of private donations is certainly one sign that publics can still care.

Yet, audiences have repeatedly said they do not want to see graphic images. Whether this is in order to feel safe from atrocity is not entirely clear. However, it would seem that there is still a considerable minority of people who actually will look at explicit images. Literature from the field of trauma studies, while still in its infancy, suggests that looking can indeed hurt, as the link between the amount of television viewing following terrorist attacks and signs of post-traumatic stress has shown.

However, as I have pointed out, there are still some methodological considerations to take account of, in particular the issue of causality. Further, the actual content of such reporting has rarely been examined. Studies of suicide reporting have consistently claimed that explicit reporting of such instances of self-harm can lead to copycat attempts. Whether reporting suicides differently and according to stricter guidelines can work to reduce the problem has also not yet been convincingly shown, although early indications are promising.

To conclude then, much work remains to be done in the area of audience effects as they relate to news reporting on death and dying. In future, researchers will need to develop more holistic frameworks for their analysis in order to better take account of the variety of reactions that people can have to graphic imagery. Trauma studies have made a good start in this area in developing frameworks to deal with the ways in which reporting of traumatic events affect people, but still need to do a better job in examining more fully the specific content under investigation. The next chapter investigates how this linking of content to long-term and cultural implications can provide some interesting insights.

7
Journalism's Role in Constructing Grief

In the previous chapters, we discussed how deaths have been represented in news reporting, both in text and images, over the past centuries to today, and some of the reasons why certain deaths are reported and others less so. These have been dominant paradigms in the scholarship of death in the news over the majority of time, but, in the past two decades, a new approach has entered the fold. This approach, which developed out of a cultural approach to the study of journalism and the media, takes a more qualitative approach and explores the way in which journalists construct meaning from current events. Scholars in this field argue that journalists legitimatize their role as authoritative storytellers in society through the way in which they shape the society's collective memory (Zelizer, 1993). In particular in relation to journalistic reports on – predominantly high-profile – death and its aftermath, many now believe that such stories are actually also shaping modern responses to death, in that they instruct audiences in the acceptable ways of dealing with grief. This form of journalism is generally referred to as 'commemorative journalism' (Kitch, 2000) or 'memorializing discourse' (Carlson, 2007).

In contrast to many of the studies we have already examined, this approach is firmly rooted in the tradition of communication as culture (Carey, 1989), which hails from a cultural studies approach to analyzing media. Here, research is focused not so much on empirical examinations of, say, the degree to which images contain graphic content. Rather, it is concerned with the way in which journalists, mostly subconsciously, imbue such messages with meanings, and how these meanings may be deciphered by audiences. Many scholars argue that the media have become the primary channel through which people experience death and, as a result, they are also now instrumental in giving out clues as to how one should deal with death. For example, Kitch and Hume (2008, p. xiv) note that the news media 'have become the primary forum for the conveyance and construction of public grief today', and, as a result, they play an important role in instructing audiences on acceptable ways of grieving. At the same time, journalism's coverage of death also tells us about life by reinforcing the values of society that are deemed most important.

Many studies of commemorative journalism were inspired by the overwhelming media coverage that tends to follow the deaths of well-known people. An important case here was the way in which journalists reported the death of Princess Diana on 31 August 1996. The way in which Diana died, and the seemingly unprecedented public reactions it engendered, turned her death into one of the stories of the decade. Particularly the English but also the world news media were replete with Diana stories for days if not weeks. The event spawned a number of scholarly books, which also placed heavy emphasis on journalism's role in mediating Diana's death to the masses. I will discuss in detail some of these analyses later in the chapter.

Firstly, it is necessary to provide a brief overview of the theoretical notions behind the scholarship in this field. In particular, we will look at how journalists are perceived as cultural producers who need to constantly legitimize their role as authoritative providers of events. This is followed by an overview of the concept of myth as it relates to news reporting of disasters and other fatal events, before I present a number of studies which have examined the concept of commemorative journalism in a variety of contexts.

Journalists as cultural producers

The study of commemorative journalism takes as its starting point the view that communication processes can be seen in terms of culture. Highly influential in this approach has been James Carey (1989), who argued for an alternative view of communication to the previously dominant transmission model. Carey believed that the transmission model's main shortcoming was that it focused on one-directional flows and cause-and-effect relationships, whereas he saw communication more as ritual. Such a view of communication is 'directed not toward the extension of messages in space but toward the maintenance of society in time; not the act of imparting information but the representation of shared beliefs' (Carey, 1989, p. 18). Newspapers thus become not merely sites for sending or receiving information, but more like attending a mass, 'a situation in which nothing new is learned but in which a particular view of the world is portrayed and confirmed' (Carey, 1989, p. 20). Communication – and this applies particularly to journalism as a form of communication – therefore becomes 'a symbolic process whereby reality is produced, maintained, repaired and transformed' (Carey, 1989, p. 23). This view of journalism as a site of the production of meaning is grounded in the semiotic approach to encoding and decoding discussed earlier, and it has become a popular way of looking at how news mediates reality. In particular, the way that Carey saw the ritual model of communication as reinforcing certain world views and values is reflected in much of the scholarship of journalism's role during times of death and other disruptions to the social order.

An analysis of how journalists achieve the task of creating (imagined) communities (Anderson, 1991) through their stories necessarily needs to be conducted by way of narrative analysis. This method enables researchers to examine the denotations and connotations of journalistic 'texts' (the term text here refers to any narrative construction, and therefore includes written and spoken words as well as images). Barbie Zelizer (1992, p. 9) has noted that journalists legitimate themselves as authoritative storytellers through their use of narratives in the news: 'Through narrative, the role of the individual, the organization/institution, and the structure of the profession become key factors in delineating the hows and whys of journalistic practice.' Journalists, thus, set themselves up as interpretive communities who are legitimated to assume the mantle of purveyors of important news. Zelizer believes that viewing journalism through a lens of traditional components of professionalism is ill-guided, as few journalists themselves adhere to such external notions. Rather than identifying themselves as professionals applying the criteria used in other professions such as medicine, journalists 'come together by creating stories about their past that they routinely and informally circulate to each other – stories that contain certain constructions of reality, certain kinds of narratives, and certain definitions of appropriate practice' (Zelizer, 1993, p. 223).

In this way, Zelizer sees journalists as assuming cultural authority, which helps them to 'use their interpretations of public events to shape themselves into authoritative communities' (Zelizer, 1992, p. 3). In their definition of the term cultural narrative, Nossek and Berkowitz (2006, p. 692) take this line of argument further when they argue that 'as part of the culture and as storytellers for that culture, journalists construct stories based on narrative conventions that are culturally resonant for themselves and their audiences'. These narratives, they note, can also be understood as myths, which act as providers of 'an often-repeated interpretation that a culture makes of itself, with common central actors and predictable outcomes' (Nossek and Berkowitz, 2006, p. 693). This notion of news as myth is important, as it will resurface again in the discussion of how journalists reaffirm values central to a culture following the death of one of their own.

The term 'myth' was already raised in relation to Barthes' (1972) definition of myth as a second order of signs, in which signs themselves become signifiers for a new signified, which in this case is intentional. Barthes discussed myths in terms of photographs, such as the myth of Frenchness in the photo of a young black soldier. In its original meaning, as defined by cultural anthropologists, myth provides the foundation for religious beliefs and practices and is concerned with the fundamentals of human existence, such as where we came from, why we are here and where we are going. Myths then serve to explain and describe an orderly universe, setting the stage for orderly behavior (Haviland, 2002, p. 394). The notion of myth extends quite easily to the practice of journalism, and a number of scholars have shown that news stories 'can be understood as the modern recurrence of myth' (Lule, 2003, p. 95). One example we have already discussed is Seaton's (2005) examination of photos that resemble the *pietá*. Such images are being used repeatedly in the news, and in this way a particular myth is extended.

According to Lule (2001, p. 150), who has examined the presence of myths in a variety of media coverage, news narratives as myths provide societies with examples of what is right and wrong or good and evil behavior, providing members of that society with 'models of social life and models for social life'. In this way, journalists are able to draw on commonly held views and attributes, and thus make sense of the world for their audiences. Zelizer (1998, 2002, 2004) has also noted the recurring nature of images of war and terrorism, which is bound up in journalistic practices developed over decades. Myth can, therefore, be understood as drawing 'upon archetypal figures and forms to offer exemplary models that represent shared values, confirm core beliefs, deny other beliefs, and help people engage with, appreciate, and understand the complex joys and sorrows of human life' (Lule, 2001, p. 15). Using a number of case studies, Lule shows how the news shared a number of traditions, and is able to identify seven master myths related to disaster coverage which constantly recur in the media and act instructively to audiences.

One reason for the perceived power of the media as the primary inter-preter and conveyor of myth is often located within television news. Goethals (1993, p. 25) has argued that the mass media have taken com-mand of the power of myth and transformed the dimensions of ritual in the live coverage of important events. He notes that various televi-sion news programs perform the function of the myth to define the world and help us to understand who we are. 'Like traditional fan-tasy, TV's ceremonial coverage of significant events are opportunities for individual feelings and sentiments to be forged into communal, shared ones' (Goethals, 1993, p. 26). In relation to the way in which journalism deals with death and dying, Kitch and Hume (2008, p. xv) argue that 'journalism conveys cultural stories employing familiar ele-ments arranged in recognizable order, stories that recur across media and over time to create a broader understanding of the meaning of death'. Whether or not these opportunities are actually taken up by audiences is an aspect that has not received a large amount of attention so far (Coonfield and Huxford, 2009).

Journalism and collective memory

The way in which journalistic narratives and myths are used in news coverage of death and dying brings us to the topic of journalism's role in collective memory. The term collective memory was established as a concept by the French sociologist Maurice Halbwachs (1992) in the 1920s. Halbwachs believed that collective memory, as separate from individual memory, was constructed and shaped as a collective process in society. 'It is in society that people normally acquire their memories. It is also in society that they recall, recognize, and localize their mem-ories' (Halbwachs, 1992, p. 38). The term has become entrenched in memory studies, with a number of scholars extending and modifying it further. The study of collective memory is of course much more compli-cated than there is space here, so we will content ourselves with a basic definition of collective memory as 'a metaphor that formulates society's retention and loss of information about its past in the familiar terms of individual remembering and forgetting' (Schwartz, 1991, p. 302). Or, as Zelizer (1992, p. 3) puts it, 'collective memory reflects a group's codified knowledge over time about what is important, preferred, and appropriate'.

The link between journalism's role as purveyor of narratives and the shaping of collective memory appears logical. Yet, journalism has not traditionally been seen by scholars as a site for memory work, to the extent that even 'decades into the systematic scholarly study of collective memory, there is still no default understanding of memory that includes journalism as one of its vital and critical agents' (Zelizer, 2008, p. 80). A major reason for this, according to Zelizer, lies in the fact that many still see journalism as only providing the first draft of history rather than doing memory work, a perception that is propagated through journalism's ideology as being concerned only with the present.

However, as a number of scholars have noted over the past two decades, journalists are actively involved in processes that create collective memory by constantly referencing the past in news. Lang and Lang (1989) have noted that in this way both the past and the future frame the news. 'Just what part of the past and what kind of future are brought into play depends on what editors and journalists believe legitimately belongs within the public domain, on journalistic conventions, and of course on personal ideologies' (Lang and Lang, 1989, p. 126). A number of studies now exist which have investigated the ways in which journalists engage in the production and shaping of collective memory (for example, Schudson, 1992; Zelizer, 1992, 1998; Edy, 1999; Kitch, 2005).

Edy's (1999) study of the mediated collective memory of the 1965 Watts riots in Los Angeles identifies three basic forms into which news stories about the past can be grouped: commemorations, historical analogies and historical contexts. Commemorative stories, she argues, are the types of stories which appear on anniversaries and commemorate certain events. Such stories are often uncontroversial, because they are usually sanctioned by a social authority. Sometimes, however, they can be about someone or something that authorities would like to create a consensus in society about or simply because it is so important that authorities cannot deny its importance (Edy, 1999, p. 74). Commemorative stories are generally located purely in the past and do not try to connect it to the present. Historical analogies, on the other hand, 'explicitly attempt to make the past relevant to the present by using a past event as a tool to analyze and predict the outcome of a current situation' (Edy, 1999, p. 77). While such stories generally contain a strongly analytical element in that they draw comparisons, they are not defined as such, in order to maintain the mantle of objectivity. Historical analogies are grounded in the belief that the past can predict the future, or at least explain the present, through the notion that history repeats itself. Edy warns that such analogies actually can be counter-productive as they may mask important differences between the historical event and the present. The third form of stories about the past, historical contexts, is actually quite rare, according to Edy. These types of stories, she says, trace parts of the past to explain current events: 'Instead of constructing some aspect of the past as similar to some aspect of the present, a historical context explains "how we got here"' (Edy, 1999, p. 80).

Edy believes that every time journalists invoke the past it affects collective memory, but that all three forms presented above may lead us to ignore aspects of the past, for different reasons. As a result, 'journalists use our collective memory as a tool to analyze and dramatize without much concern for its construction and maintenance' (Edy, 1999, p. 83). The production of collective memory is also closely linked to journalistic legitimatizations of their own cultural authority. Carlson (2007) argues that the journalistic 'memorializing discourse' about other dead journalists reinforces shared notions of an ideal-typical model of journalism: 'collective memory aids in sustaining authority in the present even as the construction of collective memory can only be made legitimate through an act of authority in the present' (Carlson, 2007, p.168).

Media events

Many studies have focused on journalism's role in memory work by looking at important historical events, such as the Watergate affair (Schudson, 1992), the assassination of John F. Kennedy (Zelizer, 1992), the Holocaust (Zelizer, 1998), the Oklahoma City bombing (Linenthal, 2001) and the events of 11 September 2001 (Kitch, 2003). Although journalists engage in memory work outside such seminal events (Kitch, 2008), it is during such 'critical incidents' (Zelizer, 1992, p. 4) that journalists' work in invoking the past is at its greatest, and arguably most apparent. These events generally consist of such drama and emotion that they tend to capture entire nations and, in more recent times, even global communities. These 'media events' provide important opportunities for journalists to use rituals and stories in order to bring society back together after extraordinary and dramatic events (Dayan and Katz, 1992). Media events can be seen through the prism of news as ritual, and while many studies have focused on the crucial role that television plays in this process, similar discourse can also be found in newspapers and magazines (Kitch, 2000).

Media events thus bring 'to the surface the values and assumptions that are most central to a particular culture, but it may also have the effect of silencing other values and alternative perspectives' (Pantti and Wieten, 2005, p. 302). Peri (1999) notes that journalists use media events to ascertain their role as cultural authorities, particularly when traumatic events are divisive and do not carry the same meaning for all groups of society. In such a case of a struggle over how to make sense of the event, the news media take a stand, which 'creates a sense of togetherness and strengthens social solidarity' (Peri, 1999, p. 107). As a result, journalists legitimate their role once more, even if audiences are often dissatisfied with them in an everyday context. Deaths are of particular relevance here, as these always present an interruption of ordered life that needs to be dealt with. Myerhoff (1984, p. 150) has argued that ritual is particularly prominent at times of uncertainty, anxiety, impotence and disorder, when its repetitive character 'provides a message of pattern and predictability'. In the wake of particularly high-profile deaths, such essentially biological events are turned into cultural drama, 'shaped to human purpose until it becomes an affirmation rather than a negation of life' (Myerhoff, 1984, p. 150).

Indeed, Pantti and Wieten point out that extraordinarily tragic events are presented in a very similar way each time: 'Typically they are represented as integrative events, moments of national consensus and unity born out of mourning together' (2005, p. 301). This combination of ritual, religion, mourning and the media is expressed in the way journalists deal with the mediation of death. Tony Walter (2006) has noted the increasingly important function which the news media play in dealing with disruptive events such as deaths, wars or disasters. In fact, he suggests that news has taken over the role of religion in dealing with death in modern societies, which makes sense in light of the notion of news as ritual. While such processes were previously controlled by official authorities, such as the church, it is now the news media that are to a large degree in the business of reinforcing rituals. Kitch and Hume (2008, p. xiv) note that the news media 'have become the primary forum for the conveyance and construction of public grief today', and, thus, play an important role in instructing audiences on acceptable processes of grieving. The following section, therefore, deals with a number of studies that relate to the way in which journalists deal with death.

Commemorative journalism

So how do journalists shape and invoke collective memory in relation to news coverage of death? How do they make sense of the sudden loss of someone in order to heal that social fabric? As this section demonstrates, journalists use a number of devices in covering high-profile media events in order to reinforce dominant values that people can find solace in. This field has received considerable attention in recent years, and I will examine a number of small case studies here so as to better understand the role that commemorative journalism plays.

While the largest amount of attention has been given to deaths as media events in the television age, the processes we observe today are actually not new. Journalists have always played an important role as narrators of national stories, ever since the arrival of a mass press. Obituaries, as we have already seen, have played a crucial function in defining how a society remembers its dead. While we have so far discussed obituaries on the more descriptive level of whose deaths are remembered, Fowler (2005) has tried to examine them at the deeper level of the meaning they construct. She is convinced that 'they are more than a series of recollections about random individuals' (Fowler, 2005, p. 53).

One important component is the way in which celebrities are described as having a number of ordinary attributes in order to make them appear 'like us'. This has been going on since the early days of obituaries and the modern-day memorializing of famous people only extends that tradition. An analysis of the British periodicals the *Post-Angel* and *Gentleman's Magazine* during the eighteenth century identified that the way in which obituaries in those times dealt with death already attempted to highlight certain values that connected celebrities to ordinary citizens (Barry, 2008). Barry (2008, p. 261) argues that all public figures, including nobles and royals 'are presented "like us" ', in order to create this connection. For example, when Queen Mary died in 1694, subsequent issues of the *Post-Angel* remembered her as having a common streak, emphasizing her humility, modesty and the fact she did not set herself above the common people (Barry, 2008, p. 265). While this appeal to their audiences can easily be seen as a sinister plot on the part of news organizations to sell more papers, Barry believes that, in the early days, it was actually part of 'a genuinely democratizing agenda, rather than the more cynical tool of consensus politics or marketing that it is now seen to be' (2008, p. 261).

Similarly, the death of leading Shakespearean actress Ellen Terry in 1928 triggered a commemorative discourse which emphasized British national identity at a time when the British Empire was losing its influence in the world (Kazmier, 2001). In many ways similar to the mourning for Princess Diana almost 70 years later, Terry's death led to mass grief in Britain, mediated through the news. In fact, she was seen as symbolizing 'the endurance of British values and institutions, which the papers ritualistically renewed' (Kazmier, 2001, p. 167). Kitch and

Hume note that, following Hartley (1982), this appearance of common people in the news serves the purpose of allowing audiences to identify with them and believe that they share common experiences and opinions. 'Characterized in death news stories as either victim or mourner, the figure of the common American makes it possible for strangers to feel involved in a tragedy, symbolically uniting the dead and the living and transforming private emotions into public ones' (Kitch and Hume, 2008, p. xx).

There is a remarkable consistency in the way that journalists have treated death over the centuries. In her study of the way in which American news magazines memorialize high-profile deaths, Kitch (2000) contends that the same processes have been going on in narratives about all the deaths she examined. She argues that the fact that Princess Diana's death generated an exceptional amount of interest in journalism's role as shaper of collective memory does not mean this hasn't happened before. 'The death of Diana and of JFK Jr. was the same journalistic story as the passing of other figures as diverse as Judy Garland, John Lennon and John Wayne' (Kitch, 2000, p. 172).

Kitch (2000) identified a three-stage process through which journalists mediate the larger cultural process of mourning, beginning with the separation through the death itself, followed by the funeral ritual characterized by a feeling of 'communitas' (Turner, 1969) and concluding with the reaffirmation of group values and acceptance of the death. It is particularly during the middle stage of the process that journalists can position themselves as the protectors of social values (Pantti and Wieten, 2005). In this process, journalists become healing spiritual leaders (Carey, 1989) and draw the community together. Journalistic notions of objectivity and distance are suddenly abandoned, with reporters continuously employing 'the subjective first-person plural, a communal "we"' (Kitch, 2000, p. 178).

Kitch also identifies the way in which magazines, much like the early news publications examined by Barry (2008), make high-profile people common again. She believes that in this way they create a sense that readers can see the real person, rather than the constructed celebrity figure. 'Reporters make heroes, even mythic figures, of well-known people, conflating fame with newsworthiness and public significance; at the same time, they explain the famous in terms of the ordinary, uniting audience members with each other and with the celebrity through "basic" values' (Kitch, 2000, p. 190). Funeral services for celebrities are thus not just passing moments, but are used by journalists to reassert their authority as storytellers, and in turn present sites for the creation of much more long-lasting meanings.

Collective memory is even shaped into consensus in the cases of controversial people. Studying the coverage of the death of highly controversial right-wing politician Pim Fortuyn in the Netherlands, Pantti and Wieten (2005) noted that television was able to contain dissent and construct the dead man in traditional Dutch values. Fortuyn had raised the ire of many with his outspoken comments and policies against immigrants in the Netherlands. The fact that he was openly homosexual and supported same-sex marriage also further complicated the issue, because such a mix of traditionally left and right political views was confusing to many. When Fortuyn was assassinated in the car park of a Hilversum radio station eight days before a national election, the event caused a considerable amount of shock in the Netherlands. The assassination was 'followed by a vast demonstration of public grief, with floral tributes, candles, notes, silent marches, and mourners lining up to view his body lying in state in a cathedral in Rotterdam' (Pantti and Wieten, 2005, p. 302). While the deaths of divisive people are usually unlikely to be turned into media events, the Dutch television coverage of the mourning for Fortuyn was able to do so by de-emphasizing the disruptive potential of his death. Instead, television broadened the definition of legitimate ritual, focusing on emotion and predominantly presenting voices of unity rather than disruption. Important, too, in this context was Dutch television's use of common people as sources to tell the rest of the nation how they felt about Fortuyn's death. Normally, common people are excluded from much of news discourse. However, in this case, it is typical of media events that deal with disasters or deaths, and it actually confers official authority on the voices of common people, thus creating a 'nationwide feeling community' (Pantti and Wieten, 2005, p. 312).

In Israel, journalists also played an important role in the way the assassination of Prime Minister Yitzhak Rabin in 1995 would enter collective memory. However, as Peri (1999) notes, this event was divisive and collective memory more contested than after events like the JFK assassination or Princess Diana's death. Rabin's policy of a peace process with Palestinians and his signing of the Oslo peace accords, which gave Palestinians partial control over the West Bank and the Gaza Strip, were highly divisive for Israeli society. His death became a site of mnemonic dispute, with different communities struggling to control the collective memory. Peri argues that journalism, and particularly television, played a pivotal role in this struggle and was eventually the most influential. Rabin was constructed in terms of a mythic war hero, which correlated with the nation-constituting myth of the state of Israel. The media framed Rabin's death by focusing particularly on the notion that the assassination came as a result of the incitement by the nationalist camp, rather than alternative frames journalists had at their disposal. Comparisons with the assassinations of other leaders around the world, particularly John F. Kennedy's, further allowed the media to frame Rabin in heroic terms. Importantly, Peri notes that the media shifted the assassination of Yitzhak Rabin from space to time in order to become the dominant agent in the shaping of collective memory.

Of course, one of the biggest media events in recent times was the week or so that followed the death of Diana, Princess of Wales on 31 August 1997. Her tragic demise in a car crash in a Paris tunnel reverberated around the world, turning the mourning for Diana into a global event based on the worldwide celebrity status she had achieved during the previous decades. The unprecedented display of public grief in traditionally reserved Britain naturally stoked the interest of a number of scholars, with particular attention paid to the role played by the media in the mourning (see, for example, Kear and Steinberg, 1999; Walter, 1999a; Thomas, 2002; Turnock, 2000). Diana's death has come to be seen as a typical media event, uniting the people of Britain (and, to a slightly smaller extent, the world) in grief for the 'people's Princess'. Diana was often described in the usual terms of commemorative journalism, which essentially made her one of us, and the news coverage was seen to have brought together the nation as a whole. Watson (1997) also observed the commemorative discourse present in eulogies of Diana. Looking at her perceived qualities of love, generosity, caring, friendship and self-sacrifice, Watson (1997, p. 7) argued that by praising those qualities in Diana, 'we indirectly praise them in ourselves: our very recognition that these are the important things in life raises our own moral status, and provides us with the strength and self-confidence to begin a new life'. But the event also created a problem for journalism, as journalistic authority was suddenly challenged due to the media's direct and indirect involvement in her death. This led to a need for journalists to defend their claim to cultural authority, meaning that both mainstream and tabloid media enacted cultural rituals to 'reassert the validity of their paradigm both to society and to themselves' (Berkowitz, 2000, p. 140).

Diana's death became predominantly associated with the 'unprecedented' public mourning in Britain. While there is no denying the mass demonstrations of grief in public places like Kensington Palace and Buckingham Palace, Walter (1999c) acknowledges that such commemorations were actually not that new, with precedents to be found some years earlier. However, he believes that events like the mourning for Diana are a sign of perhaps the beginning of a return to public mourning, a new kind of interaction between 'folk custom, grief, and the mass media' (Walter, 1999c, p. 274). He believes that, as people have little direct experience with death anymore, they rely on depictions in the media. 'How do I learn how to behave when there is a tragedy? In part through observing how the media portray other people behaving' (Jupp and Walter, 1999, p. 277). Other studies of public mourning after events such as the Oklahoma City bombing (Linenthal, 2001) and 9/11 (Kitch, 2003) confirm this development in wider society. Such mediated mourning, then, Linenthal (2001, p. 111) claims, helps construct imagined 'nationwide bereaved communities'.

It would certainly appear that the news media are having some influence on the way in which people mourn in the twenty-first century. It seems much more common these days to have impromptu displays of mass public grief, such as the laying of flowers at the scene of death or the deceased's home. Peri (1999) notes that television's reporting of the aftermath of the assassination of Yitzhak Rabin even changed traditional Jewish mourning patterns. Instead of remaining in the privacy of her home for the week of mourning, as is customary, the deceased's widow, Leah Rabin, actually participated in a live television broadcast from her home. Rabin's grandchildren even took part in a television talk show, which was filmed at a studio. This appears to have led to a general change in mourning protocols, as 'since the assassination, television cameras did not hesitate to enter mourners' homes' (Peri, 1999, p. 111).

Nevertheless, communities of mourners for deceased celebrities have existed for quite some time. Wolffe (1996) has noted that even during the nineteenth century, there were mass reactions to the deaths of royals such as Princess Charlotte and the Duke of Wellington, who died in 1817 and 1852 respectively, a time when the reach of news media was much smaller. Yet, people still expressed their solidarity through attending, in much larger numbers than usual, services in churches around the country. This attendance 'gave them a meaningful point of contact with the distant funeral and a mechanism for publicly identifying with perceived national grief' (Wolffe, 1996, p. 285).

However, as I will discuss later in this chapter, there is also still considerable disagreement as to whether the amount of mediated mourning is actually an accurate reflection of people's real grief. First, however, it is necessary to contextualize some of the main arguments in this chapter by way of examining a small case study.

How commemorative journalism works: A case study

Commemorative journalism's propensity to construct the dead within mythical terms was also evident in the saturation coverage in Australia which followed the death of Steve Irwin, better known to global audiences as the 'Crocodile Hunter'. I will here refer to the way in which his death was reported in the Australian news media in order to highlight some of the specific ways in which commemorative journalism works.

Irwin had achieved worldwide fame for his daredevil antics with nature's most deadly animals. In a way, his death from a stingray barb while filming for his show on Australia's Great Barrier Reef in September of 2006 was an irony, given that he had cheated death so many times before with much more dangerous animals than this 'pussycat of the sea' (Miles, 2006, p. 3). Irwin's demise generated front-page coverage in newspapers from America to Europe, Latin America and Asia, given his celebrity status. However, while global audiences were shocked at his death, they still went back to normality shortly afterwards. This was not the case in his native country of Australia, where newspapers, television, radio and the Internet were replete with eulogies and tales of his life. The death also led to makeshift memorials at Australia Zoo, the place he had spent a lifetime trying to establish as an international tourist attraction. Australian journalism, in much the same tradition as we have seen occur elsewhere, was quick to frame Irwin within traditional Australian myths (Hanusch, 2009).

In fact, journalists invoked one notable Australian myth, that of the 'Australian legend' (Ward, 1958). It describes the bushman, who is down to earth and close to nature, willing to try out anything, non-religious, egalitarian and anti-elitist, independent and against authority (a 'larrikin') and who proves himself a good mate to anyone around him. While it is acknowledged that most Australians would not subscribe to this image of the typical Australian in the twenty-first century, aspects of this national myth still circulate in public discourse today (Elder, 2007). From the beginning, Irwin was constructed in the terms of this myth, which also came at a time when the conservative then-Prime Minister John Howard was attempting to instill traditional values in society (Hanusch, 2009). News stories described the dead Crocodile Hunter as an 'ordinary bloke', a traditional larrikin and a down-to-earth Australian who embodied everything that's good about the country. The political sphere also joined in this discourse, with Prime Minister Howard describing the Crocodile Hunter as a typical 'knock-about' Australian bloke, even claiming that he died in 'some respects in quintessentially Australian circumstances' (cited in Karvelas, 2006, p. 5). Considering that only three people had died from stingray barbs in Australian waters until then, this may have been a somewhat dubious claim, yet it signified how much Irwin's death became intertwined with Australian mythology.

Irwin was also identified through the myth of mateship, which holds 'an exceptionally important place in the Australian national mystique' (Wierzbicka, 1997, p. 101). In fact, the term 'mate' was identified in 15 per cent of articles in Australian newspapers during the week following the death (Hanusch, 2009). Similarly, descriptions of the deceased as a 'larrikin' also abounded. In his description of the Australian legend, Ward (1958, p. 2) speaks of this typical Australian as 'a fiercely independent person who hates officiousness and authority'. While the term was originally used to describe a young hooligan or thug, it has in recent years come to engender a much more positive meaning. Nowadays the term is used to describe someone who is 'cheeky, outrageous, youthful, energetic, iconoclastic, flouting authority and convention at every turn' (Kapferer, 1996, p. 62).

The commemorative journalism employed by Australian news workers, then, made use of a number of specific national myths, which combined to a larger discourse on social values. Steve Irwin was constructed as 'one of us' and was presented as someone who was emblematic of what Australians should aspire to be. The actor Russell Crowe, a friend of Steve Irwin's, expressed these sentiments adequately when he called Irwin 'the Australian we all aspire to be' (in Bodey, 2006, p. 1). This is quite similar to much of the press coverage of the death of Princess Diana discussed earlier.

As the general literature on journalistic authority and commemorative journalism shows, journalists invoke the past to make sense of the present. This was no different in the news coverage of Steve Irwin's death, which often compared the mass outpouring of grief to that following the death of Princess Diana. A number of commentators even compared it directly with Diana's death, speculating over an Australian Diana moment (Barkham, 2006; Birmingham, 2006; Connolly, 2006). In fact, at Irwin's memorial service, Australian singer John Williamson, in a scene reminiscent of Elton John's rewrite of *Candle in the Wind* in honor of the late Princess Diana, included references to Steve Irwin in a rendition of his traditional folk song *True Blue*. Another Australian singer even penned a complete song in Irwin's honor, replete with references to Irwin's down-to-earth character (Buchanan, 2006).

As we can see, Australian journalists, as well as the political and artistic sphere, framed the deceased Steve Irwin in mythical terms in order to make sense of his death and, thus, heal the wounds in the community of mourners. Yet, the Irwin case was also one where, albeit for a fleeting moment, an alternative discourse surfaced when the Australian expatriate intellectual Germaine Greer published – one day after the death – a column in the *Guardian* that was strongly critical of the Crocodile Hunter. Greer said she had felt embarrassed by his loudmouth antics and believed he had got what he deserved:

> The animal world has finally taken its revenge on Irwin, but probably not before a whole generation of kids in shorts seven sizes too small has learned to shout in the ears of animals with hearing ten times more acute than theirs, determined to become millionaire animal-loving zoo-owners in their turn . . . .
>
> (Greer, 2006, p. 7)

As I have discussed previously, it is rare that commemorative journalism allows dissenting voices which are contrary to the dominant memorializing discourse. Kitch (2000) and Pantti and Wieten (2005) have pointed out that commemorative journalism silences opposing views, yet due to the actual absence of alternative discourses in their studies, could not shed much light on how this issue is dealt with when an alternative does arise. This intervention by Greer, therefore, provides an interesting example of how journalism deals with such an interruption. Of course, speaking ill of the dead so soon after their demise breaks a social rule, which demands that 'whatever you personally feel, you do not undermine the prime mourners by publicly saying the deceased is not worth mourning' (Walter, 1999b). So in this context, Greer's comments were ill-timed, even if many Australians themselves had previously regarded Irwin as embarrassing, and he had also been attacked in the media on a few occasions.

However, rather than merely silencing Greer's comments, much of the Australian journalism community did something interesting: It actually co-opted her comments into the mythological frame. While newspapers of course denounced her comments, they also used them to demonstrate how Greer stood for everything that was contrary to the 'proper' social values. She was portrayed as the elitist who represented everything that

Steve Irwin and other 'ordinary Australians' stood against. This aspect of an Australian culture that wants to be 'popular' rather than 'elite' is well demonstrated (Fiske *et al.*, 1987). In fact, then-Tourism Minister, Fran Bailey, underlined this aspect when she said about Greer's piece: 'This article, as well as being so offensive, very firmly plants her as a cultural elitist who is completely out of touch with the average Australian' (quoted in Buttler and Rose, 2006). Further, Greer was of course a traitor who had left her country of birth to live in Britain of all places, making her criticism less legitimate as she surely wouldn't know what she was talking about. And, of course, above everything Greer was a woman in a mythological discourse which placed supreme emphasis on male attributes (Hanusch, 2009).

As we can see, all the elements of commemorative journalism which have been identified in past studies, such as the use of historical analogies and invoking the past to assert journalism's cultural authority as shaper of collective memory, were present in the news coverage that followed the death of the Crocodile Hunter. The ritualistic coverage of high-profile deaths is well-documented; however, there also exist some criticisms which pertain to this analysis in the way that it may overestimate the effects of such coverage.

Critiques of commemorative journalism's effects

A primary criticism of the commemorative journalism approach has been that just because the dominant news media discourse after the death of a famous person is generally homogenous and reinforcing of certain values, this does not mean that all audience members also react in the same way to it. This draws into question the argument that news representations of death and mourning rituals are actually changing wider patterns in society. While this argument is certainly persuasive and we can find some evidence for it (see, for example, Walter, 1999c), the empirical base for such a claim is relatively small. Particularly following the death of Princess Diana, there was considerable debate in academic circles about the extent to which the British people actually grieved. It has generally been argued that people learn their mourning behavior from the media, in particular during high-profile media events (Dayan and Katz, 1992). However, others have begun to claim that often such mourning is actually only portrayed as uniform through the media, and public mourning rituals are thus more constructed rather than necessarily manifest in the wider population (Couldry, 2003). In fact, as Thomas (2002) found in an analysis of the mourning for Diana, according to opinion polls, 75 per cent of people in Britain did not participate in the public mourning, while 50 per cent did not even watch the funeral. Turnock (2000) found a similar reaction in television viewers interviewed by the British Film Institute. The study concluded that the event left half of the respondents unaffected. Nevertheless, Walter (1999b) has argued that even though there was indeed a variety of moods, there was also no denying that a significant number of people were affected, as evidenced in those who did participate in the public mourning. But the function of media rituals in this context is that they silence opposing views – which may actually constitute a majority – in favor of portraying a single public mood that enables them to draw on a wider discourse of national grief in order to unite people, and, ultimately, assert their authority as storytellers (Zelizer, 1993).

Thomas (2008) also notes that, while it is certainly true that common people, who are usually excluded from media spaces, are given a voice at times of public expressions of grief, those who are interviewed are often, in the words of Liebes (1998, p. 80) 'the people who scream the most … the louder, the less controlled, the better'. If these people are presented as being 'like us', then surely their reactions must be representative of the wider community. As a result, other voices who may not comply with the particular mood journalists aim to construct are largely excluded from representation in the news. Thomas (2008) also believed there was a brief period of 'liminality' shortly after Diana's death, which saw people unsure of how to act. Once an accepted mourning pattern was established, those who dissented did so quietly, so as not to be seen to go against the perceived dominant emotion; a behavioral pattern that has been well-established in Noelle-Neumann's (1993) so-called 'spiral of silence'. Indeed, this dominant journalistic discourse even developed somewhat of a life of its own, with some journalists themselves later admitting that they had engaged in self-censorship so as not to appear unpatriotic or unfeeling (Thomas, 2008, p. 372).

Coonfield and Huxford (2009) have also criticized the tendency of media events studies to focus on the production and content, and that these studies have not sufficiently examined what audiences actually do at such times beyond merely gathering to witness an event. They believe that too often there has been a perception in scholarly work on news as ritual that 'the ritual effect is regarded as uniform and occurs somehow simply because the news is viewed or read' (Coonfield and Huxford, 2009, p. 461). This they see as dangerous, because it grants 'media self-sufficiency by contravening their socio-cultural contexts' (p. 474). As a result, as the chapter on audience research has already argued, it is essential that we pay more attention to the ways in which audiences actually react during times of media events that relate to death.

Many studies have also neglected to sufficiently examine the conditions of production when looking at how the media deal with death. In fact, an overwhelming majority of literature focuses on the content of media messages, but does not sufficiently engage with the behavior of journalists at such times. A more holistic method would be needed to examine more in depth the processes that journalists go through when covering death on the scale of a media event. Berkowitz (2000) admits that most assumptions about production are based on the resulting content, but also believes that it would be difficult to observe the actual news-making process. Referring to the Diana story, he says: 'Although much could have been learned from observing and interviewing journalists at work as the story broke, developed, and waned, it would also be quite challenging to see beyond their professional ideology' (Berkowitz, 2000, p. 140). Nevertheless, he also believes that it would be useful to take into account at least some of the broader demands and working constraints of television journalism through officially available data.

Conclusion

Death is always a disruptive event. And in a world where everyone's life is affected to at least some degree by the news media, the death of someone famous or important presents an even bigger challenge for modern societies. This chapter has examined the way in which journalists assert their cultural authority as storytellers and the way in which they deal with the task of reporting a disruptive event that is elevated to the status of media event. We have seen that, if viewed through the prism of news as ritual, journalism can present a unifying force for society to deal with the death of someone that few knew personally, yet many considered close to them as a result of their media presence in life. So while commemorative journalism can be seen as a positive thing (Peri, 1999), it also can be seen as anti-democratic in that it excludes discourses which run counter to the chosen frame of reporting. Whether they were the deaths of Princess Diana, Pim Fortuyn or Steve Irwin, journalism presented them as 'one of us' and invoked particular types of myths in order to present to society a model way of how to live their lives. These myths are usually national myths and they build upon ideal social values that members of a nation should have. Even if contrary discourse is allowed, as seen in the case of Germaine Greer's comments about the Crocodile Hunter Steve Irwin, these are quickly incorporated into the mythic discourse in order to demonstrate what it means not to be a part of the community.

Some controversy still exists over the effects of the memorializing discourse of such media events. It appears logical that in a society where few have had direct exposure to death, and therefore may not be sure about appropriate practices of mourning, many take their cue from the mourning displayed in the news media. Yet to assume that all members of society will do so is simplistic. Responses to seeing death in general in the news are quite varied. This is also the case at times of media events such as the death of Princess Diana. Those who do not follow the frame chosen by the news media are typically excluded from much of the discourse, or are too afraid to voice their opinion for fear of being seen as tasteless or without empathy. Yet, as a number of studies discussed here have shown, at least in the case of Diana a considerable number of people did not mourn for her the way it was constructed in the news. Clearly, more research is needed on this counter flow in order to find out whether, to what degree, and in which conditions commemorative journalism can have an effect on audiences.

There certainly is some evidence to suggest that mourning rituals are changing, at least for some people. This is in line with the commonly-held belief that Western society is moving toward a renewed acceptance of death and a resulting move back into the public sphere. As news media redefine death rituals, the way in which societies deal with news about death may indeed be undergoing a change. We can see this happening particularly when we examine how death is visible in an increasingly pervasive new medium, the Internet, which is the focus of the next chapter.

8
Representing Death in the Online Age

As death moves back into the public sphere in the early twenty-first century, many people in the Western world are presumably beginning to feel more comfortable talking about their grief. A large part of this development may be thanks to the rapid development of new media technologies over the past couple of decades or so. New technologies, particularly the Internet, have allowed the audience to reclaim part of the public sphere in that ordinary people are now able to publish their own news for the consumption of a worldwide audience. This trend has affected traditional news media in an enormous way, to the extent that some now argue that newspapers, and even television, will die within a relatively short time-frame. What role new media may be playing in how death is reported in the news, how visible it is in the public sphere and in what way they affect the way societies are dealing with death, are all aspects addressed in this chapter.

As very few in-depth studies of how the Internet is affecting news representations of death exist, much of what follows here relies on individual case studies as well as contextual evidence. Nevertheless, we can make out a number of different ways in which new media impact quite strongly on the way journalists are able to report death. As anyone with an Internet connection is able to publish news, traditional media are not the only ones anymore who are able to broadcast news of accidents, disasters and wars to the masses. As a result, old barriers to publishing graphic imagery are being eroded by a medium that allows users, on the one hand, to publish all kinds of photos without the media's usual checks and balances. On the other hand, audiences are empowered to make a conscious decision about whether they want to see a certain image, and should therefore have less reason to complain.

Unfortunately, few studies have sufficiently examined this new dynamic in relation to how it changes the coverage of death in the news.

New technologies and the news media

The arrival of new technologies such as the Internet has over the past two decades had a tremendous impact on the way in which news organizations gather and report news. The Internet in particular has opened up numerous opportunities for improved news coverage, while at the same time leading to a decrease in newspaper readership and circulation figures. Newspapers are struggling to survive in a number of Western countries, predominantly due to the fact that much of the advertising revenue – which newspapers have so depended on in the past – has moved across to the Internet. On the Internet, everyone now expects news and information to be free, which has left many traditional media organizations struggling to find a business model that can help them to survive. In a widely-cited book about the decline of newspapers, Philip Meyer (2004) analyzed newspaper readership trends between 1967 and 2002 and detailed the financial problems newspapers were having. Famously, he predicted that newspapers would die in the year 2043 if declines were to continue along the same trend line.

There is no doubt that newspapers are in trouble in most Western societies. In 2009, 142 newspapers closed in the United States, and it has been estimated that nowadays only 13 per cent of Americans buy a daily newspaper, as opposed to 31 per cent in 1940 (Ahrens, 2009). Circulation for US newspapers has been falling dramatically since the turn of the millennium, while online news has experienced unprecedented growth. This highlights an important issue in the debate over the decline of newspapers: it is not that people are not interested in news anymore, but rather the way they choose to receive it has changed. Audit figures have shown that the websites of such venerable newspapers like the *New York Times* and *Washington Post* have increased the number of their unique visitors, but their advertising revenues have fallen considerably. This, Ahrens (2009, p. A15) points out, is due to the fact that 'ads on newspaper Internet sites sell for pennies on the dollar compared with ads in their ink-on-paper cousins'. Trends in many European countries are similar to those in the United States, though perhaps not as stark.

So while the arrival of the Internet has coincided with a dramatic decline in newspaper sales, the new technology has at the same time opened up a number of important new avenues for gathering, presenting and receiving news. Advantages exist for all involved in the communication of news. Journalists are able to research and cover stories much more quickly than they were able to in the past. Because of this, news about events in even the most far-flung corners of the world can be at a user's fingertips within minutes. Similarly, there are few restrictions on space on the Internet, allowing news organizations to post many more stories than they would be normally able to fit into a news bulletin or a newspaper. A number of scholars have argued that these developments can lead to some kind of parity in the flow of international news, allowing previously less-reported countries to be more present (see, for example, Deuze, 2003; Wu, 2007). Others, however, believe that such ideas are wishful thinking, and in fact the Internet is exacerbating the gap between the information 'haves' and the 'have-nots' (Castells, 1996; O'Sullivan, 2005). In fact, there is some evidence to suggest that while the amount of news available on mainstream news websites has certainly increased, there are questions about whether usually neglected countries and issues are now more present. A comparison of the websites of the *New York Times* and CNN with their respective parent publications has shown that there is very little difference in the way foreign news is reported in the new medium (Wu, 2007). In fact, as Wu found, traditional gatekeepers such as the international news agencies seem to have experienced a resurgence as they provide increasing amounts of material to news websites. Similarly, a study of the framing of the Iraq War on 26 online news sites in the United States found that stories largely followed the same framing that existed in their parent publications (Schwalbe, 2006).

Such findings notwithstanding, there are still great expectations for the Internet to act as a democratizing tool of communication. Such beliefs are grounded in a further fundamental shift in the production of news online, which allows ordinary people to become involved in the process. This phenomenon, generally known as 'participatory journalism' or 'citizen journalism', is seen particularly by scholars critical of mainstream media as having the potential to bring balance to the presentation of news online (Bruns, 2005). In this way, the Internet may provide a space through which the 'public sphere' (Habermas, 1989) can be reclaimed from what are deemed all-powerful media corporations. The average person with an Internet connection can now be a journalist, and have their story accessed by anyone in the world within seconds, potentially bypassing any news organization. Here, much attention has been paid to the potential of weblogs and social networking sites to bypass traditional media processes in order to get news out that may otherwise not make it past the gates of news organizations. Additionally, social networking sites such as Myspace, Facebook and Twitter are creating new online communities for special interests.

However, the process works both ways. These so-called citizen journalists are not only challenging the dominance of media organizations, they are also being co-opted by news media to help in the newsgathering process. Numerous websites around the world have established citizen journalism sections in which they recruit news from their audiences. This has especially been the case during times of large-scale disasters. For example, following the 2004 Boxing Day tsunami in the Indian Ocean, few mainstream media outlets had reporters in the region, and covering the disaster was immensely difficult. As a result, many of the first images of the tsunami to come out of the region had been recorded on tourists' mobile phones and video cameras. These were quickly rebroadcast by television stations around the world. In fact, the speed with which such images from the tsunami were available to mainstream media was astonishing. Ottosen (2007) has reported that the Norwegian newspaper *VG* had received a message about the disaster from a reader on a roof in Phuket 45 minutes before the Norwegian News Agency NTB sent out its first message. Websites administered by amateurs were also able to send out information from regions the mainstream media had no access to. At the same time, mainstream media, most notably the BBC website, aggregated blogs and gave ordinary people affected by the disaster a voice in the mainstream (Allan, 2006, pp. 7–9). Citizen journalism as a tool for crisis communication had well and truly arrived, a development Allan (2006, p. 9) has described as a 'tipping point'. Indeed, citizen journalists have played important roles in the coverage of the July 2005 London Underground bombings, as well as Hurricane Katrina only a few months later. Importantly, the news media, through aggregating other sites and providing forums for people affected by a disaster, can actively become engaged in helping a crisis and change the way it may affect people (Kodrich and Laituri, 2005).

Over the following pages, I examine the ways in which such processes are affecting a number of aspects of the representation of death. These include the role that citizen journalists may play in the presentation of particularly graphic death, the way journalists are making use of social networks in reporting death, as well as the formation of virtual bereavement sites and new ways of dealing with death online. There exists relatively little empirical research in the area of the representation of death online, so as a result much of the work here is restricted to case studies. Nevertheless, it will become apparent that the Internet is playing an important role in what many regard as shifting attitudes to death in Western societies.

Online representations of death

The nature of the Internet has enabled users to either post or actively seek out information that mainstream news organization may not provide for a variety of reasons discussed earlier. This is particularly evident in the visibility of graphic death, where anyone is now able to access gory images previously withheld from public view. This has implications in a number of ways. Previously, newspaper readers had little opportunity to decide whether they wanted to see a certain image because it was thrust upon them. And while on television, news readers could give a warning to viewers that reports would contain graphic images so that those who did not want to see them had to actively avoid them by changing channels. These days, however, news websites will usually only provide links to graphic images, together with a suitable warning. Therefore, it becomes less an issue of actively *avoiding* graphic images of death and now readers need to actively *seek them out*. On the part of news organizations, it provides them with an ethical way out as it transfers the decision whether or not to view these images to the audience.

In addition, due to the global nature of the Internet, it is now much easier to follow news from countries where the display of horrific images may be a more normalized affair than in the West. Thus, images that are censored in the Western media are more accessible from alternative media sources (Cottle, 2006). This can also include the websites of news organizations in other countries. For example, when the actor David Carradine was found hanged in his Bangkok hotel room in June 2009, a leaked photo of the scene was quickly published in the local *Thai Rath* newspaper (Li, 2009). Interestingly, a poll taken by the tabloid *New York Daily News* found that 40 per cent of respondents admitted they were curious enough to want to look at the photos if they could (*New York Daily News*, 2009). Of course, readers did not have to wait very long, as the image was soon reproduced on the Internet, even though they would have to click through a number of links to find it. What this example demonstrates, however, is how the Internet has eliminated distance in the reporting of news of death. Whereas 20 years ago, the photo of a dead David Carradine would have been unlikely to make it from a Thai newspaper to a worldwide audience, the Internet now enables this access. This can also create difficult ethical conundrums for journalists who try to take into account the sensibilities of their audiences. Often, local television stations or newspapers have avoided showing local dead out of respect for their grieving families. News organizations further away from the incident did not usually exercise such restraint, arguably because their audiences were unlikely to have known the dead. Now, however, news media are local and international at the same time, which means the footage or image published across the country can easily feed back to the local community (Keith *et al.*, 2006, p. 256). To complicate such matters further, the fact that journalists exercise restraint and follow police requests in relation to the identification of, for example, accident victims does not necessarily mean that news won't get out in other ways. In a case in Australia in October 2009, information about a fatal car crash was uploaded so quickly to the social media site Facebook that the family of the victim found out about their daughter's death through the site before police were able to inform them (Styles, 2009).

The publication of amateur images of death on the Internet need not be sensational by definition, but can also serve a more political purpose. One good example here is the way in which official Pentagon policy was circumvented in April 2004. We saw earlier how the US Government between 1991 and 2009 had restricted the media from taking photographs of coffins of US soldiers returning from war zones, allegedly out of respect for the grieving families. In 2004, however, a civilian working at Kuwait airport had taken photos of rows of coffins draped in US flags inside an air force cargo plane about to depart for Germany (Matheson and Allan, 2009, p. 141). The pictures were emailed to a friend in America who forwarded it to the *Seattle Times*, which promptly printed one on the front page. The publication of the photos, which led to the sacking of the civilian working in Kuwait, created a storm of controversy in the United States, as 'appeals to freedom of expression clashed with protests that the photo was undermining the war effort' (Matheson and Allan, 2009, p. 143). The debate reached the highest echelons of American politics, with presidential candidate John Kerry believing that people had a right to see the images, and President Bush arguing the case for a continued ban. Matheson and Allan note that while such images have been taken since the earliest days of photography, the digital era appears to fundamentally transform the practice as it is now much easier to send such images out to mass publics. The infamous images of Iraqi prisoners being tortured and abused by American military personnel at Abu Ghraib prison in Iraq are perhaps even more important in affecting political discourse in this regard, particularly as previous mistreatment claims from human rights organizations had been ignored by the mainstream media, who only became involved when the digital images surfaced (Matheson and Allan, 2009).

The video-hosting website YouTube has also played an important role in allowing amateur footage to scoop mainstream news organizations by publishing moving images of controversial deaths. One of the most famous in this regard was posted during the violent protests following the contested Iranian elections in June 2009. The protests had erupted when supporters of opposition leader Mir-Hossein Moussavi took to the streets to accuse President Mahmoud Ahmadinejad's government of widespread fraud during the elections. The suppressed revolution was particularly notable for the use of social media sites to get information from Iran to the outside world, leading many to nickname it the Twitter Revolution, although we should probably be careful with such a term as, after all, the revolution wasn't immediately successful (Burns and Eltham, 2009). At the height of the demonstrations and amid news that the government was trying to violently beat down the protests, two videos of the shooting and subsequent death of a young Iranian woman made it onto YouTube, from where they quickly spread around the world and were shown, despite the graphic nature, even on some mainstream news sites (Booth, 2009). The woman, Neda Agha-Soltan, immediately became a rallying point for opposition supporters in Iran, and the videos also alerted the international community to what was going on in the country, leading to widespread condemnation (Fathi, 2009). The Iranian government quickly prohibited public mourning ceremonies for the woman, realizing the potential for an upsurge in unrest. Instead, it attempted to divert attention by claiming that the CIA must have killed Agha-Soltan to destabilize Iran (Malcolm, 2009).

Other videos have received notoriety in recent years both for their particularly graphic imagery as well as their political implications. For example, when the former Iraqi dictator Saddam Hussein was executed in December 2006, official video of the hanging was broadcast on TV channels around the world. The BBC made certain choices about broadcasting the video, cutting out the scene where the noose was placed around his neck for the breakfast news, while leaving it unedited after 9 pm. (Matheson and Allan, 2009). Soon after the release of the official video, however, a grainy video, shot on a mobile phone, appeared on the Internet, showing that there was much more to the story. While the official video had no sound and appeared almost like a dignified execution, stopping as the noose was placed around Saddam's neck, 'the unofficial version documented his verbal exchanges with his captors (who were clearly determined to torment him) followed by the moment of his demise as the trapdoor opens and drops out of the gallows platform' (Matheson and Allan, 2009, p. 161). At the end of the clip, the viewer even gets to see a close-up of Saddam's broken neck, together with the sound of cheering among his executioners.

The ability of anyone to post material involving death and dying online is beginning to affect journalism's authority as the provider of narratives about war. Anden-Papadopoulos (2008) observes that the increasing number of videos posted by US military personnel, civilians and insurgents in Iraq on websites such as YouTube is contributing to the way the Internet is challenging the mainstream media's control over images. Castells (2001) has argued that citizen journalism has the potential to undermine propaganda efforts by governments, and, as we have seen in past chapters, mainstream media have, particularly during wartime, followed official policies. Online, however, we can now see images which show exactly the things the mainstream media do not show their audiences. In her analysis, Anden-Papadopoulos is able to show that while a number of videos posted by soldiers enforce the dominant war narrative of the United States as liberators, they also show the dark side of war, thus arguably portraying it in more realistic ways. Dead bodies abound in many such videos, as well as other graphic images of suicide bombings and the narratives of the soldiers themselves. Anden-Papadopoulos believes that such videos can provide unmediated, raw footage which has the potential to balance official narratives. 'Contrary to the myths of national glory, macho heroism, and clinical warfare manufactured by military and media elites, the firsthand testimonials by soldiers actually living the war offer the public uncensored insights into the mundane, violent, and even depraved faces of warfare' (2008, p. 25).

Further cases that have attracted attention in recent years include videos of the beheadings of Daniel Pearl (in Afghanistan) and Nicholas Berg (Iraq) at the hands of their captors in 2002 and 2004 respectively. While mainstream media showed excerpts from the execution videos, they never showed the actual moments of death, as doing so would obviously have contravened the bounds of taste and decency. However, the videos were quickly available online at websites devoted to showing graphic imagery, and their relative popularity demonstrated that, for better or worse, people wanted to see documentary footage of killings. Before it closed, the website Ogrish.com archived 19 beheading videos, with each one having been viewed several million times. The Berg video alone was downloaded more than 15 million times (Tait, 2008).

Certainly the arrival of the Internet has led to a considerable increase in the availability of explicit images of death and dying. It is not that such images never existed before, but they are now accessible by everyone, with established news media unable to control what audiences can see. Of course, this raises similar questions to those discussed in relation to the compassion fatigue thesis. While certainly enabling a more democratic access to factual portrayals of death, does the viewing of such images equate to pornography, or do they actually provide a true opportunity for audiences to bear witness? Or, as Sue Tait (2008) has argued in one of the few studies to examine this phenomenon online, does neither of these descriptions really fit what is actually going on?

Tait examined user comments about explicit footage on the website Ogrish.com, which has since closed and transferred much of its content to LiveLeak.com. Ogrish had promoted itself as a documentary, anti-propaganda site, where Internet users could access truths about the wars in Iraq and Afghanistan that they would not be able to get through the mainstream media. In this way, the website set itself up in the form of a citizen journalist-type venture. Tait found that viewers actually accessed the material on the site for a variety of reasons, and she argued that descriptions of such forms of looking could not be adequately described as pornography. Instead, looking was framed by 'a range of factors including a taste for morbid material that may extend to fandom, prior experience of trauma or the expectation of involvement in traumatic situations, personal contexts that may orient the viewer to the suffering of others, or a commitment to freedom of expression' (Tait, 2008, p. 106). As a result, Tait believes that it is dangerous to simply foreclose any debate over how graphic images of body horror are used online by dismissing viewers as purely voyeurs and labeling them as pornographic. She also warns, however, that uncensored video hosting sites do not function, unlike the news media, to enable viewers to become moral witnesses, as there is no instruction attached in terms of how to feel: 'Without the provision of political and social context for imagery, the viewing of graphic material may be an experience of bodily response or the expression of an imagined entitlement rather than an ethical engagement' (Tait, 2008, p. 108). However, she acknowledges that from user comments it would appear that at least some viewers do feel motivated to act upon viewing graphic content. Nevertheless, further work is required to better understand why people view graphic content on online video-sharing websites, as well as how such viewing affects them. It is clear that scholarship still has some way to go in this regard. A further area, which has also only recently begun to attract more attention from scholars, is the way in which user-generated content is being co-opted by journalists in their reporting and the ethical concerns this may entail.

The ethics of co-opting user-generated material

A number of scholars have observed that part of the appeal of user-generated videos and images of death and dying lies in the nature of the quality. Videos taken with mobile phones are often grainy and shaky productions, which may give them a certain appearance of authenticity over the sometimes slick footage produced by major media corporations. However, there are questions about the truth claims some images and videos make.

Traditional journalistic ideas of ethics, a muddy concept at the best of times, are constantly being challenged in the new media environment, where citizen journalists may not work to, or even be aware of established journalistic codes of ethics. Yet, the pull of such user-generated content has been so strong that mainstream news organizations have come to routinely co-opt it on their websites. As a result, these websites have become 'a shared space, filled with constantly changing content produced by a broad range of individuals and informed by relationships among those contributors' (Singer and Ashman, 2009, p. 3). But of course journalists still act as gatekeepers for content that goes on their websites, and even though they are committed to upholding traditional standards and ethics the fast-paced online environment as well as the downsizing of many news organizations mean it becomes increasingly difficult to ensure all user-generated material is genuine (Arant and Anderson, 2001). As a result, it is sometimes difficult for viewers to ascertain whether footage they are presented with has been reviewed by journalists for its legitimacy (although of course that is not to say that journalists have not also been guilty of passing off fake material as real in the past). One such case occurred during the 2004 tsunami in the Indian Ocean, when what appeared to be real-time photographs of people being swamped by the wave were published in news media around the world (Chakrawertti, 2005). However, it quickly emerged that the photos were actually of a tidal bore on the Qiantangjiang River in China in 2002. By that time, the images had been published by newspapers in Canada, Germany, India and South Africa, as well as by television stations in Australia.

Similarly, soon after a devastating earthquake struck Haiti in January 2010, social media sites began publishing a number of images which purported to be from the scene of the disaster. But some of the pictures were not the real deal, with everything from previous earthquakes in China and Japan to even regular photos of Haiti being passed off as photos of the disaster (Mahar, 2010). Journalists who use social media sites for their coverage thus need to be extremely careful in examining such images and, due to the aforementioned pressures, this is not always possible. At least, the fact that news images are scrutinized by Internet users also means that they can quickly tip off publishers, which, according to news executives, implies that if news media do get it wrong, at least they don't get it wrong for long (Mahar, 2010).

Additionally, the growing popularity of social networking sites such as MySpace and Facebook, as well as personal blogs, means that the Internet constitutes a treasure trove of publicly available but essentially private information about individuals. This has come in handy for journalists in order to at least partially gather information about the dead without doing the dreaded death knock discussed earlier. Previously, reporters needed to be able to get inside the house of a grieving family and then tactfully ask for a photograph of the deceased. Now this process is as easy as a click of the mouse. Journalists are able to access public profiles (and, increasingly, even gain access to private ones) where they will find photos as well as useful personal information and even quotes (Fletcher, 2007). Such techniques have come to be increasingly used, with many news stories nowadays reporting personal information from Facebook or MySpace. For example, when an English student died after a party, a British newspaper reported that he had boasted of his drinking on his MySpace site and that his profile also included pictures of him drinking (Fletcher, 2007). Similarly, the suicides of two 16-year-old girls in Melbourne, Australia during April 2007 attracted immense media attention, not least because newspapers were able to pull massive amounts of information and photographs from their MySpace sites (Blood *et al.*, 2008). The Virginia Tech massacre in the United States in that same month also resulted in the publication of many of the victims' details as reported on their social networking sites (Wigley and Fontenot, 2009). Naturally associated with such practices are ethical concerns, as the dead cannot be asked for permission to use their ramblings on the Internet. But as a journalist, Fletcher sees reporting from such sites as entirely legitimate, noting that public websites do not fall under privacy legislation, and to him they represent a dream come true:

These Internet sites fulfill a fantasy many of us have had from our first days as cub reporters. Suddenly no one shuts the door in our face;

no grey-faced, grief-stricken relative tells us we are ghouls and makes us think worse of ourselves. Now there is no need for that awkward speech of introduction. The door is wide open and a friendly figure is beckoning: 'Come in, come in. Make yourself at home. I don't know if any of it is any use to you, but you will find lots of pictures and some last words and several tributes from friends. Just help yourself'.

(Fletcher, 2007, p. 46)

It isn't always this easy, however, as a German newspaper's exposé on the coverage of the death of the Iranian protester Neda Agha-Soltan has shown (Schraven, 2010). When the student at the Islamic Azad University was shot in a Tehran street and the video of her death began circulating on the Internet, bloggers and news organizations around the world began searching for photos of her. In the video, the name Neda was audible, and soon the surname, Soltan, and the fact that she was a university student also became available. At some point, someone came across a Facebook entry for a Neda Soltani, a lecturer at the same university whose profile photo looked somewhat similar to the available images of Agha-Soltan. Her Facebook profile was restricted so only friends could see her entries, but the profile photo was publicly available. Quickly, the image of Soltani was circulated on the Internet, eventually reaching the mainstream media, all of whom published it, believing it to be Agha-Soltan. A day later, the photo was used in demonstrations in Iran, and it became an icon for the opposition movement in that country. But it was the wrong photo. It took on a life of its own and certainly had a life-changing impact for Neda Soltani, who was, of course, quite alive. When she found out her image had been used, it was too late. She wrote to Voice of America to let them know there had been an error and attached a further photo of herself to prove it. But the organization instead circulated the image as a new photo of the dead Agha-Soltan. Other corporations like CBS then also broadcast it. When she deleted her photo from her Facebook account, bloggers, believing the Iranian censors were behind it, quickly copied it and distributed it on hundreds of Facebook sites and on Twitter. By this time, Soltani had no further opportunities to set the record straight. The blogosphere would not believe her friends who tried to right the wrong, instead accusing them of wanting to take away their 'angel'. The Iranian government pressured Soltani because it wanted to use her for its own ideological ends, to expose what it saw as Western forgery. Eventually Soltani had to flee her country, and now lives as an asylum seeker in

Germany. Some news organizations have acknowledged the case, yet the wrong photo and even name are still regularly used in news reports. This case shows that, sometimes, news media do get it wrong for a long time. And it also demonstrates how difficult it becomes to stop a story once it reaches the Internet, where it is duplicated with amazing speed across a sheer immeasurable number of websites. Of course, as Schraven (2010) notes, it also says a lot about journalism in times of hysteria.

How the Internet impacts grieving behavior

As we have seen so far, the Internet is having a profound effect on the way in which journalists are able to report news stories involving death. Similarly, the participatory nature of the web allows ordinary people to upload material into the public sphere that would otherwise likely have been censored by mainstream media. This participatory aspect also has the potential to affect the discourse of commemorative journalism that was discussed earlier. In order to improve communication with their readers and viewers, many news organizations have added comment functions to their sites. This allows readers of websites to respond to and challenge news stories, as well as engage in a conversation with the author and other readers. This function has had an interesting effect when famous people have died in recent years. For example, when Australia's Crocodile Hunter Steve Irwin died in 2006, Australian news site news.com.au recorded more than 6000 comments on its Irwin story within the first 24 hours. Comments consisted mostly of tributes to the Crocodile Hunter, from within Australia and also from more than 20 countries around the world (Ramadge, 2006). Similarly, the news of the death of Michael Jackson caused numerous websites to crash due to the strong demand from Internet users (Rawlinson and Hunt, 2009).

So what do such developments mean about the way in which people deal with death online? Condolence books can historically be seen as providing a platform for the social expression of grief (Brennan, 2008). Online tribute sites, then, are an extension of such books, but, I would argue, they represent an important departure, also. Firstly, it is now easier for people to express their grief over someone's death by simply going online, when previously they may have had to stand in line for hours. Additionally, and more significantly, their comments can now be seen by potentially millions of people around the world. The relatively private expression of grief has thus moved further into the public sphere. Because comments are usually linked to specific news stories, such sites also present an opportunity to challenge the dominant discourse of collective memory. Thus, 'the use of web memorial discourse fundamentally empowers and strengthens the vernacular voices of commemorating communities' (Hess, 2007, p. 828). This aspect has been very little researched, although anecdotal evidence would suggest that there may not be much deviation from the collective memory produced by journalists, not least because even online those with a dissenting view may feel it inappropriate or tasteless to voice their dissent.

Nevertheless, death appears to be such a hot topic on the Internet that a number of online memorial sites have sprung up in recent years. Internet users are now able to write tributes to their loved ones on numerous websites dedicated to the memory of the dead. Memorial websites allow users to create individual pages including pictures, video and other tributes. Many also offer options for users to express their condolences. Some sites have attracted the ire of critics who see such developments as problematic, however. The website MyDeathSpace.com, for example, has come under attack for invading the privacy of the dead and their families, as well as trivializing death and aiding voyeurism (Aitken, 2009). The site, which archives news stories and online obituaries of deceased MySpace members, allows Internet users to leave comments about the dead. Yet, as the families of the dead are usually not asked when deaths are registered, many have complained about the site, leading the owner to, in his own words, receive 75 per cent hate mail and 25 per cent fan mail (Sofka, 2009). Similar to news coverage of death, it is also mainly those who have died prematurely and often senselessly that are represented on the page.

Nevertheless, the opportunity for friends to leave comments on memorial sites and archived profiles on social networking sites means that for the Internet generation, 'the printed obituary written by a newspaper with limited input from the family or a paid death notice is being replaced by online shrines where friends, family, and strangers can all remember the deceased together' (Goodstein, 2007, p. 61). Certainly, such sites offer the bereaved opportunities to express their feelings and talk about death in ways that have often been denied during the twentieth century (Roberts, 2006). Most recently, family members can also choose to have the funeral webcast to an audience. Viewers are then able to watch the service from their home live or download the file to view it later. One benefit of this is that now people who may otherwise not have been able to come to a funeral for reasons of time and distance are able to participate at least virtually (Veale, 2009).

Arguably, then the Internet is leading the charge in driving social change towards a renewed acceptance and public discussion of death. And as early studies show, dealing with their grief through such sites can have quite beneficial effects for the bereaved (Roberts, 2004, 2006). In fact, Roberts' survey of Internet users who participated in online memorials found that 91 per cent felt the process had helped them in their grief. However, there is still a very limited amount of research on the topic; and in particular the way in which people may grieve through news websites is virtually unexplored.

Conclusion

The arrival of the Internet has certainly heralded a number of significant changes in a news industry which has taken some time to come to terms with the promise of a more democratic flow of information. Citizen journalism is having a profound effect on the way mainstream journalism is practiced, and this shows not least in the area of the news coverage of death. Images which used to be censored by news organizations for fear of upsetting audiences are now freely available, and there are strong indications that such images are widely accessed. For mainstream media, this presents a dilemma for commercial reasons. Often, images are chosen also on the basis of what the competition may have. Now, journalists need to take into account what may appear on Twitter or LiveLeak.com. In the interests of disclosing all information to the public, they may feel the pressure to either include such images in their coverage, or at least link to it, with an appropriate warning. What implications does this have for wider attitudes to death in society? May such developments lead to changes in standards and increasingly graphic coverage even in mainstream media? Some observers are certainly suggesting that the coverage of death is becoming ever more explicit (Seaton, 2005), yet there have been very few empirical studies to support this argument. Was the coverage of the January 2010 earthquake in Haiti more graphic than that after the 2004 tsunami? How do these compare to even earlier disasters? Without comparative studies, we will not be able to have a definitive answer.

Of course, if there is indeed a trend toward more detailed visual coverage, what is driving such change? It may well be that the ability of ordinary people to make such images available to the wider public is a part of such a development, if it does exist. Goldberg (1998) has noted that the progressive disappearance of explicit images in the illustrated press during the late nineteenth century coincided with a shift in general attitudes toward hiding death. Perhaps the increased availability of images online and the establishment of online grieving sites are similar indications of a greater shift back towards a more public acknowledgment of and engagement with the end of life, as some have argued (Bradbury, 1999; Walter, 2006). On the other hand, it may just be the case that social scientists have been too busy uncovering hidden death that they have neglected to acknowledge existing public death in the past (Howarth, 2007).

The study of the Internet's influence on news representations of death is certainly in its infancy and will need to grow considerably in coming years in order to properly examine the shifts which may be taking place. A number of aspects which have been raised throughout this book in relation to traditional media also apply to online studies. We firstly need to ascertain whether news organizations actually are displaying more graphic images, or at least are linking to them. Secondly, and even more importantly, we need to examine the motivations and experiences of Internet users when uploading and viewing such images as displayed on so-called 'death porn' sites. Tait's (2008) study presents an important blueprint, but we need to go beyond it and include wider news audiences.

We need to examine whether the viewing of more graphic imagery may actually lead to compassion fatigue and complacency or if such images, because they are ostensibly perceived as more realistic, actually may have the power to spur audiences into action. Similarly, does the viewing of graphic imagery lead to increased signs of post-traumatic stress? The only studies to examine this aspect have looked at traditional media, while studies which examine Internet users may be even more useful. This is because, on the Internet, users often actively choose to view certain images, thus placing the responsibility for selection back on audiences. It would be interesting to find out whether this may result in different levels of PTSD or even compassion.

9
Conclusion

If the majority of scholars are to be believed we are on the cusp of entering a new era in our relationship with death. A topic that was taboo for most of the twentieth century now seems to be experiencing somewhat of a renaissance. All of a sudden death is becoming a mentionable subject again, whereas it had been largely avoided previously, something to be hidden away rather than publicly discussed. Only during the latter part of the past century did death begin to make its reappearance, and the news media are believed to have played a role in this. We don't know for certain whether increased public discussion of death is caused by increased media coverage, or vice versa. Other social developments are likely to play their part also. Yet, undoubtedly, we are now exposed to a multitude of mediated representations of death through newspapers, news broadcasts and, especially, the Internet.

This is not to say that death was never before present in the news media. A look at the history of the representation of death in the public sphere shows that death in all its forms has long been an integral component of journalism. What has changed since the latter part of the twentieth century is that news media, aided by the arrival of new technologies such as the Internet, have become even more present in our day-to-day lives. One hundred years ago, the only medium through which most people received news about the outside world – apart from face-to-face communication – was the newspaper. News was therefore manageable, as people sat down with the paper at a given time to take in the information at their leisure. Now, we are literally bombarded with messages all through the day, which means we need to process a much larger amount of information. On a basic level, this obviously means there are more representations of death. Newspapers, television and online news all have the potential to display different aspects of a fatal event, supplying us with a much wider variety of images and knowledge than we may have previously had access to.

Yet, while death is arguably more present, the historical context also shows that the types of representations have not changed much over the centuries. Sensational images or descriptions about people who encounter an untimely fate have been part and parcel of journalism ever since the first newsbooks arrived in Europe. If we count official collections like the Roman *Acta*, human interest stories have been around for even longer. Etchings and woodcuts, as well as photographs, have all depicted death in its most gruesome detail, and the only thing that has changed is that photographs are able to lay claim to a higher credibility in terms of what they represent. Written accounts of sixteenth and seventeenth century deaths were in no way less horrific than modern day news stories. If anything, they may have been more gruesome, even if their veracity may have been questionable.

An increased resurgence of death in the public sphere therefore does not necessarily mean that mainstream news media are becoming more liberal in their visual display of death. In fact, the empirical evidence so far suggests that for the most part, news still sanitizes death to a very large degree. Similarly, audiences are still squeamish when it comes to graphic representations of death, as is evident in the perennial opinion surveys when graphic images do surface in the news. We don't seem to mind written descriptions so much, but most draw the line at visual depictions of the dead, particularly when they leave nothing to the imagination. But the representation of death in the news is much more complex than that.

This book set out to map the quickly expanding field of the study of death in the news, in order to identify the main paradigms, ideas and arguments which relate to the way in which journalism deals with the end of life. In order to provide an overview, the existing body of research in the field was examined along the lines of the production, content and reception of journalistic work on death. In doing so, it was possible to unearth the main patterns that have characterized scholarly work, and particularly to highlight the, at times, considerable gaps that still exist in our knowledge. The study of news representations of death has been located within a number of paradigms, such as journalism and communication studies, cultural studies, sociology, literature, anthropology, psychiatry and psychology. Most studies have stayed within their respective paradigms, rarely venturing outside into other fields in order to inform a more comprehensive assessment of the state of the field. Similarly, few have combined quantitative and qualitative approaches, or even attempted to include all components of the communication process in one study.

The result is that our understanding of the way in which journalism deals with death is hampered by narrow foci that can only offer us a glimpse of the bigger picture. Nowhere is this more evident than in the debate over a perceived glut of graphic images and compassion fatigue among audiences. Here, Moeller's (1999) and originally Sontag's (1977) work has run on the assumption that increasingly graphic and stereo-typed coverage of wars, disasters and diseases have led audiences to care less about the fate of others. Yet, as this book has shown repeatedly, the normative assumptions are difficult to prove in empirical research. Mainstream news media, for the most part at least, show extremely few graphic images of death, and whether we are seeing an increase is diffi-cult to say as few comparative studies have looked at this issue. Similarly, the notion that a surfeit of photography necessarily leads to compassion fatigue is not borne out in more detailed research, which has actually shown that audiences experience such coverage in a variety of ways and, therefore, extract widely differing meanings from it (Kinnick *et al.*, 1996; Perlmutter, 1998; Tait, 2008). Nevertheless, there is no doubt that some journalists as well as audience members experience compassion fatigue, particularly in the form of secondary traumatic stress. But the short-coming here is that research on traumatic stress in television viewers of deadly terrorist attacks has so far only been able to show a correla-tion between the amount of exposure to news coverage and the level of stress. Whether it is the case that seeing images of horror leads to trau-matic stress or simply that people who are more affected by an event watch more television is not entirely clear.

Also, while a majority of news consumers generally say they do not want to see graphic imagery, the appearance of more graphic visuals online has offered a significant number of people the opportunity to see what the mainstream media usually censors from public display. On the Internet, those who are curious enough (and whose stomach can handle it) are able to view real death as it happens, courtesy of mostly amateur footage which can be uploaded by anyone. This is a relatively recent development, and it is still too early to say what effect it may have on wider representations of death in the news. However, the fact that this material is available and is accessed by a considerable segment of society means that at least a part of the audience wants to be able to see it. What impact may this trend have on compassion fatigue?

It becomes obvious that, when trying to answer some of these impor-tant questions, we are going around in circles a little. It is difficult to piece together a comprehensive picture of representations of death in the news not only because their production, content, distribution and reception are extremely complex, but also because much of the existing literature is fragmented and concerned with only parts of the whole. It is therefore important that future research attempts to address some of these issues by taking into account three main considerations, which are important for any research on communication but are even more crucial in the study of death in the news. In the following, I shall sketch these out by examining them in terms of where existing research has failed to provide a more differentiated perspective, as well as areas which may provide useful sites for future analyses.

The aspects to be considered include the need for:

- holistic approaches that can take account of the various stages of the communication process as well as inter-disciplinary contexts;
- a combination of quantitative and qualitative methods in order to enhance the depth of analysis;
- comparative approaches that track the representations of death over time, across media and against different cultural backgrounds.

Holistic approaches

The example above of what we know about compassion fatigue and what may cause it demonstrates an urgent need to more comprehensively address the way in which journalism deals with death. This includes a consideration of all stages of the communication process, as well as taking into account insights from inter-disciplinary contexts. The scholarship on the social history of death proved immensely useful as a contextual background against which we can situate the display of death in the news media. As a result, it was possible to see certain developments in representations as being in line with wider societal changes, as well as technological progress in journalism. During the late nineteenth century, graphic displays of death became more numerous in the penny press, quite likely a function of economic motives. But this was also a time when many people's direct experiences of death began to become less frequent and more people started to come into contact with death only through the news media (Goldberg, 1998). The more ubiquitous availability of graphic imagery in recent years has been linked to a wider shift towards a recognition of death, away from the concealment that had been so dominant during much of the twentieth century (Staudt, 2009a). In a similar way, journalism's role in mediating grief may be having an impact on how people grieve for the dead. The mass mediation of public displays of grief may be giving increasing numbers of people the confidence to show their emotions freely, and engendering longer-term social change (Walter, 2006).

Additionally, while political and economic motives may feature strongly in the background of a significant amount of news decisions, there may be additional factors, such as cultural grounds. This has been evident in the literature on the values that are placed on deaths from other countries. Often, particularly during wartime, political economy arguments can be very persuasive, as they are able to take account of the connection between news as business and journalism's close association with politics. News media simply do not want to appear as unpatriotic and lose their most valuable asset for attracting income, which is their audience. But at other times, political and economic links may not be as important as more overarching cultural bonds, as evidenced in studies that have looked at the coverage of news from abroad (Adams, 1986; Christensen, 2004; Hanusch, 2008a). In these cases, how much the dead are like us becomes the important criterion. This is evident in journalists' throw-away lines such as: 'One dead fireman in Brooklyn is worth five English bobbies, who are worth 50 Arabs, who are worth 500 Africans' (cited in Moeller, 1999, p. 22).

At the same time, approaches from the field of psychiatry have had a profound impact on journalism studies' understanding of the ways in which reporting on traumatic events such as death can impact on journalists as well as audiences. Journalists suffer real consequences from being exposed to accidents, murders and other fatal events on a regular basis. Until not very long ago, there was little appreciation of this circumstance within the journalistic profession. Journalists were supposed to be able to separate their experiences from their work and not be affected by such events. But, as journalists are only human, a significant number do suffer as a result of their work. Further, many studies of journalism's role in mediating death have neglected to look more closely at journalists' decision-making and instead have concentrated on the content of stories. Sometimes, findings from such content studies were used to infer certain decisions that would have been made by journalists. Journalists themselves, however, were rarely involved in the research, and there is an urgent need to bolster our knowledge about this part of the process. Studies such as the one by Beam and Spratt (2009) are certainly a step in the right direction.

In a similar way, examinations of traumatic stress in audiences have ignored more in-depth assessments of the content these audiences were exposed to (Cantrell, 2005). Of course this area of the field is still in its infancy, so future research here should be able to shine more light on the ways in which audiences can react to seeing traumatic images in the news, as long as it takes wider processes into account. Perhaps the largest amount of attention has been given to the way in which news represents death, be it in text or visual form. But even here, analyses could be more refined, even in clarifying what we mean by pictures of death. Zelizer (in press) has added another important category for the scholarship of news representations of death by adding the category of 'about-to-die' images. Most studies of the past have regarded many of the photos Zelizer discusses as photos of death, when technically they may not have been. It will therefore be important to more closely distinguish differing degrees of death portrayed visually in the news, in order to arrive at a more comprehensive picture of the representation of death.

Further, much like studies that have focused on producers or audiences alone, content studies have often inferred journalistic decision-making or audience reactions. While it would by necessity demand a comprehensive approach and labor-intensive study, there is no reason why we should not aim to combine the three aspects of the process – production, content and reception – into one study. Doing so would provide us with a significantly more holistic outcome that may be able to highlight other connections between previously fragmented studies.

Combining methodologies

Beyond the need to look at all stages of the communication process, it is also necessary to take a holistic approach when it comes to methodological concerns. This particularly relates to the combination of quantitative as well as qualitative approaches and a triangulation of results. The literature on representations of death in the news is marked by studies which could have benefitted from a mixture of methods. For example, we have seen that, in a quantitative sense, newspapers are more likely to report certain types of deaths, depending on the location, circumstances and people involved. However, there has been a lack of more textual approaches which could have examined more closely the discourse that is prevalent in such reporting. Scholarly work on the role of the media in mediating high-profile deaths by way of commemorative techniques has shown that a qualitative approach can be immensely beneficial in order for us to understand some of the wider processes around the mediation of grief. Yet, few studies have extended qualitative work to the reporting of the deaths of ordinary people. On a similar level, we have seen that there exists somewhat of a disconnection in the work on the visual representation of death in the news. Studies at the denotative level have been able to examine how prevalent especially the display of graphic death is in the mainstream media. It has been shown repeatedly that graphic imagery of death is quite rare, both in wars and disasters as well as on a more general level (Singletary and Lamb, 1984; Taylor, 1998; Fishman, 2001; Hanusch, 2008a). On the other hand, appraisals of the visual coverage of death, which weren't so much grounded in empirical research, have ascertained that we are exposed to a glut of graphic imagery (Sontag, 1977; Moeller, 1999). Such studies, undertaken on the more connotative level, have nevertheless provided useful insights and arguments about the potential effects of stereotyped reporting, which quantitative assessments have rarely taken into account. As a result, two streams of research that really have much in common have tended to work along a similar path without talking to each other. Combining such approaches may enable us to arrive at more profound insights into how journalism portrays the end of life.

The field of trauma studies has also provided helpful insights into the ways in which journalists and audiences respond to death in the news. There are signs that a correlation does exist between covering and viewing traumatic events and the presence of post-traumatic stress symptoms. However, such studies have tended to focus perhaps too much on quantitative assessments as to how many people might be affected rather than additionally engaging in more depth with the actual content that journalists produce. This is where textual analyses of news stories about death can come in useful. Similarly, the definitions of compassion fatigue, as employed by media scholars and the field of psychiatry, have differed quite considerably, and a more wholesome approach may be able to align some of those sentiments. Trauma researchers have applied their criteria to the study of audiences through quantitative surveys and found that a significant number of people do experience traumatic stress while watching news footage of terrorist attacks. Yet, few studies have examined compassion fatigue as defined in the media studies literature in a similar way. Certainly trauma studies provide more stringent criteria, but they do not connect with the sentiment of compassion fatigue as defined by scholars such as Moeller (1999). Kinnick *et al.* (1996) employed criteria to measure the latter definition and arrived at some interesting results, which may prove useful for future studies. Here, too, the combination of quantitative surveys with in-depth interviews of audiences may provide interesting insights into the ways in which representations of death may affect various segments of the population.

Comparative approaches

Another area of concern, which often appears in studies such as this as only an afterthought, is the fact that the vast majority of work in the field has been restricted to Western, and particularly Anglo-American contexts. By necessity, this book has also focused heavily on the representation of death in those countries. While non-Western material was included where available, a comprehensive body of work simply does not exist outside of the West yet. The overwhelming majority of research has been conducted in the United States, the United Kingdom and Australia, and there has been a tendency in research to extrapolate, even if only implicitly, the results on at least the rest of the Western if not the entire world. But news coverage of death does not only differ within national contexts depending on the circumstances, it also varies even more widely across cultures. Northern European and North American countries tend to shy away from showing graphic images of death most of the time. Yet, anecdotal evidence shows that this is not necessarily the case elsewhere. The predominantly Catholic countries of Southwestern Europe and Latin America may be more open to seeing death in their newspapers than Protestant countries. Some countries in the Middle East as well as Southeast Asia seem to confront their audiences with more gruesome images also. There is no one representation of death in the news, and cultural contexts may play a large part in variances. Yet, there are hardly any noteworthy comparative approaches. Employing such lines of inquiry may tell us more about our own attitudes to dealing with death by looking at the way in which others handle the end of life. Other aspects of the coverage would also be worth comparing across cultures, for example, the portrayal of others' deaths as opposed to the deaths of our countrymen and women. Do news media around the world pay attention to their own dead to a different degree as much as seems to be the case in the West? Further, we need to view such differences against comparative studies of audiences, which are also still to be developed.

There are also differences among the countries considered to constitute the 'West', as the comparison between German and Australian newspapers has shown (Hanusch, 2008a). Even across these very similar cultural backgrounds there appeared to be considerable differences as to what is acceptable to show and what isn't: German newspapers were even more squeamish than their already restrained Australian counterparts. While Australian journalists also freely admitted that different rules applied to Australian deaths than foreign deaths, German journalists were much more balanced in their comments and seemed to take a more humanistic perspective. Anecdotal evidence also shows that within Latin America, for example, different countries have different perspectives on what is permissible to show. As globalization advances, a comprehensive comparative analysis may also be able to shed light on the extent to which representations of death in the news may have universally relevant aspects, in order to find out how global developments may play a role.

There is, further, a need for comparative approaches to the study of death in the news within countries themselves. Here, future research must address the various types of news delivery systems, in order to more fully capture the level of death audiences are exposed to in news reporting. It is intuitive to believe that news media at the more consumer-oriented end of the market may be more likely to sensationalize death and show a larger number of graphic images than publications that focus more on providing their audiences with news stories that are essential for them to make decisions in a democracy. Yet, as Fishman's (2001) study has demonstrated, American tabloids like the *New York Post* and *Philadelphia Daily News* have actually shown fewer graphic images of death than broadsheets like the *New York Times* and *Washington Post*. We need to find out whether these results can be replicated in other countries as well.

However, rather than merely focusing on newspapers, future studies need to involve other media as well, as the more recent studies of the coverage of the Iraq War have tended to do (Silcock *et al.*, 2008). This is increasingly crucial as the Internet presents journalism with a significant challenge to its role as society's storytellers, which has an impact on the availability of graphic images of death and dying. Social media allow individuals to upload dramatic images containing any imaginable degree of horror, as has been apparent in the presence of many videos and photographs of death online which had been censored in the mainstream media for fear of contravening the rules of decency and taste. A significant number of people are accessing such material online and, if research in the field wants to look to the future, such developments must be taken into account. Early studies show that mainstream media do not differ significantly in their online coverage of wars compared to the traditional media (Schwalbe, 2006; Silcock *et al.*, 2008). Whether this will continue to be the case as participatory journalism further impacts on traditional journalism practices is a question that needs to be answered.

Such comparisons may give us further insight into the workings of the various levels of influences, which range from macro levels such as cultural, political and economic factors through mid-level constraints of news organizations down to individual influences. Existing research has been able to make out various influences, but a comprehensive appraisal of how these influences play out specifically in journalism's work is still missing. We know that political, economic and cultural factors can play a significant role in deciding whether and how to report death, particularly when it comes to high-profile events. Yet, there are also important organizational influences, such as individual publications' preferences about the coverage of death and resulting, albeit implicit, newsroom policies. These can be simply down to an editor who believes that graphic death should not be shown under any circumstances. But individual journalists can, in special circumstances, bypass official policies. For example, an Australian journalist who said his editor did not want to show death in the news, but who himself was more open to doing so, noted that from time to time he had been able to slip an image into the paper when the editor was away (Hanusch, 2008b, p. 141).

A final comparative dimension that is needed in the study of the way in which death is reported in the media is the tracking of representations over time. Such longitudinal studies may enable us to better relate news coverage to wider societal development. Seaton (2005) reported an unpublished study in Britain which found an increase in graphic images of death on the front page over time, yet very little details were available about that particular study. While individual case studies of high-impact events such as the 2004 tsunami or the Iraq War are useful in extracting attitudes to reporting death, we would need to find out how these compare to the reporting of other disasters and wars. What is further needed here is a wider representative comparison of the display of death in day-to-day news coverage. Such analyses would also need to take account of not just the number of graphic images *per se*, but also the percentage of the overall number of photographs, in order to control for the general trend to include more images in the news. This could give us a more adequate picture of how death is represented outside the extreme examples.

At the same time, in order to better triangulate such results, comparative research would also need to look at audience attitudes to, and perhaps even effects of, the news coverage of death. The evidence so far suggests that the majority of people in the West still do not like to see graphic imagery, while exploratory work in the Middle East suggests other cultures may have different views (Fahmy and Johnson, 2007). What is needed, then, is a comparative study of such attitudes that allows us to track, within the one framework, what the differences are and, more importantly, the determinants of any such differences.

The recommendations for advancing the study of news representations of death presented here are substantial. What is proposed may appear difficult to achieve. In a way, I am suggesting studies should investigate the production, content, distribution channels and reception of death in the news, across time and across cultures, using a mix of quantitative and qualitative methodologies and with input from as many paradigms and disciplines as relevant. This is, of course, an ideal scenario, which would require the involvement of many researchers, substantial amounts of funding and some time to complete. And perhaps it is unachievable in one project. But what is obvious from reflecting on the wide variety of scholarship that is concerned with the presence (or lack) of death in the news is that we cannot go on producing research that does not take account of wider contexts. Too often research in the field has been restricted by narrow approaches that, while useful in shedding light on some particular aspect, have neglected relevant insights, be they related to different paradigms or simply methodological aspects. The field, therefore, needs a collaborative approach that can benefit from the variety of scholars' expertise in the different fields discussed here. Only then will we be able to more fully understand the complexities of news representations of death. And to do so should always be the main objective.

Bibliography

Adams, William C. (1986) 'Whose lives Count? TV coverage of natural disasters', *Journal of Communication*, 36(2), pp. 113–22.

Aday, Sean (2005) 'The real war will never get on television: Casualty imagery in American television coverage of the Iraq War', in Seib, Philip (ed.) *Media and Conflict in the Twenty-first Century*, pp. 141–56. New York, Palgrave Macmillan.

Adoni, Hanna and Sherrill Mane (1984) 'Media and the social construction of reality: Toward an integration of theory and research', *Communication Research*, 11(3), pp. 323–40.

Ahern, Jennifer, Sandro Galea, Heidi Resnick, Dean Kilpatrick, Michael Bucuvalas, Joel Gold and David Vlahov (2002) 'Television images and psychological symptoms after the September 11 terrorist attacks', *Psychiatry*, 65(4), pp. 289–300.

Ahrens, Frank (2009) 'The accelerating decline of newspapers', *The Washington Post*, 27 October, p. A15.

Aitken, Amanda (2009) 'Online life after death', *Bereavement Care*, 28(1), pp. 34–5.

Alford, Roger (2004) 'Panel: U.S. newspapers running more tragic photos in wake of 9/11', *Associated Press*, 15 October.

Allan, Stuart (2006) *Online News: Journalism and the Internet*, Buckingham, Open University Press.

Alonso, J., M. C. Angermeyer, S. Bernert, R. Bruffaerts, T. S. Brugha, H. Bryson, G. Girolamo, R. Graaf, K. Demyttenaere, I. Gasquet, et al. (2004) 'Prevalence of mental disorders in Europe: Results from the European Study of the Epidemiology of Mental Disorders (ESEMeD) project', *Acta Psychiatrica Scandinavica*, 109(s420), pp. 21–7.

Altheide, David L. (2003) 'Notes towards a politics of fear', *Journal for Crime, Conflict and the Media*, 1(1), pp. 37–54.

American Psychiatric Association (2000) *Diagnostic and Statistical Manual of Mental Disorders*, 4th edn, Washington, DC, American Psychiatric Association.

Anden-Papadopoulos, Kari (2008) 'The Abu Ghraib torture photographs: News frames, visual culture, and the power of images', *Journalism*, 9(1), pp. 5–30.

Andersen, Robin (1989) 'Images of war: Photojournalism, ideology and Central America', *Latin American Perspectives*, 16(2), pp. 96–114.

Anderson, Benedict (1991) *Imagined Communities: Reflections on the Origin and Spread of Nationalism*, London, Verso.

Arant, M. David and Janna Quitney Anderson (2001) 'Newspaper online editors support traditional standards', *Newspaper Research Journal*, 22(1), pp. 57–69.

Aries, Philippe (1974) *Western Attitudes Toward Death: From the Middle Ages to the Present*, Baltimore, MD, Johns Hopkins University Press.

Arnason, Arnar, Sigurjon Baldur Hafsteinsson and Tinna Gretarsdottir (2003) 'Letters to the dead: Obituaries and identity, memory and forgetting in Iceland', *Mortality*, 8(3), pp. 268–84.

Artwick, Claudette Guzan (1996) 'Blood, body bags & tears', *Visual Communication Quarterly*, 3(2), pp. 14–19.

Australian Press Council (2003) 'Statement of Principles', *Australian Press Council*, viewed 10 April 2010, www.presscouncil.org.au/pcsite/complaints/sop.
html

Ball, John C. and Jill Jonnes (2000) *Fame at Last: Who Was Who According to The New York Times Obituaries*, Kansas City, MO, Andrews McMeel.

Barkham, Patrick (2006) 'It's like a part of Australia has died', *Guardian*, 5 September, viewed 10 April 2010, http://www.guardian.co.uk/print/0„3295 68748-110732,00.html

Barry, Elizabeth (2008) 'From epitaph to obituary: Death and celebrity in eighteenth-century British culture', *International Journal of Cultural Studies*, 11(3), pp. 259–75.

Barthes, Roland (1967) *Elements of Semiology*, London, Cape.

Barthes, Roland (1972) *Mythologies*, New York, Hill and Wang.

Barthes, Roland (1977) *Image-Music-Text*, London, Fontana.

Barthes, Roland (1981) *Camera Lucida: Reflections on Photography*, New York, Hill and Wang.

Beam, Randal A. and Meg Spratt (2009) 'Managing vulnerability: Job satisfaction, morale and journalists' reactions to violence and trauma', *Journalism Practice*, 3(4), pp. 421–38.

Bennett, Ellen M., Jill Dianne Swenson and Jeff S. Wilkinson (1992) 'Is the medium the message? An experimental test with morbid news', *Journalism Quarterly*, 69(4), pp. 921–28.

Bennett, Paul, Yvette Williams, Nicola Page, Kerenza Hood, Malcolm Woollard and Norman Vetter (2005) 'Associations between organizational and incident factors and emotional distress in emergency ambulance personnel', *British Journal of Clinical Psychology*, 44(2), pp. 215–26.

Bennett, W. L. (1990) 'Toward a theory of Press-State Relations in the United States', *Journal of Communication*, 40(2), pp. 103–25.

Berger, Peter L. and Thomas Luckmann (1966) *The Social Construction of Reality: A Treatise in the Sociology of Knowledge*, London, Allen Lane.

Berkowitz, Dan (2000) 'Doing double duty: Paradigm repair and the Princess Diana what-a-story', *Journalism*, 1(2), pp. 125–43.

Berrington, Eileen and Ann Jemphrey (2003) 'Pressures on the press: Reflections on reporting tragedy', *Journalism*, 4(2), pp. 225–48.

Birmingham, John (2006) 'Greer's feral attack reflects elitist conceit', *The Australian*, 7 September, p. 12.

Blanchard, Edward B., Eric Kuhn, Dianna L. Rowell, Edward J. Hickling, David Wittrock, Rebecca L. Rogers, Michelle R. Johnson and Debra C. Steckler (2004) 'Studies of the vicarious traumatization of college students by the September 11th attacks: Effects of proximity, exposure and connectedness', *Behaviour Research and Therapy*, 42(2), pp. 191–205.

Blood, R. Warwick, Andrew Dare, Kerry McCallum, Kate Holland and Jane Pirkis (2008) 'Enduring and competing news frames: Australian newspaper coverage of the deaths by suicide of two Melbourne girls', Paper presented at the Australian and New Zealand Communication Association Conference, Wellington, 9–11 July.

Blood, R. Warwick, Jane Pirkis and Kate Holland (2007) 'Media reporting of suicide methods: An Australian perspective', *Crisis: The Journal of Crisis Intervention and Suicide Prevention*, 28(Suppl. 1), pp. 64–9.

Blood, R. Warwick, Peter Putnis, Jane Pirkis, Trish Payne and Catherine Francis (2001) 'Monitoring media coverage of suicide: Theory and methodology', *Australian Journalism Review*, 23(1), pp. 57–80.

Blumenthal, Sol and Lawrence Bergner (1973) 'Suicide and newspapers: A replicated study', *American Journal of Psychiatry*, 130(4), pp. 468–71.

Bodey, Michael (2006) 'The Australian we all aspire to be', *The Australian*, 5 September, p. 1.

Booth, Jenny (2009) 'Iranian authorities scramble to negate Neda Soltan "martyrdom" ', *The Times*, 23 June, viewed 10 April 2010, http://www.timesonline.co.uk/tol/news/world/middle_east/article6561253.ece

Borg, Alan (1991) *War Memorials: From Antiquity to the Present*, London, Leo Cooper.

Bradbury, Mary (1999) *Representations of Death: A Social Psychological Perspective*, London, Routledge.

Brennan, Michael (2008) 'Condolence books: Language and meaning in the mourning for Hillsborough and Diana', *Death Studies*, 32(4), pp. 326–51.

Breslau, Naomi, Ronald C. Kessler, Howard D. Chilcoat, Lonni R. Schultz, Glenn C. Davis and Patricia Andreski (1998) 'Trauma and posttraumatic stress disorder in the community: The 1996 Detroit area survey of Trauma', *Archives of General Psychiatry*, 55(7), pp. 626–32.

British Broadcasting Corporation (2005) *Editorial Guidelines: The BBC's Values and Standards*, London, BBC.

Brosius, Hans-Bernd (1993) 'The effects of emotional pictures in television news', *Communication Research*, 20(1), pp. 105–24.

Brothers, Caroline (1997) *War and Photography: A Cultural History*, London, Routledge.

Bruns, Axel (2005) *Gatewatching: Collaborative Online News Production*, New York, Peter Lang.

Buchanan, Colin (2006) Goodbye Crocodile Hunter. Universal Music.

Burant, Jim (1984) 'The visual world in the Victorian Age', *Archivaria*, 19, pp. 110–21.

Burdach, Konrad J. (1988) 'Reporting on deaths: The perspective coverage of accident news in a German tabloid', *European Journal of Communication*, 3, pp. 81–9.

Burns, Alex and Ben Eltham (2009) 'Twitter free Iran: An evaluation of Twitter's role in public diplomacy and information operations in Iran's 2009 election crisis', in Papandrea, Franco and Mark Armstrong (eds) *Record of the Communications Policy & Research Forum 2009*, pp. 298–310. Sydney, Network Insight Institute.

Burns, Stanley (1990) *Sleeping Beauty: Memorial Photography in America*, Altadena, CA, Twelvetrees Press.

Buttler, Danny and Kate Rose (2006) 'Outrage over Greer pot shots', *Herald Sun*, 6 September, p. 6.

Bytheway, Bill and Julia Johnson (1996) 'Valuing lives? Obituaries and the life course', *Mortality*, 1(2), pp. 219–34.

Campbell, David (2004) 'Horrific blindness: Images of death in contemporary media', *Journal for Cultural Research*, 8(1), pp. 55–74.

Cantrell, Christina (2005) 'Covering trauma: Impact on the public', viewed 10 April 2010, http://dartcenter.org/content/trauma-coverage-impact-on-public

Carey, James W. (1989) *Communication as Culture: Essays on Media and Society*, Winchester, MA, Unwin Hyman.

Carlson, Matt (2007) 'Making memories matter: Journalistic authority and the memorializing discourse around Mary McGrory and David Brinkley', *Journalism*, 8(2), pp. 165–83.

Carruthers, Susan L. (2000) *The Media at War*, London, Macmillan.

Castanos, Angel J. and Amor Muñoz (2005) 'Covering Terrorism: 911 versus 311 in American and Spanish Newspaper Front Pages', Paper presented at the Media in Transition Conference, MIT, Cambridge, MA, May 6–8.

Castells, Manuel (1996) *The Rise of the Network Society*, Malden, MA, Blackwell.

Castells, Manuel (2001) *The Internet Galaxy: Reflections on the Internet, Business and Society*, Oxford, Oxford University Press.

Castle, Philip (1999) 'Journalism and trauma: Proposals for change', *Asia Pacific Media Educator*, 1(7), pp. 143–50.

Chakrawertti, Samiran (2005) 'After the deadly tsunami, a photo hoax wave', *The Times of India*, 8 January, viewed 10 April 2010, http://timesofindia.india times.com/india/After-the-deadly-tsunami-a-photo-hoax-wave/articleshow/ 984253.cms

Chang, Chia-Ming, Li-Ching Lee, Kathryn M. Connor, Jonathan R. T. Davidson, Keith Jeffries and Te-Jen Lai (2003) 'Posttraumatic distress and coping strategies among rescue workers after an earthquake', *Journal of Nervous and Mental Disease*, 191(6), pp. 391–8.

Christensen, Christian (2004) 'Political victims and media focus: The killings of Laurent Kabila, Zoran Djindjic, Anna Lindh and Pim Fortuyn', *Journal for Crime, Conflict and the Media*, 1(2), pp. 23–40.

Cohen, Y. (1986) *Media Diplomacy: The Foreign Office in the Mass Communications Age*, London, F. Cass.

Combs, Barbara and Paul Slovic (1979) 'Newspaper coverage of causes of death', *Journalism Quarterly*, 56(4), pp. 837–43, 49.

Connolly, Steve (2006) 'Diana and the Croc Hunter: An odd couple in death', *Australian Associated Press*, 7 September.

Cook, Bernie (2001) 'Over my dead body: The ideological use of dead bodies in network news coverage of Vietnam', *Quarterly Review of Film and Video*, 18(2), pp. 203–16.

Cooke, Jennifer (2008) 'Why I took drugs: A reporter's war with his demons', *Sydney Morning Herald*, 8 November.

Coonfield, Gordon and John Huxford (2009) 'News images as lived images: Media ritual, cultural performance, and public trauma', *Critical Studies in Media Communication*, 26(5), pp. 457–79.

Copeland, David (1997) *Colonial American Newspapers: Character and Content*, Newark, NJ, University of Delaware Press.

Coté, William and Roger Simpson (2000) *Covering Violence: A Guide to Ethical Reporting about Victims and Trauma*, New York, Columbia University Press.

Cottle, Simon (2006) *Mediatized Conflict*, Maidenhead, Open University Press.

Couldry, Nick (2003) *Media Rituals: A Critical Approach*, London, Routledge.

Coyle, Joanne and Doreen MacWhannell (2002) 'The importance of "Morality" in the social construction of suicide in Scottish newspapers', *Sociology of Health and Illness*, 24(6), pp. 689–713.

Davis, Lennard J. (1983) *Factual Fiction: The Origins of the English Novel*, New York, Columbia University Press.

Dayan, Daniel and Elihu Katz (1992) *Media Events: The Live Broadcasting of History*, Cambridge, MA, Harvard University Press.

de Jong, Joop T. V. M., Ivan H. Komproe and Mark Van Ommeren (2003) 'Common mental disorders in postconflict settings', *The Lancet*, 361(9375), pp. 2128–30.

de Saussure, Ferdinand (1983) *Course in General Linguistics*, London, Duckworth.

De Vries, Leonard (1967) *Panorama 1842–1865: The World of the Early Victorians as Seen Through the Eyes of the Illustrated London News*, London, Murray.

De Vries, Leonard (1973) *History as Hot News, 1865–1897: The Late Nineteenth Century World as Seen through the Eyes of the 'Illustrated London News' and 'The Graphic'*, London, John Murray.

Deutscher Presserat (2005) *Publizistische Grundsätze (Pressekodex)*, Bonn, Deutscher Presserat.

Deuze, Mark (2003) 'The web and its journalisms: Considering the consequences of different types of news media online', *New Media & Society*, 5(2), pp. 203–30.

Domke, David, David D. Perlmutter and Meg Spratt (2002) 'The primes of our times? An examination of the 'power' of visual images', *Journalism*, 3(2), pp. 131–59.

Donsbach, Wolfgang (2003) 'Journalist', in Noelle-Neumann, Elisabeth, Winfried Schulz and Jürgen Wilke (eds) *Publizistik-Massenkommunikation (Fischer Lexikon)*, 2nd edn, pp. 78–125. Frankfurt am Main, Fischer.

Dworznik, Gretchen (2006) 'Journalism and Trauma: How reporters and photographers make sense of what they see', *Journalism Studies*, 7(4), pp. 534–53.

Dworznik, Gretchen and Max Grubb (2007) 'Preparing for the worst: making a case for trauma training in the journalism classroom', *Journalism and Mass Communication Educator*, 62(2), pp. 190–210.

Edy, Jill A. (1999) 'Journalistic uses of collective memory', *Journal of Communication*, 49(2), pp. 71–85.

Elder, Catriona (2007) *Being Australian: Narratives of National Identity*, Sydney, Allen and Unwin.

Entman, Robert M. (1991) 'Framing U.S. coverage of International News: Contrasts in narratives of the KAL and Iran Air Incidents', *Journal of Communication*, 41(4), pp. 6–27.

Esser, Frank (1998) *Die Kräfte hinter den Schlagzeilen. Englischer und deutscher Journalismus im Vergleich*, Freiburg, Alber.

Ettema, James E., D. Charely Whitney and Daniel D. Wackman (1987) 'Professional mass communicators', in Berger, Charley R. and Steven H. Chaffee (eds) *Handbook of Communication Science*, pp. 747–80. Beverley Hills, CA, Sage.

Etzersdorfer, Elmar and Gernot Sonneck (1998) 'Preventing suicide by influencing mass-media reporting: The Viennese experience 1980–1996', *Archives of Suicide Research*, 4(1), pp. 64–74.

Eytan, Ariel, Marianne Gex-Fabry, Letizia Toscani, Lisa Deroo, Louis Loutan and Patrick A. Bovier (2004) 'Determinants of postconflict symptoms in Albanian Kosovars', *Journal of Nervous and Mental Disease*, 192(10), pp. 664–71.

Fahmy, Shahira (2005) 'Photojournalists' & photoeditors' attitudes and perceptions: The visual coverage of 9/11 & the Afghan War', *Visual Communication Quarterly*, 12(3&4), pp. 146–63.

Fahmy, Shahira, Sooyoung Cho, Wayne Wanta and Yonghoi Song (2006) 'Visual agenda-setting after 9/11: Individuals' emotions, image recall, and concern with terrorism', *Visual Communication Quarterly*, 13(1), pp. 4–15.

Fahmy, Shahira and Thomas J. Johnson (2007) 'Show the truth and let the audience decide: A web-based survey showing support among viewers of Al-Jazeera for use of graphic imagery', *Journal of Broadcasting & Electronic Media*, 51(2), pp. 245–64.

Fahmy, Shahira and Daekyung Kim (2008) 'Picturing the Iraq war: Constructing the image of war in the British and US Press', *International Communication Gazette*, 70(6), pp. 443–62.

Fahmy, Shahira and Wayne Wanta (2007) 'What visual journalists think others think: The perceived impact of news photographs on public opinion formation', *Visual Communication Quarterly*, 14(1), pp. 16–31.

Fairbrother, Gerry, Jennifer Stuber, Sandro Galea, Alan R. Fleischman and Betty Pfefferbaum (2003) 'Posttraumatic stress reactions in New York city children after the September 11, 2001, terrorist attacks', *Ambulatory Pediatrics*, 3(6), pp. 304–11.

Farhood, Laila, Hani Dimassi and Tuija Lehtinen (2006) 'Exposure to war-related traumatic events, prevalence of PTSD, and general psychiatric morbidity in a civilian population from Southern Lebanon', *Journal of Transcultural Nursing*, 17(4), pp. 333–40.

Fathi, Nazila (2009) 'In a death seen around the world, a symbol of Iranian protests', *The New York Times*, 23 June, p. 1.

Fedler, Fred (2004) 'Insiders' stories: coping with newsroom stress: An historical perspective', *American Journalism*, 21(3), pp. 77–106.

Feinstein, Anthony (2003) *Dangerous Lives: War and the Men and Women Who Report It*, Toronto, Thomas Allen.

Feinstein, Anthony (2006) *Journalists Under Fire: The Psychological Hazards of Covering War*, Baltimore, MD, The Johns Hopkins University Press.

Feinstein, Anthony and Dawn Nicholson (2005) 'Embedded journalists in the Iraq war: Are they at greater psychological risk?', *Journal of Traumatic Stress*, 18(2), pp. 129–32.

Feinstein, Anthony, John Owen and Nancy Blair (2002) 'A hazardous profession: War, journalists and psychopathology', *American Journal of Psychiatry*, 159, pp. 1507–75.

Figley, Charles R. (ed.) (1995) *Compassion Fatigue: Coping with Secondary Traumatic Stress Disorder in those Who Treat the Traumatized*, New York, Brunner/Mazel.

Fishman, Jessica Morgan (2001) *Documenting Death: Photojournalism and Spectacles of the Morbid in the Tabloid and Elite Newspaper*, PhD Thesis. Philadelphia, PA, University of Pennsylvania.

Fishman, Jessica Morgan (2003) 'News norms and emotion: Pictures of pain and metaphors of distress', in Gross, Larry, John Stuart Katz and Jay Ruby (eds) *Image Ethics in the Digital Age*, pp. 53–69. Minneapolis, MN, University of Minnesota Press.

Fiske, John (1990) *Introduction to Communication Studies*, 2nd edn, London, Routledge.

Fiske, John, Bob Hodge and Graeme Turner (1987) *Myths of Oz*, Sydney, Allen and Unwin.

Fletcher, Kim (2007) 'Why blogs are an open door', *British Journalism Review*, 18(2), pp. 41–6.

Foltyn, Jacque Lynn (2008) 'Dead famous and dead sexy: Popular culture, forensics, and the rise of the corpse', *Mortality*, 13(2), pp. 153–73.

Fowler, Bridget (2005) 'Collective memory and forgetting: Components for a study of obituaries', *Theory, Culture & Society*, 22(6), pp. 53–72.

Fowler, Bridget (2007) *The Obituary as Collective Memory*, Abingdon, Routledge.

Franklin, Bob (2008) 'The future of newspapers', *Journalism Studies*, 9(5), pp. 630–41.

Frans, Örjan, Per-Arne Rimmö, Lars Åberg and Mats Fredrikson (2005) 'Trauma exposure and post-traumatic stress disorder in the general population', *Acta Psychiatrica Scandinavica*, 111(4), pp. 291–9.

Fraser, Derek (1992) 'Media re-define reality of death', *Media Development*, 39(4), p. 24.

Freinkel, Andrew, Cheryl Koopman and David Spiegel (1994) 'Dissociative symptoms in media eyewitnesses of an execution', *The American Journal of Psychiatry*, 151(9), pp. 1335–9.

Frost, Karen, Erica Frank and Edward Maibach (1997) 'Relative risk in the news media: a quantification of misrepresentation', *American Journal of Public Health*, 87(5), pp. 842–5.

Galtung, Johan and Mari Holmboe Ruge (1965) 'The structure of foreign news: The presentation of the Congo, Cuba and Cyprus crises in four Norwegian newspapers', *Journal of Peace Research*, 2(1), pp. 64–90.

Garcia, Mario R. and Pegie Stark (1991) *Eyes on the News*, St. Petersburg, FL, Poynter Institute.

Gerbner, George (1980) 'Death in prime time: Notes on the symbolic functions of dying in the mass media', *Annals of the American Academy of Political and Social Science*, 447, pp. 64–70.

Giddens, Anthony (1991) *Modernity and Self-Identity: Self and Society in the Late Modern Age*, Cambridge, Polity.

Giffard, C. Anthony (1975) 'Ancient Rome's daily gazette', *Journalism History*, 2(4), pp. 32, 106–9.

Goethals, Gregor (1993) 'Media mythologies', in Arthur, C. J. (ed.) *Religion and the Media: An Introductory Reader*, pp. 25–39. Cardiff, University of Wales Press.

Goethe, Johann Wolfgang von (1989) *The Sorrows of Young Werther [1774]*, London, Penguin.

Goldberg, Vicky (1998) 'Death takes a holiday, sort of', in Goldstein, Jeffrey (ed.) *Why We Watch: The Attractions of Violent Entertainment*, pp. 27–52. New York, Oxford, Oxford University Press.

Goodstein, Anastasia (2007) *Totally Wired: What Teens and Tweens Are Really Doing Online*, New York, St. Martin's Press.

Gorer, Geoffrey (1965) *Death, Grief and Mourning in Contemporary Britain*, London, Cresset.

Gould, Madelyn S. (2001) 'Suicide and the media', *Annals of the New York Academy of Sciences*, 932(1), pp. 200–24.

Graber, Doris A. (1987) 'Television news without pictures?', *Critical Studies in Mass Communication*, 4(1), pp. 74–8.

Graber, Doris A. (1990) 'Seeing is remembering: How visuals contribute to learning from television news', *Journal of Communication*, 40(3), pp. 134–55.

Greer, Germaine (2006) 'That sort of self-delusion is what it takes to be a real Aussie larrikin', *Guardian*, 5 September, pp. 6–7.

Griffin, Michael (1999) 'The great war photographs: Constructing myths of history and photojournalism', in Brennen, Bonnie and Hanno Hardt (eds) *Picturing the Past: Media, History, and Photography*, pp. 122–57. Urbana, IL, University of Illinois.

Griffin, Michael and Jongsoo Lee (1995) 'Picturing the Gulf War: Constructing an image of war in *Time*, *Newsweek*, and *US News & World Report*', *Journalism and Mass Communication Quarterly*, 72(4), pp. 813–25.

Guo, Ya-Jun, Chin-Hung Chen, Mong-Liang Lu, Happy Kuy-Lok Tan, Huei-Wen Lee and Tsu-Nai Wang (2004) 'Posttraumatic stress disorder among professional and non-professional rescuers involved in an earthquake in Taiwan', *Psychiatry Research*, 127(1–2), pp. 35–41.

Habermas, Jürgen (1989) *The Structural Transformation of the Public Sphere: An Inquiry into a Category of Bourgeois Society*, Cambridge, Polity.

Hachten, William A. (1999) *The World News Prism: Changing Media of International Communication*, 5th edn, Ames, Iowa State University Press.

Halbwachs, Maurice (1992) *On Collective Memory*, Chicago, IL, University of Chicago Press.

Hall, Stuart (1973) 'The determinations of news photographs', in Cohen, Stanley and Jock Young (eds) *The Manufacture of News: Deviance, Social Problems and the Mass Media*. London, Constable.

Hallin, Daniel C. (1986) *The Uncensored War: The Media and Vietnam*, New York, Oxford University Press.

Hammond, William M. (1989) 'The press in Vietnam as agent of defeat: A critical examination', *Reviews in American History*, 17(2), pp. 312–23.

Hammond, William M. (1998) *Reporting Vietnam: Media and Military at War*, Lawrence, KS, University Press of Kansas.

Hanitzsch, Thomas (2009) 'Zur Wahrnehmung von Einflüssen im Journalismus: Komparative Befunde aus 17 Ländern [On Perceived Influences on Journalism: Evidence from 17 countries]', *Medien & Kommunikationswissenschaft*, 57(2), pp. 153–73.

Hanusch, Folker (2007) 'Publishing the perished: The visibility of foreign death in Australian quality newspapers', *Media International Australia*, 125, pp. 29–40.

Hanusch, Folker (2008a) 'Valuing those close to us: A study of German and Australian quality newspapers' reporting of death in foreign news', *Journalism Studies*, 9(3), pp. 341–56.

Hanusch, Folker (2008b) *Distant Deaths: How Newspapers Report Fatal Events from Abroad*, Saarbrücken, VDM Verlag.

Hanusch, Folker (2008c) 'Graphic death in the news media: present or absent?', *Mortality*, 13(4), pp. 301–17.

Hanusch, Folker (2008d) 'The impact of cultural dimensions on language use in quality newspapers', *Estudos de Comunicação (Communication Studies)*, 3, pp. 51–78.

Hanusch, Folker (2009) ' "The Australian we all aspire to be": Commemorative journalism and the death of the Crocodile Hunter', *Media International Australia*, 130, pp. 28–38.

Hanusch, Folker (2010) 'Death on the front page', in Fuller, Linda K. (ed.) *Tsunami Communication: (Inter)personal/Intercultural, Media, Technical, Ethical,*

Philanthropic, Development, and Personal Responses, Cresskill, NJ, Hampton Press. In Press.

Harcup, Tony and Deirdre O'Neill (2001) 'What is news? Galtung and Ruge revisited', *Journalism Studies,* 2(2), pp. 261–80.

Hartley, John (1982) *Understanding News,* London, Methuen.

Hartley, John (1996) *Popular Reality: Journalism, Modernity, Popular Culture,* London, Arnold.

Haviland, William A. (2002) *Cultural Anthropology,* 10th edn, Fort Worth, TX, Harcourt College Publishers.

Hawley, Charles (2007) 'New TV channel takes on death and dying', 22 June, viewed 10 April 2010, http://www.spiegel.de/international/zeitgeist/0,1518, 490174,00.html

Herman, Edward S. (1993) 'The media's role in U.S. foreign policy', *Journal of International Affairs,* 47(1), pp. 23–45.

Herman, Edward S. (1996) 'The propaganda model revisited', *Monthly Review,* 48(3), pp. 115–28.

Herman, Edward S. and Noam Chomsky (1988) *Manufacturing Consent: The Political Economy of the Mass Media,* New York, Pantheon Books.

Herman, Jack R. (2002) 'Distasteful images', *Australian Press Council News,* 14(4), viewed 10 April 2010, http://www.presscouncil.org.au/pcsite/apcnews/nov02/ images.html

Heron, Melonie, Donna L. Hoyert, Sherry L. Murphy, Jiaquan Xu, Kenneth D. Kochanek and Betzaida Tejada-Vera (2009) Deaths: Final Data for 2006. *National Vital Statistics Report.* US Department of Health and Human Services, Centers for Disease Control and Prevention.

Hess, Aaron (2007) 'In digital remembrance: vernacular memory and the rhetorical construction of web memorials', *Media, Culture and Society,* 29(5), pp. 812–30.

Hight, Joe and Frank Smyth (2003) *Tragedies and Journalists: A Guide for More Effective Coverage,* New York, Dart Center for Journalism and Trauma.

Hittner, James B. (2005) 'How robust is the Werther effect? A re-examination of the suggestion-imitation model of suicide', *Mortality,* 10(3), pp. 193–200.

Hoge, Charles W., Carl A. Castro, Stephen C. Messer, Dennis McGurk, Dave I. Cotting and Robert L. Koffman (2004) 'Combat duty in Iraq and Afghanistan, mental health problems, and barriers to care', *New England Journal of Medicine,* 351(1), pp. 13–22.

Höijer, Birgitta (2004) 'The discourse of global compassion: the audience and media reporting of human suffering', *Media, Culture and Society,* 26(4), pp. 513–31.

Hollings, James (2005) 'Reporting the Asian tsunami: The ethical issues', Paper presented at the Journalism Education Association New Zealand Conference, Hamilton, New Zealand, 7–9 December.

Howarth, Glennys (2007) *Death and Dying: A Sociological Introduction,* Cambridge, Polity Press.

Hume, Janice (2000) *Obituaries in American Culture,* Jackson, University Press of Mississippi.

Hume, Janice (2003) ' "Portraits of Grief," reflectors of values: *The New York Times* remembers victims of September 11', *Journalism & Mass Communication Quarterly,* 80(1), pp. 166–82.

Irby, Kenneth (2004) 'Beyond taste: Editing truth', 30 March, viewed 10 April 2010, http://www.poynter.org/content/content_view.asp?id=63131

Jalland, Pat (1999) 'Victorian death and its decline: 1850–1918', in Jupp, Peter and Clare Gittings (eds) *Death in England: An Illustrated History*, pp. 230–55. Manchester, Manchester University Press.

Johnson, Michelle (1999) 'Aftershock: Journalists and trauma', *Quill*, 87(9), pp. 14–19.

Josephi, Beate, Christine Müller and Hans-Jürgen Friske (2007) 'How private a death? Obituaries in Australia and Germany', *Hungarian Journal for English and American Studies*, 12(1–2), pp. 29–42.

Jupp, Peter and Tony Walter (1999) 'The healthy society: 1918–98', in Jupp, Peter and Clare Gittings (eds) *Death in England: An Illustrated History*, pp. 256–82. Manchester, Manchester University Press.

Kapferer, Judith (1996) *Being All Equal: Identity, Difference and Australian Cultural Practice*, Oxford, Berg.

Karvelas, Patricia (2006) 'Seal of approval for quintessential larrikin', *The Australian*, 6 September, p. 5.

Kastenbaum, Robert, Sara Peyton and Beatrice Kastenbaum (1977) 'Sex discrimination after death', *Omega*, 7(4), pp. 351–59.

Kazmier, Lisa (2001) 'Her final performance: British culture, mourning and the memorialization of Ellen Terry', *Mortality*, 6(2), pp. 167–90.

Keane, John (1996) *Reflections on Violence*, London, Verso.

Kear, Adrian and Deborah Lynn Steinberg (eds) (1999) *Mourning Diana: Nation, Culture and the Performance of Grief*, London, Routledge.

Keith, Susan, Carol B. Schwalbe and B. William Silcock (2006) 'Images in ethics codes in an era of violence and tragedy', *Journal of Mass Media Ethics*, 21(4), pp. 245–64.

Kellehear, Allan (2007) *A Social History of Dying*, Cambridge, Cambridge University Press.

Kellner, Douglas (1992) *The Persian Gulf TV War*, Boulder, CO, Westview Press.

Kepplinger, Hans Matthias (1979) 'Paradigm change in communications research', *Communication*, 4, pp. 163–82.

Kepplinger, Hans Martin (1991) 'The impact of presentation techniques: Theoretical aspects and empirical findings', in Biocca, Frank (ed.) *Television and Political Advertising: Volume 1: Psychological Processes*, pp. 173–94. Hillsdale, NJ, Lawrence Erlbaum Associates.

Kessler, Ronald C., Geraldine Downey, J. Ronald Milavsky and Horst Stipp (1988) 'Clustering of teenage suicides after television news stories about suicides: a reconsideration', *The American Journal of Psychiatry*, 145(11), pp. 1379–83.

Kessler, Ronald C, Amanda Sonnega, Evelyn Bromet, Michael Hughes and Christopher B Nelson (1995) 'Posttraumatic stress disorder in the National Comorbidity Survey', *Archives of General Psychiatry* 52(12), pp. 1048–60.

King, Cynthia and Paul Martin Lester (2005) 'Photographic coverage during the Persian Gulf and Iraqi wars in three U.S. newspapers', *Journalism and Mass Communication Quarterly*, 82(3), pp. 623–37.

Kinnick, Katherine, Dean Krugman and Glen Cameron (1996) 'Compassion fatigue: Communication and burnout toward social problems', *Journalism & Mass Communication Quarterly*, 73(3), pp. 687–707.

Kitch, Carolyn (2000) "A news of feeling as well as fact': Mourning and memorial in American newsmagazines', *Journalism*, 1(2), pp. 171–95.

Kitch, Carolyn (2003) 'Mourning in America: Ritual, redemption, and recovery in news narrative after September 11', *Journalism Studies*, 4(2), pp. 213–24.

Kitch, Carolyn (2005) *Pages from the Past: History and Memory in American Magazines*, Chapel Hill, NC, University of North Carolina Press.

Kitch, Carolyn (2008) 'Placing journalism inside memory – and memory studies', *Memory Studies*, 1(1), pp. 311–20.

Kitch, Carolyn and Janice Hume (2008) *Journalism in a Culture of Grief*, New York, Routledge.

Klaehn, Jeffery (2002) 'A critical review and assessment of Herman and Chomsky's "propaganda model"', *European Journal of Communication*, 17(2), pp. 147–82.

Knightley, Phillip (1975) *The First Casualty. From the Crimea to Vietnam: The War Correspondent as Hero, Propagandist, and Myth Maker*, New York, Harcourt Brace Jovanovich.

Kodrich, Kris and Melinda Laituri (2005) 'The formation of a disaster community in cyberspace: The role of online news media after the 2001 Gujarat earthquake', *Convergence: The International Journal of Research into New Media Technologies*, 11(3), pp. 40–56.

Konstantinidou, Christina (2007) 'Death, lamentation and the photographic representation of the other during the Second Iraq War in Greek newspapers', *International Journal of Cultural Studies*, 10(2), pp. 147–66.

Koponen, Juhani (2003) 'The structure of foreign news revisited', in Malmelin, Nando (ed.) *Välittämisen tiede. Viestinnän näkökulmia yhteiskuntaan, kulttuuriin jakansalaisuuteen. [The science of mediation and caring. Communicational viewpoints of society, culture and citizenship].* pp. 144–66. Helsinki, Helsingin yliopisto.

Kratzer, Renee Martin and Brian Kratzer (2003) 'How newspapers decided to run disturbing 9/11 Photos', *Newspaper Research Journal*, 24(1), pp. 34–47.

Kübler-Ross, Elisabeth (1973) *On Death and Dying*, New York, Collier.

Kulka, Richard A., William E Schlenger, John A Fairbanks, Richard L Hough, B. Kathleen Jordan, Charles R Marmar, Daniel S Weiss and David A Grady (1990) *Trauma and the Vietnam War Generation: Report of Findings from the National Vietnam Veterans Readjustment Study*, New York, Brunner/Mazel.

Kunczik, Michael and Astrid Zipfel (2005) *Publizistik*, Köln, Böhlau Verlag.

Lang, Annie (2000) 'The limited capacity model of mediated message processing', *Journal of Communication*, 50(1), pp. 46–70.

Lang, Annie, Kulijinder Dhillon and Qingwen Dong (1995) 'Arousal, emotion, and memory for television messages', *Journal of Broadcasting & Electronic Media*, 39(3), pp. 313–27.

Lang, Kurt and Gladys Engel Lang (1989) 'Collective memory and the news', *Communication*, 11, pp. 123–39.

Li, David K. (2009) ' "Kung Fu" Kin Rip Death-Site Pix', *New York Post*, 8 June, p. 3.

Lie, Rico (2003) *Spaces of Intercultural Communication: An Interdisciplinary Introduction to Communication, Culture, and Globalizing/Localizing Identities*, Cresskill, NJ, Hampton Press.

Liebes, Tamar (1998) 'Television disaster marathons: A danger for the democratic process?', in Curran, James and Tamar Liebes (eds) *Media, Ritual and Identity*, pp. 71–86. London, Routledge.

Linenthal, Edward T. (2001) *The Unfinished Bombing: Oklahoma City in American Memory*, New York, Oxford University Press.

Lomnitz, Claudio (2005) *Death and the Idea of Mexico*, New York, Zone Books.

Loyd, Anthony (1999) *My War Gone By, I Miss It So*, New York, Atlantic Monthly Press.

Loyd, Anthony (2007) *Another Bloody Love Letter*, London, Headline Review.

Lule, Jack (2001) *Daily News, Eternal Stories: The Mythological Role of Journalism*, New York, Guilford.

Lule, Jack (2003) 'Waters of death in Central America', in Anokwa, Kwadwo, Carolyn A. Lin and Michael B. Salwen (eds) *International Communication: Concepts and Cases*, pp. 91–109. Belmont, CA, Wadsworth/Thomson Learning.

MacKellar, Landis (2006) *The "Double Indemnity" Murder: Ruth Snyder, Judd Gray, & New York's Crime of the Century*, Syracuse, NY, Syracuse University Press.

Macleod, Scott (1994) 'The life and death of Kevin Carter', *Time*, 12 September, pp. 70–3.

Mahar, Jessica (2010) 'Bloggers jump gun with wrong photos', *Sydney Morning Herald*, 15 January, p. 7.

Malcolm, Andrew (2009) 'Iran ambassador suggests CIA could have killed Neda Agha-Soltan', *Los Angeles Times*, 25 June, viewed 10 April 2010, http://latimesblogs.latimes.com/washington/2009/06/neda-cia-cnn-killing.html

Marais, A. and A. Stuart (2005) 'The role of temperament in the development of post-traumatic stress disorder amongst journalists', *South African Journal of Psychology*, 35(1), pp. 89–105.

Marzuk, Peter M., Kenneth Tardiff, Charles S. Hirsch, Andrew C. Leon, Marina Stajic, Nancy Hartwell and Laura Portera (1994) 'Increase in suicide by asphyxiation in New York City after the publication of *Final Exit*', *Publishing Research Quarterly*, 10(4), pp. 62–8.

Matheson, Donald and Stuart Allan (2009) *Digital War Reporting*, Cambridge, Polity.

Maxson, Jan (1999) 'Training journalism students to deal with trauma', Paper presented at the Annual Meeting of the Association for Education in Journalism and Mass Communication, New Orleans, LA, August 4–7.

McCabe, Eamonn (1991) 'The stuff of nightmares', *British Journalism Review*, 2(3), pp. 23–6.

McIntyre, Jamie (2009) 'Documenting the return of war dead at Dover', *American Journalism Review*, 31(3), pp. 8–9.

McMahon, Cait (2001) 'Covering disaster: a pilot study into secondary trauma for print media journalists reporting on disaster', *Australian Journal of Emergency Management*, 16, pp. 52–6.

McMahon, Cait (2005) 'Journalists and trauma: The parallel worlds of growth and pathology', in Katsikitis, Mary (ed.) *Proceedings of the 40th APS Annual Conference*, pp. 188–92. Melbourne, Australia, Australian Psychological Society.

McMahon, Cait and Trina McLellan (2008) 'Journalists reporting for duty: Resilience, trauma and growth', in Gow, Kathryn and Douglas Paton (eds) *The Phoenix of Natural Disasters: Community Resilience*, pp. 101–22. New York, Nova.

McQuail, Denis (2005) *McQuail's Mass Communication Theory*, 5th edn, London, Sage.

Meech, Peter (1992) 'Death in a Scottish tabloid', *Media Development*, 39(4), pp. 14–16.

Mellor, Philipp A. and Chris Shilling (1993) 'Modernity, self identity and the sequestration of death', *Sociology*, 27, pp. 411–32.

Meyer, Philip (2004) *The Vanishing Newspaper: Saving Journalism in the Information Age*, Columbia, University of Missouri Press.

Michel, Konrad, Conrad Frey, Thomas E. Schlaepfer and Ladislav Valach (1995) 'Suicide reporting in the Swiss print media: Frequency, form, and content of articles', *European Journal of Public Health*, 5(3), pp. 199–203.

Miles, Janelle (2006) 'Unlikely creature proved deadliest', *The Courier-Mail*, 5 September, p. 3.

Mitchell, Greg (2008) *So Wrong, So Long: How the Press, the Pundits – and the President – Failed on Iraq*, New York, Sterling.

Moeller, Susan D. (1989) *Shooting War: Photography and the American Experience of Combat*, New York, Basic Books.

Moeller, Susan D. (1999) *Compassion Fatigue: How the Media Sell Disease, Famine, War and Death*, London, Routledge.

Moremen, Robin and Cathy Cradduck (1998/1999) 'How will you be remembered after you die? Gender discrimination after death twenty years later', *Omega*, 38(4), pp. 241–54.

Morrison, David E. (1992) *Television and the Gulf War*, London, John Libbey.

Mosco, Vincent (1996) *The Political Economy of Communication: Rethinking and Renewal*, London, Sage.

Motto, Jerome A. (1967) 'Suicide and suggestibility: The roles of the press', *American Journal of Psychiatry*, 124(2), pp. 252–56.

Mowlana, Hamid (1997) *Global Information and World Communication: New Frontiers in International Relations*, 2nd edn, London, Sage.

Murdock, Graham and Peter Golding (1977) 'Capitalism, communication and class relations', in Curran, James, Michael Gurevitch and Janet Woollacott (eds) *Mass Communication and Society*, pp. 12–43. London, Edward Arnold.

Myerhoff, Barbara G. (1984) 'A death in time: Construction of self and culture in ritual drama', in MacAloon, J.J. (ed.) *Rite, Drama, Festival, Spectacle*, pp. 102–31. Philadelphia, PA, Institute for the Study of Human Issues.

Nabi, Robin L. (2003) ' "Feeling" resistance: Exploring the role of emotionally evocative visuals in inducing inoculation', *Media Psychology*, 5(2), pp. 199–223.

Neuman, Johanna (1996) *Lights, Camera, War: Is Media Technology Driving International Politics?*, New York, St. Martin's Press.

New York Daily News (2009) 'Your verdict', *New York Daily News*, 10 June, p. 20.

Newhagen, John E. (1998) 'TV news images that induce anger, fear and disgust: Effects on approach-avoidance and memory', *Journal of Broadcasting & Electronic Media*, 42(2), pp. 265–76.

Newman, Elana, Roger Simpson and David Handschuh (2003) 'Trauma exposure and post-traumatic stress disorder among photojournalists', *Visual Communication Quarterly*, 10(1), pp. 4–13.

Noelle-Neumann, Elisabeth (1993) *The Spiral of Silence*, Chicago, IL, University of Chicago Press.

Nordin, Kenneth D. (1979) 'The entertaining press: Sensationalism in eighteenth-century Boston newspapers', *Communication Research*, 6(3), pp. 295–320.

Nossek, Hillel and Dan Berkowitz (2006) 'Telling "our" story through news of terrorism: Mythical newswork as journalistic practice in crisis', *Journalism Studies*, 7(5), pp. 691–707.

Noys, Benjamin (2005) *The Culture of Death*, Oxford, Berg.

O'Brien, Sue (1993) 'Eye on Soweto: A study of factors in news photo use', *Journal of Mass Media Ethics*, 8(2), pp. 69–87.

O'Dowd, Cathy (1996) 'The blood of photojournalism', *Visual Communication Quarterly*, 3(1), p. 3.

O'Sullivan, John (2005) 'Delivering Ireland: Journalism's search for a role online', *International Communication Gazette*, 67(1), pp. 45–68.

Ottosen, Rune (2007) 'Emphasising images in peace journalism: theory and practice in the case of Norway's biggest newspaper', *Conflict & Communication Online*, 6(1), pp. 1–16.

Ozen, Sakir and Aytekin Sir (2004) 'Frequency of PTSD in a group of search and rescue workers two months after 2003 Bingol (Turkey) earthquake', *Journal of Nervous and Mental Disease*, 192(8), pp. 573–5.

Palgi, Phyllis and Henry Abramovitch (1984) 'Death: A cross-cultural perspective', *Annual Review of Anthropology*, 13, pp. 385–417.

Pantti, Mervi and Jan Wieten (2005) 'Mourning becomes the nation: television coverage of the murder of Pim Fortuyn', *Journalism Studies*, 6(3), pp. 301–13.

Parsons, Patrick R. and William E. Smith (1988) 'R. Budd Dwyer: A case study in newsroom decision making', *Journal of Mass Media Ethics*, 3(1), pp. 84–94.

Paschalidis, Gregory (1999) 'Images of war and the war of images', *Gramma: Journal of Theory and Criticism*, 7, pp. 121–52.

Peri, Yoram (1999) 'The media and collective memory of Yitzhak Rabin's remembrance', *Journal of Communication*, 49(3), pp. 106–24.

Perkonigg, Axel, Ronald C. Kessler, S. Storz and Hans-Ulrich Wittchen (2000) 'Traumatic events and post-traumatic stress disorder in the community: Prevalence, risk factors and comorbidity', *Acta Psychiatrica Scandinavica*, 101(1), pp. 46–59.

Perlmutter, David D. (1998) *Photojournalism and Foreign Policy: Icons of Outrage in International Crises*, Westport, CT, Praeger.

Peterson, April and Meg Spratt (2005) 'Choosing graphic visuals: How picture editors incorporate emotion and personal experience into decision making', *Visual Communication Quarterly*, 12(1), pp. 4–19.

Petley, Julian (2003) 'War without death: Responses to distant suffering', *Journal for Crime, Conflict and the Media*, 1(1), pp. 72–85.

Pfarr, Kristina (1983) *Die Neue Zeitung: Emprische Untersuchung eines Informationsmediums der frühen Neuzeit unter besonderer Berücksichtigung von Gewaltdarstellungen*, PhD Thesis. Mainz, University of Mainz.

Pfau, Michael, Michel M. Haigh, Theresa Shannon, Toni Tones, Deborah Mercurio, Raina Williams, Blanca Binstock, Carlos Diaz, Constance Dillard, Margaret Browne, et al. (2008) 'The influence of television news depictions of the images of war on viewers', *Journal of Broadcasting & Electronic Media*, 52(2), pp. 303–22.

Pfefferbaum, Betty, Sara Jo Nixon, Rick D. Tivis, Debby E. Doughty, Robert S. Pynoos, Robin H. Gurwitch and David W. Foy (2001) 'Television exposure in children after a terrorist incident', *Psychiatry*, 64(3), pp. 202–11.

Pfefferbaum, Betty, Thomas W. Seale, Edward N. Jr. Brandt, Rose L. Pfefferbaum, Debby E. Doughty and Scott M. Rainwater (2003) 'Media exposure in children one hundred miles from a terrorist bombing', *Annals of Clinical Psychiatry*, 15(1), pp. 1–8.

Phillips, David P. (1974) 'The influence of suggestion on suicide: Substantive and theoretical implications of the Werther effect', *American Sociological Review*, 39(3), pp. 340–54.

Phillips, David P. (1979) 'Suicide, motor vehicle fatalities, and the mass media: Evidence toward a theory of suggestion', *American Journal of Sociology*, 84(5), pp. 1150–74.

Phillips, David P. (1985) 'The Werther effect: Suicide and other forms of violence are contagious', *The Sciences*, 7/8, pp. 32–9.

Phillips, David P. and Lundie L. Carstensen (1986) 'Clustering of teenage suicides after television news stories about suicide', *New England Journal of Medicine*, 315(11), pp. 685–9.

Phillips, David P. and Lundie L. Carstensen (1988) 'The effect of suicide stories on various demographic groups, 1968–1985', *Suicide and Life-Threatening Behavior*, 18(1), pp. 100–14.

Pine, Daniel S., Jane Costello and Ann Masten (2005) 'Trauma, proximity, and developmental psychopathology: The effects of war and terrorism on children', *Neuropsychopharmacology*, 30(10), pp. 1781–92.

Pirkis, Jane and R. Warwick Blood (2001) *Suicide and the Media: A Critical Review*, Canberra, Commonwealth Department of Health and Aged Care.

Pirkis, Jane, R. Warwick Blood, Annette Beautrais, Philip Burgess and Jaelea Skehan (2006) 'Media guidelines on the reporting of suicide', *Crisis: The Journal of Crisis Intervention and Suicide Prevention*, 27(2), pp. 82–7.

Pirkis, Jane, R. Warwick Blood, Catherine Francis, Peter Putnis, Philip Burgess, Belinda Morley, Andrew Stewart and Trish Payne (2002) *The Media Monitoring Project: A Baseline Description of How the Australian Media Report and Portray Suicide and Mental Health and Illness*, Canberra, Commonwealth Department of Health and Aged Care.

Pirkis, Jane, Philip Burgess, R. Warwick Blood and Catherine Francis (2007) 'The newsworthiness of suicide', *Suicide and Life-Threatening Behavior*, 37(3), pp. 278–83.

Pollard, Nick (2005) 'Diary of a disaster', *British Journalism Review*, 16(1), pp. 7–12.

Preston, Paschal (2009) *Making the News: Journalism and News Cultures in Europe*, London, Routledge.

Prigge, Matt (2006) 'Upward Christian soldier', *Philadelphia Weekly*, 3 May, viewed 10 April 2010, http://www.philadelphiaweekly.com/news-and-opinion/upward_christian_soldier-38414669.html

Pyevich, Caroline, Elana Newman and Eric Daleiden (2003) 'The relationship among cognitive schemas, job-related traumatic exposure and post-traumatic stress disorder in journalists', *Journal of Traumatic Stress*, 16, pp. 325–8.

Rainey, James (2005) 'Portraits of war: When words weren't enough', *Los Angeles Times*, 21 May.

Ramadge, Andrew (2006) 'Irwin comments overwhelming', News Limited, 5 September, viewed 10 April 2010, http://blogs.news.com.au/news/news/index.php/news/comments/irwin_comments_overwhelming

Ramey, Jessie (2004) 'The bloody blonde and the marble woman: Gender and power in the case of Ruth Snyder', *Journal of Social History*, 37(3), pp. 625–50.

Randell, Karen and Sean Redmond (eds) (2008a) *The War Body on Screen*, New York, Continuum.

Randell, Karen and Sean Redmond (2008b) 'Introduction: Setting the screen', in Randell, Karen and Sean Redmond (eds) *The War Body on Screen*, pp. 1–13. New York, Continuum.

Rawlinson, Linnie and Nick Hunt (2009) 'Jackson dies, almost takes Internet with him', CNN, 26 June, viewed 10 April 2010, http://www.cnn.com/2009/TECH/06/26/michael.jackson.internet/index.html

Ray, Munni and Prahbhjot Malhi (2005) 'Reactions of Indian adolescents to the 9/11 terrorist attacks', *Indian Journal of Pediatrics*, 72(3), pp. 217–29.

Roberts, Pamela (2004) 'Here today and cyberspace tomorrow: Memorials and bereavement support on the web', *Generations*, 28(2), pp. 41–6.

Roberts, Pamela (2006) 'From My Space to our space: The functions of web memorials in bereavement', *The Forum*, 32(4), pp. 1, 3–4.

Robertson, Lori (2004) 'Images of war', *American Journalism Review*, 26(5), pp. 44–51.

Robinson, Piers (2001) 'Theorizing the influence of media on world politics: Models of media influence on foreign policy', *European Journal of Communication*, 16(4), pp. 523–44.

Robinson, Piers (2002) *The CNN Effect: The Myth of News, Foreign Policy and Intervention*, London, Routledge.

Rohter, Larry (2009) 'New doubts raised over famous war photo', *The New York Times*, 18 August, p. 1.

Romei, Stephen (2004) 'Foreign bodies', *The Walkley Magazine*, (December/January), p. 5.

Roth, Andrew, Zoe Huffman, Jeffrey Huling, Kevin Stolle and Jocelyn Thomas (2008) 'Covering war's victims: A content analysis of Iraq and Afghanistan war photographs in *The New York Times* and the *San Francisco Chronicle*', Project Censored, viewed 10 April 2010, http://www.projectcensored.org/assets-managed/pdf/covering-wars-victims.pdf

Ruby, Jay (1995) *Secure the Shadow: Death and Photography in America*, Cambridge, MA, MIT Press.

Rushdy, Ashraf (1999) 'Exquisite corpse', *Transition*, 83, pp. 70–7.

Saylor, Conway F., Brian L. Cowart, Julie A. Lipovsky, Crystal Jackson and A. J. Finch Jr (2003) 'Media exposure to September 11: Elementary school students' experiences and posttraumatic symptoms', *American Behavioral Scientist*, 46(12), pp. 1622–42.

Schiller, Gertrud (1971) *Iconography of Christian Art*, London, Lund Humphries.

Schiller, Herbert (1969) *Mass Communications and American Empire*, New York, A.M. Kelley.

Schlenger, William E., Juesta M. Caddell, Lori Ebert, B. Kathleen Jordan, Kathryn M. Rourke, David Wilson, Lisa Thalji, J. Michael Dennis, John A. Fairbank and Richard A. Kulka (2002) 'Psychological reactions to terrorist attacks: Findings from the national study of Americans' reactions to September 11', *Journal of the American Medical Association*, 288(5), pp. 581–8.

Schraven, David (2010) 'Das zweite Leben der Neda Soltani', *Süddeutsche Zeitung Magazin*, 6 February, viewed 10 April 2010, http://sz-magazin.sueddeutsche.de/texte/anzeigen/32571/das-zweite-leben-der-neda-soltani

Schudson, Michael (1992) *Watergate in American Memory: How We Remember, Forget and Reconstruct the Past*, New York, Basic Books.

Schudson, Michael (1995) *The Power of News*, Cambridge, MA, Harvard University Press.

Schulz, Winfried (1976) *Die Konstruktion von Realität in den Nachrichtenmedien: Analyse der aktuellen Berichterstattung*, Freiburg, München, Alber Verlag.

Schuster, Mark A., Bradley D. Stein, Lisa H. Jaycox, Rebecca L. Collins, Grant N. Marshall, Marc N. Elliott, Annie J. Zhou, David E. Kanouse, Janina L. Morrison and Sandra H. Berry (2001) 'A national survey of stress reactions after the September 11, 2001, terrorist attacks', *New England Journal of Medicine*, 345(20), pp. 1507–12.

Schwalbe, Carol B. (2006) 'Remembering our shared past: Visually framing the Iraq War on U.S. news websites', *Journal of Computer-Mediated Communication*, 12, pp. 264–89.

Schwartz, Barry (1991) 'Iconography and collective memory: Lincoln's image in the American mind', *Sociological Quarterly*, 32(3), pp. 301–9.

Scott, Janny (2001) 'Closing a scrapbook full of life and sorrow', *The New York Times*, 31 December, p. B6.

Seale, Clive (1998) *Constructing Death: The Sociology of Dying and Bereavement*, Cambridge, Cambridge University Press.

Seaton, Jean (2005) *Carnage and the Media: The Making and Breaking of News About Violence*, London, Allen Lane.

Sharkey, Jacqueline E (2004) 'Al Jazeera under the gun', *American Journalism Review*, 26(5), pp. 18–19.

Shoemaker, Pamela J. and Stephen D. Reese (1996) *Mediating the Message: Theories of Influences on Mass Media Content*, 2nd edn, White Plains, NY, Longman.

Silcock, B. William, Carol B. Schwalbe and Susan Keith (2008) ' "Secret" casualties: Images of injury and death in the Iraq war across media platforms', *Journal of Mass Media Ethics*, 23(1), pp. 36–50.

Simon, Adam F. (1997) 'Television news and international earthquake relief', *Journal of Communication*, 47(3), pp. 82–93.

Simpson, Michael A. (1972) *The Facts of Death: A Complete Guide for Being Prepared*, London, Prentice Hall.

Simpson, Roger and James Boggs (1999) 'An exploratory study of traumatic stress among newspaper journalists', *Journalism and Communication Monographs*, 1, pp. 1–26.

Simpson, Roger and William Coté (2006) *Covering Violence: A Guide to Ethical Reporting About Victims and Trauma*, 2nd edn, New York, Columbia University Press.

Sinclair, John (2002) 'Media and communications: theoretical traditions', in Cunningham, Stuart and Graeme Turner (eds) *The Media and Communications in Australia*, pp. 23–34. Sydney, Allen and Unwin.

Singer, Eleanor, Phyllis Endreny and Marc B. Glassman (1991) 'Media coverage of disasters: effect of geographic location', *Journalism Quarterly*, 68(1/2), pp. 48–58.

Singer, Jane B. and Ian Ashman (2009) ' "Comment is free, but facts are sacred": User-generated content and ethical constructs at the *Guardian*', *Journal of Mass Media Ethics*, 24(1), pp. 3–21.

Singletary, Michael W. and Chris Lamb (1984) 'News values in award-winning photos', *Journalism Quarterly*, 61(1), pp. 104–8, 233.

Smith, River (2008) *Trauma and Journalism: Exploring a Model of Risk and Resilience*, PhD Thesis. Oklahoma, University of Tulsa.

Smith, River and Elana Newman (2009) 'Covering trauma: Impact on journalists', Dart Center for Journalism and Trauma, viewed 10 April 2010, http://dartcenter.org/content/covering-trauma-impact-on-journalists

Sofka, Carla J. (2009) 'Adolescents, technology, and the Internet: Coping with loss in the digital world', in Balk, David E. and Charles A. Corr (eds) *Adolescent Encounters with Death, Bereavement, and Coping*. New York, Springer.

Sontag, Susan (1977) *On Photography*, New York, Farrar, Straus and Giroux.

Sontag, Susan (2002) 'Looking at war: Photography's view of devastation and death', *The New Yorker*, pp. 82–98.

Sontag, Susan (2003) *Regarding the Pain of Others*, New York, Farrar, Straus and Giroux.

Sorenson, Susan B., Julie G. Peterson Manz and Richard A. Berk (1998) 'News media coverage and the epidemiology of homicide', *American Journal of Public Health*, 88(10), pp. 1510–4.

Spratt, Meg (2005) 'Unraveling media and trauma connections', viewed 10 April 2010, http://dartcenter.org/content/unraveling-media-and-trauma-connections

Spratt, Meg, April Peterson and Taso Lagos (2005) 'Of photographs and flags: Uses and perceptions of an iconic image before and after September 11, 2001', *Popular Communication*, 3(2), pp. 117–36.

Sreberny-Mohammadi, Annabelle, Kaarle Nordenstreng and Robert L. Stevenson (1984) 'The world of the news study', *Journal of Communication*, 34(1), pp. 134–8.

Stack, Steven (1987) 'Celebrities and suicide: A taxonomy and analysis, 1948–1983', *American Sociological Review*, 52(3), pp. 401–12.

Stack, Steven (1990) 'A reanalysis of the impact of non celebrity suicides', *Social Psychiatry and Psychiatric Epidemiology*, 25(5), pp. 269–73.

Stack, Steven (1996) 'The effect of the media on suicide: Evidence from Japan, 1955–1985', *Suicide and Life-Threatening Behavior*, 26(2), pp. 132–42.

Stack, Steven (2005) 'Suicide in the media: A quantitative review of studies based on non-fictional stories', *Suicide and Life Threatening Behavior*, 35(2), pp. 121–33.

Starck, Nigel (2004) *Writes of Passage: A Comparative Study of Newspaper Obituary Practice in Australia, Britain, and the United States*, PhD Thesis. Flinders University of South Australia.

Starck, Nigel (2005) 'Posthumous parallel and parallax: The obituary revival on three continents', *Journalism Studies*, 6(3), pp. 267–83.

Starck, Nigel (2006) *Life After Death: The Art of the Obituary*, Melbourne, Melbourne University Press.

Starck, Nigel (2007) 'Revelation, Intrusion, and Questions of Taste', *Journalism Practice*, 1(3), pp. 372–82.

Starck, Nigel (2008a) 'Death can make a difference: A comparative study of "Quality Quartet" obituary practice', *Journalism Studies*, 9(6), pp. 911–24.

Starck, Nigel (2008b) 'Obituaries for sale: Wellspring of cash and unreliable testimony', *Journalism Practice*, 2(3), pp. 444–52.

Staudt, Christina C. (2001) *Picturing the Dead and Dying in the Nineteenth-Century L'Illustration*, PhD Thesis. Columbia University, New York.

Staudt, Christina C. (2009a) 'From concealment to recognition: The discourse on death, dying, and grief', in Bartalos, Michael K. (ed.) *Speaking of Death: America's New Sense of Mortality*, pp. 3–41. Westport, CT, Praeger.

Staudt, Christina C. (2009b) 'Covering (Up?) death: A close reading of Time Magazine's September 11, 2001, special issue', in Bartalos, Michael K. (ed.) *Speaking of Death: America's New Sense of Mortality*, pp. 152–82. Westport, CT, Praeger.

Stephens, Mitchell (2007) *A History of News*, 3rd edn, New York, Oxford University Press.

Stevenson, Robert L. (1997) 'Remapping the world', viewed 10 April 2010, http://www.ibiblio.org/newsflow/results/Newsmap.htm

Stone, Philip and Richard Sharpley (2008) 'Consuming dark tourism: A thanatological perspective', *Annals of Tourism Research*, 35(2), pp. 574–95.

Strobel, Warren P. (1996) 'The CNN effect', *American Journalism Review*, 18(4), pp. 32–8.

Styles, Aja (2009) 'Girl's death posted on Facebook before family informed', *Sydney Morning Herald*, 9 October, viewed 10 April 2010, http://www.smh.com.au/technology/technology-news/girls-death-posted-on-facebook-before-family-informed-20091009-gq5x.html

Sullivan, Gerard (2007) 'Should suicide be reported in the media? A critique of research', in Mitchell, Margaret (ed.) *Remember Me: Constructing Immortality – Beliefs on Immortality, Life, and Death*, pp. 149–58. New York, Routledge.

Tait, Sue (2008) 'Pornographies of violence? Internet spectatorship on body horror', *Critical Studies in Media Communication*, 25(1), pp. 91–111.

Taylor, John (1991) *War Photography: Realism in the British Press*, London, Routledge.

Taylor, John (1998) *Body Horror: Photojournalism, Catastrophe, and War*, New York, Manchester University Press.

Taylor, Philip M. (1992) *War and the Media: Propaganda and Persuasion in the Gulf War*, Manchester, Manchester University Press.

Teegen, Frauke and Maike Grotwinkel (2001) 'Traumatische Erfahrungen und Posttraumatische Belastungsstörung bei Journalisten: Eine internet-basierte Studie [Traumatic exposure and post-traumatic stress disorder of journalists. An internet-based study]', *Psychotherapeut*, 46(3), pp. 169–75.

Terr, Lenore C., Daniel A. Bloch, Beat A. Michel, Hong Shi, John A. Reinhardt and SuzAnne Metayer (1999) 'Children's symptoms in the wake of challenger: A field study of distant-traumatic effects and an outline of related conditions', *American Journal of Psychiatry*, 156(10), pp. 1536–44.

Tester, Keith (2001) *Compassion, Morality and the Media*, Buckingham, Open University.

Thomas, James (2002) *Diana's Mourning: A People's History*, Cardiff, University of Wales Press.

Thomas, James (2008) 'From people power to mass hysteria: Media and popular reactions to the death of Princess Diana', *International Journal of Cultural Studies*, 11(3), pp. 362–76.

Thompson, John B. (1995) *The Media and Modernity: A Social Theory of the Media*, Cambridge, Polity Press.

Thompson, Susan (2004) *The Penny Press: The Origins of the Modern News Media, 1833–1861*, Northport, AL., Vision Press.

Tsang, Kuo-jen, Yean Tsai and Scott S. K. Liu (1988) 'Geographic Emphases of International News Studies', *Journalism Quarterly*, 65(1), pp. 191–4.

Tsang, Kuo-Jen (1984) 'News photos in *Time* and *Newsweek*', *Journalism Quarterly*, 61(3), pp. 578–84, 723.

Tucker, Phebe, Betty Pfefferbaum, Sara Jo Nixon and Warren Dickson (2000) 'Predictors of post-traumatic stress symptoms in Oklahoma City: Exposure, social support, peri-traumatic responses', *Journal of Behavioral Health Services and Research*, 27(4), pp. 406–16.

Turner, Victor (1969) *The Ritual Process: Structure and Anti-Structure*, London, Routledge.

Turnock, Robert. (2000) *Interpreting Diana: Television Audiences and the Death of a Princess*, London, BFI Publishing.

Veale, Kylie (2009) 'Online memorialisation', in Earle, Sarah, Carol Komaromy and Caroline Bartholomew (eds) *Death and Dying: A Reader*, pp. 147–205. Milton Keynes, The Open University.

Walter, Tony (1991) 'Modern death – taboo or not taboo?', *Sociology*, 25(2), pp. 293–310.

Walter, Tony (1994) *The Revival of Death*, London, Routledge.

Walter, Tony (1996) 'Facing death without tradition', in Howarth, Glennys and P. Jupp (eds) *Contemporary Issues in the Sociology of Death, Dying and Disposal*, pp. 193–204. Basingstoke, Macmillan.

Walter, Tony (ed.) (1999a) *The Mourning for Diana*, Oxford, Berg.

Walter, Tony (1999b) 'The questions people asked', in Walter, Tony (ed.) *The Mourning for Diana*, pp. 19–47. Oxford, Berg.

Walter, Tony (1999c) 'And the consequence was...', in Walter, Tony (ed.) *The Mourning for Diana*, pp. 271–8. Oxford, Berg.

Walter, Tony (2006) 'Disaster, modernity, and the media', in Garces-Foley, K. (ed.) *Death and Religion in a Changing World*, pp. 265–82. Armonk, NY, M.E. Sharpe.

Walter, Tony, Jane Littlewood and Michael Pickering (1995) 'Death in the news: the public invigilation of private emotion', *Sociology*, 29(4), pp. 579–96.

Ward, Russel (1958) *The Australian Legend*, Melbourne, Oxford University Press.

Wasserman, Ira M. (1984) 'Imitation and suicide: A reexaminaton of the Werther Effect', *American Sociological Review*, 49(3), pp. 427–36.

Watson, C. W. (1997) ' "Born a lady, became a princess, died a saint": The reaction to the death of Diana, Princess of Wales', *Anthropology Today*, 13(6), pp. 3–7.

Weaver, David H. (1998) *The Global Journalist: News People Around the World*, Cresskill, NJ, Hampton Press.

Weidmann, Anke, Lydia Fehm and Thomas Fydrich (2008) 'Covering the tsunami disaster: Subsequent post-traumatic and depressive symptoms and associated factors', *Stress and Health*, 24(2), pp. 129–35.

Weischenberg, Siegfried (1992) *Journalistik. Theorie und Praxis aktueller Medienkommunikation. Bd 1: Mediensysteme, Medienethik, Medieninstitutionen*, Opladen, Westdeutscher Verlag.

White, David Manning (1950) 'The "Gate Keeper": A case study in the selection of news', *Journalism Quarterly*, 27, pp. 383–96.

Whitney, Charles D., Randall S. Sumpter and Denis McQuail (2004) 'News media production: Individuals, organizations, and institutions', in Downing, John D. H., Denis McQuail, Philip Schlesinger and Ellen A. Wartella (eds) *The Sage Handbook of Media Studies*, pp. 393–409. Thousand Oaks, CA, Sage.

Wierzbicka, Anna (1997) *Understanding Cultures through Their Key Words: English, Russian, Polish, German, and Japanese*, New York, Oxford University Press.

Wigley, Shelley and Maria Fontenot (2009) 'Where media turn during crises: A look at information subsidies and the Virginia Tech shootings', *Electronic News*, 3(2), pp. 94–108.

Wilke, Jürgen (1984) *Nachrichtenauswahl und Medienrealität in vier Jahrhunderten: Eine Modellstudie zur Verbindung von historischer und empirischer Publizistikwissenschaft*, Berlin, De Gruyter.

Wilke, Jürgen (2005) 'Krieg als Medienereignis: Zur Geschichte seiner Vermittlung in der Neuzeit', in Preußer, Heinz-Peter (ed.) *Krieg in den Medien*, pp. 83–104. Amsterdam, Rodopi.

Williams, Kevin (1992) 'AIDS stories covered up', *Media Development*, 39(4), pp. 9–11.

Wiltenburg, Joy (2004) 'True crime: The origins of modern sensationalism', *American Historical Review*, 109(5), pp. 1377–404.

Wolfe, Jessica, Darin J. Erickson, Erica J. Sharkansky, Daniel W. King and Lynda A. King (1999) 'Course and predictors of posttraumatic stress disorder among Gulf War veterans: A prospective analysis', *Journal of Consulting and Clinical Psychology*, 67(4), pp. 520–8.

Wolffe, John (1996) 'Responding to national grief: Memorial sermons on the famous in Britain 1800–1914', *Mortality*, 1(3), pp. 283–96.

Wu, H. Denis (2007) 'A brave new world for international news? Exploring the determinants of the coverage of foreign nations on US websites', *International Communication Gazette*, 69(6), pp. 539–51.

Zelizer, Barbie (1992) *Covering the Body: The Kennedy Assassination, the Media, and the Shaping of Collective Memory*, Chicago, IL, University of Chicago Press.

Zelizer, Barbie (1993) 'Journalists as interpretive communities', *Critical Studies in Mass Communication*, 10(3), pp. 219–37.

Zelizer, Barbie (1995) 'Words against images: Positioning newswork in the age of photography', in Hardt, Hanno and Bonnie Brennen (eds) *Newsworkers: Towards a History of the Rank and File*, pp. 135–59. Minneapolis, MN, University of Minnesota Press.

Zelizer, Barbie (1998) *Remembering to Forget: Holocaust Memory Through the Camera's Eye*, Chicago, IL, University of Chicago Press.

Zelizer, Barbie (2002) 'Photography, journalism, and trauma', in Zelizer, Barbie and Stuart Allan (eds) *Journalism after September 11*, pp. 48–68. London, Routledge.

Zelizer, Barbie (2004) 'When war is reduced to a photograph', in Allan, Stuart and Barbie Zelizer (eds) *Reporting War: Journalism in Wartime*, pp. 115–35. London, Routledge.

Zelizer, Barbie (2008) 'Why memory's work on journalism does not reflect journalism's work on memory', *Memory Studies*, 1(1), pp. 79–87.

Zelizer, Barbie (2010) *About to Die: How News Images Move the Public*, New York, Oxford University Press, In press.

Index